Early praise for *Effective Testing with RSpec 3*

Ruby embraces the old Lisp idea that you should "build up a language" to address your problem, and RSpec carries this approach into the world of testing. But RSpec is a big toolbox, and in order to harness its full power you need a guide. This is that guide: the bridge you need to take you from writing tests, to expressing your design requirements in code.

➤ **Avdi Grimm**
   Author of *Confident Ruby* and *Exceptional Ruby* and Head Chef, RubyTapas

Effective Testing with RSpec 3 does a great job of explaining both the main features of RSpec as well as its lesser known, powerful, and often overlooked features. It's an essential resource for Rubyists looking to learn RSpec, or for those who use it every day. I've already started using it regularly as a resource.

➤ **Noel Rappin**
   Author of *Rails 4 Test Prescriptions* and Director of Development, Table XI

Myron and Ian have written the essential "missing" manual for modern RSpec, connecting all the latest best practices for TDD and BDD. If you were having trouble mastering modern testing with RSpec, this book will sort you out.

➤ **Sam Joseph**
   Co-instructor on the BerkeleyX Agile Development using Ruby on Rails MOOC and co-founder, AgileVentures Charity

Myron has been the driving force behind RSpec development for years. He is an expert on testing practices and getting the most out of the RSpec suite. His care and attention to detail are impeccable, and it shows in both the codebase and this book.

➤ **Xavier Shay**
   RSpec core team member and Payments Engineering Lead, Square

Having worked with Myron for many years on the RSpec core team, I'm very pleased to see *Effective Testing with RSpec 3*. This book contains everything you need to learn not only how RSpec works, but how to test effectively with the framework. If you're working with RSpec on a daily basis and looking to get better at working with the framework, I could not recommend this book more heartily.

➤ **Sam Phippen**
   RSpec core team member and engineer, Digital Ocean

The exercises are illustrative and challenging. The final chapter on test doubles really synthesizes the best way to use these tools. You'll write far more readable and robust specs after reading this book, especially when interfacing with the shifting sands of third-party APIs.

➤ **Nigel Lowry**
   Company Director and Principal Consultant, Lemmata

Effective Testing with RSpec 3 is well worth a read: it is much more than a technical reference and will make you a better developer by teaching you how to write more expressive, robust, and maintainable tests.

➤ **Alessandro Bahgat**
   Professional software developer

Effective Testing with RSpec 3

Build Ruby Apps with Confidence

Myron Marston

Ian Dees

The Pragmatic Bookshelf

Raleigh, North Carolina

Many of the designations used by manufacturers and sellers to distinguish their products are claimed as trademarks. Where those designations appear in this book, and The Pragmatic Programmers, LLC was aware of a trademark claim, the designations have been printed in initial capital letters or in all capitals. The Pragmatic Starter Kit, The Pragmatic Programmer, Pragmatic Programming, Pragmatic Bookshelf, PragProg and the linking *g* device are trademarks of The Pragmatic Programmers, LLC.

Every precaution was taken in the preparation of this book. However, the publisher assumes no responsibility for errors or omissions, or for damages that may result from the use of information (including program listings) contained herein.

Our Pragmatic books, screencasts, and audio books can help you and your team create better software and have more fun. Visit us at *https://pragprog.com.*

The team that produced this book includes:

Publisher: Andy Hunt
VP of Operations: Janet Furlow
Executive Editor: Susannah Davidson Pfalzer
Development Editor: Jacquelyn Carter
Indexing: Potomac Indexing, LLC
Copy Editor: Liz Welch
Layout: Gilson Graphics

For sales, volume licensing, and support, please contact *support@pragprog.com.*

For international rights, please contact *rights@pragprog.com.*

Printed in the United States of America.
ISBN-13: 978-1-68050-198-8
Printed on acid-free paper.
Book version: P1.0—August 2017

Contents

Part II — Building an App With RSpec 3

Part III — RSpec Core

Part IV — RSpec Expectations

Part V — RSpec Mocks

Foreword

Making software is hard, and it's difficult to know how to get better at it. There's always so much stuff to learn, and so many competing opinions about the right way to do things. And yet somehow here you are, about to read another book full of ideas you're apparently supposed to remember.

Well, the truth is that you can make software just fine without writing tests, and you can write tests just fine without using RSpec, so you'll be okay if you stop reading now. But if you decide to keep going, you'll discover something interesting: writing tests with RSpec is a great way to get really good at making software.

That's because RSpec isn't just a testing framework. It's a tool for learning how to think critically, patiently, and systematically about the design of your code, and how to make software in a methodical way so you have confidence that it's well organized, clear, and correct.

It's also the product of an ongoing experiment. Over the last decade or so, RSpec's users have refined the way they write programs and the strategies they use to test them, and RSpec itself has continually changed to reflect these emerging decisions. In recent years it's settled down into a stable, crystalline form: a kind of executable document of what all those programmers learned from their iterated successes and failures.

As a result, each feature in RSpec is there for a good reason. It was put there by a developer like you, to address a problem like the ones you face every time you write code. There's an art to appreciating this gallery of features as a unified whole and settling into the state of mind it wants you to adopt. You could spend months memorizing all of RSpec's methods and options and fiddly bits, yet still be none the wiser about how to use your tests to drive your implementation decisions and steer your design toward simplicity.

After all, the big challenge of test-driven development isn't knowing how to *write* tests, but knowing how to *listen* to them. For your tests to be worth the bytes they're written in, they must be able to speak to you about how well the underlying program is designed and implemented—and, crucially, you must be able to hear them. The words and ideas baked into RSpec are carefully chosen to heighten your sensitivity to this kind of feedback. As you play with its expressive little pieces you'll develop a taste for what a good test looks like, and the occasional stumble over a test that now seems harder or uglier or way more annoying than necessary will start you on a journey of discovery that leads to a better design for that part of your codebase.

Myron and Ian have excellent taste and a keen ear for the feedback that tests can provide. This book unpacks the hard-won wisdom of RSpec's feature set and translates it into gentle, practical, actionable advice for your own code. By the time you've completely internalized everything here, you'll have acquired that elusive meta-skill: judgment, the ability to make your own decisions about how to do things right.

Tom Stuart

London, May 2017

Author of *Understanding Computation*

Acknowledgments

To our early readers of this book: you are amazing. You challenged us to do a better job explaining and connecting concepts. You found errors that had made it past us. You gave us specific feedback that we could act on (and did!) to improve the book.

We'd like to mention a few early readers by name. First, our technical reviewers: Alessandro Bahgat, Katie Bosch, John Fearnside, Derek Graham, Avdi Grimm, Jeff Holland, Rebecca Holzschuh, Sam Joseph, Ben Kirzhner, Nigel Lowry, Matt Margolis, Noel Rappin, Nell Shamrell, Xavier Shay, Travis Spangle, and Tom Stuart. Next, the alert readers who discovered errata in the beta book: Shisong Chen, Kenrick Chien, James Jefferies, Josh Justice, Bernard Kaiflin, Richard Murnane, Victor Paolo Reyes, Masaki Suketa, and Tony Ta. Last but not least, the readers who discussed the book with us in the forums: Manuel E Vidaurre Arenas, Askarbek Karasaev, Mark, and Edwin Meyer. Thank you all!

To Jackie, our development editor: thank you for your endless patience with us on this herculean project. You've constantly kept us focused on one question: "How does this material help the reader?" To Susannah, our executive editor: thank you for your expert advice on the big-picture questions of project scope and sequence. To the Pragmatic Bookshelf: thank you for publishing this book. We're proud of what we've made, and we're honored to see the Pragmatic banner gracing the cover.

As we've written this book, we've relied on the efforts of software developers all over the world. Thank you for building the tools we've relied on to create this project. Special thanks to Zachary Scott and the rest of the Sinatra core team for releasing Sinatra 2.0 just in time for this book—doing so helped us keep our book's content fresh and up-to-date.

Tom Stuart wrote a brilliant foreword for us. We smile every time we read it. Thank you, Tom!

Finally, we'd like to thank the Ruby and RSpec communities. We wish you well, and we hope this book helps you build amazing software.

From Myron Marston

To my wife Lori and children Coen, Daphne, and Crosby: thank you for supporting me through all the late nights and busy weekends so we could complete the book. I couldn't have done it without your love and support!

To my co-author Ian: thanks for being such a pleasure to work with. You handled my thousands of review comments with such graciousness. You're able to put concepts into words so much better than I ever could. I'm convinced this book is much better than what either of us could have come up with on our own!

To the RSpec core team (Jon Rowe, Sam Phippen, Xavier Shay, Yuji Nakayama, and Bradley Schaefer): thanks for supporting me as I write this book, and for working on RSpec all these years. RSpec is what it is today only because of the community we've built around it, and you all are a key part of that.

To David Chelimsky: thanks for shepherding RSpec so well for so many years, and for trusting me enough to hand the reins of the project over to me.

Finally, thanks to my employer, Moz, for supporting me in working on RSpec and writing this book, and generally being such an amazing place to work.

From Ian Dees

To my co-author Myron: this book has been the hardest technical project I've ever done—in the best possible way! There's no word other than *exhilarating* to describe the feeling of watching a chapter take shape over days of back-and-forth commentary on the changes. We each brought our own obsessions to the project, and I think it shows in the usefulness of the finished work.

To my wife Lynn and my children Avalon, Robin, and Damien: thank you for putting up with a shuffling zombie after all those late nights and early mornings spent writing. You are all creative, inspiring, kind people, and I love you. Now that this book is wrapped up, let's all hang out on the couch and watch some *Parks and Recreation*!

To my colleagues at work who have built RSpec projects with me, especially Rachael, Liss, Ben, Zoe, Noelle, and Katie: thank you for always pushing me to write better, more readable specs.

Introduction

"Our tests are broken again!" "Why does the suite take so long to run?" "What value are we getting from these tests anyway?"

The years go by and the technologies change, but the complaints about automated tests are the same. Teams try to improve the code and end up fighting test failures. Slow test times drag down productivity. Poorly written tests do a bad job communicating, guiding the software design, or catching bugs.

No matter whether you're new to automated tests or have been using them for years, this book will help you write more effective tests. By *effective*, we mean tests that give you more value than the time spent writing them.

We'll be using the RSpec 3 framework to explore the art of writing tests. Every aspect of RSpec was designed to solve some problem that developers have encountered in the wild. With it, you can build Ruby apps with confidence.

How to Use This Book

With this book, you'll learn RSpec 3 in three phases:

- Part I: Introductory exercises to get you acquainted with RSpec

- Part II: A worked example spanning several chapters, so that you can see RSpec in action on a meaningfully sized project

- Parts III–V: A series of deep dives into specific aspects of RSpec, which will help you get the most out of RSpec

We wrote this book to be read cover to cover. Whatever your level of expertise, reading the chapters in order will give you the most value. However, if you're pressed for time and want to know where to look first, we can make a few suggestions.

If you're familiar with other test frameworks but new to RSpec, we recommend that you read the first two parts of the book, and then try RSpec out in one of your own projects. As you do so, you'll likely have questions that you can consult specific deep-dive chapters for.

If you're a long-time user of RSpec, you can start with Parts III, IV, and V. These contain detailed recipes for situations you've likely encountered in the wild. Later on, you can return to the beginning of the book for a refresher on RSpec's philosophy.

Finally, if you use RSpec 3 every day, keep the deep-dive parts of this book nearby. You'll find them handy to refer to in specific situations—we do, and we've been using RSpec for years!

Code Snippets

We have provided code snippets throughout the book that show how RSpec is used in real-world situations. Most of these examples are intended for you to follow along with on your computer, particularly those in Part I and Part II.

A typical snippet will contain one or more lines of Ruby code meant for you to type into your text editor so that you can run them later. Here is an example:

```
00-introduction/01/type_me_in.rb
puts "You can type me in; it's okay!"
```

We'll show each code file a few lines at a time. If you need more context for any given snippet, you can click the filename banner (in the eBook) or open the book's source code (linked at the end of this chapter) to view the entire file at once.

Some code examples have no banner; these typically represent a session at your terminal, either in interactive Ruby (IRB) or in a shell like Bash. For IRB snippets, you'll run the irb terminal command and then type in just the parts after the green >> prompt:

```
>> %w[Type in just the bit after the prompt].join(' ')
=> "Type in just the bit after the prompt"
```

We'll represent shell sessions with a green $ prompt instead. As with IRB sessions, you won't type in the prompt or the output lines, just the commands *after* the prompt:

```
$ echo 'RSpec is great!'
RSpec is great!
```

Later on in the book, we sometimes show isolated snippets from a larger project; these are *not* meant for you to run on your computer. If you're interested in running them on your own, you can download all the project files from the book's source code repository.

Most chapters have a "Your Turn" section with exercises for you to try. Don't skip these! Practicing on your own will ensure that each chapter builds on the skills you've honed over the course of the book.

RSpec and Behavior-Driven Development

RSpec bills itself as a behavior-driven development (BDD) test framework. We'd like to take a moment to talk about our use of that term, along with a related term, test-driven development (TDD).

Without TDD, you might check your program's behavior by running it manually or by writing a one-off test harness. In situations where you intend to scrap the program shortly afterward, these approaches are all right. But when long-term maintenance is a priority, TDD provides important benefits.

With TDD, you write each test case just before implementing the next bit of behavior. When you have well-written tests, you wind up with more maintainable code. You can make changes with the confidence that your test suite will let you know if you've broken something.

The term TDD is a bit of a misnomer, though. Despite the fact that it has the word "test" in the name, TDD isn't just about your tests. It's about the way they enable fearless improvements to your design. For this reason, Dan North coined the term behavior-driven development in 2006 to encapsulate the most important parts of TDD.[1]

BDD brings the emphasis to where it's supposed to be: your code's *behavior*. The community stresses the importance of expressiveness in your tests, something that we'll be talking about a lot in this book. BDD is also about treating your software requirements with the same kind of care, since they're yet another expression of behavior. It's about involving all of your stakeholders in writing acceptance tests.

---

1. https://dannorth.net/introducing-bdd/

As a test framework, RSpec fits into a BDD workflow quite well. RSpec helps you "get the words right" and specify exactly what you mean in your tests. You can easily practice the outside-in approach favored in BDD, where you start with acceptance tests and move inward to unit tests.[2] At every level, your expressive tests will guide your software design.

However, RSpec and BDD are not synonymous. You don't have to practice BDD to use RSpec, nor use RSpec to practice BDD. And much of BDD is outside the scope of RSpec; we won't be talking in this book about stakeholder involvement, for instance.

Who We Are

Myron Marston started using RSpec in 2009 and began contributing to it in 2010. He's been its principal maintainer since late 2012. Here are just of the few major improvements he's made to RSpec:

- Composable matchers, which express exactly the pass/fail criteria you need
- rspec --bisect, which finds the minimal set of test cases to reproduce a failure
- Integrating RSpec's assertions and mocking libraries with the Minitest framework that ships with Ruby
- The --only-failures and --next-failure options that let you rerun just your failing tests so that you can fix bugs more quickly

With the insider knowledge Myron provides in this book, you'll learn all of these techniques and more. By the end, you'll be able to get free of just about any problems you run into with your test suite.

Ian Dees stumbled on an old beta of RSpec in 2006. It was just what he needed to build the automated acceptance tests for an embedded touchscreen device. Since then, he's used and taught RSpec for testing everything from tiny microcontrollers to full-featured desktop and web apps.

Who You Are

We hope this book is useful to a wide range of developers, from people who are just getting started with RSpec to those who have written thousands of tests with it. That said, we have made a few assumptions in order to keep the book from getting too bogged down with introductory material.

---

2. https://dannorth.net/whats-in-a-story/

First, we assume you're familiar with Ruby. You don't need to be an expert. We stick to the basics of classes, methods, and blocks for the most part. We will be directing you to install several Ruby gems, so it'll be useful to be familiar with that process as well. If you're new to Ruby, we recommend you first learn the language a bit using resources like Zed Shaw's *Learn Ruby the Hard Way* eBook or the Ruby tutorials at exercism.io.[3,4]

Although you'll be building a web service over the course of several chapters, we don't assume that you're already a web developer. Lots of folks use RSpec to test command-line apps, GUI apps, and so on. We'll explain a few web development concepts as they come up during the discussion.

When we have content that's meant for a specific audience—such as people coming from an older version of RSpec or folks who are new to web development—we'll put that content in a sidebar.

A Note on Versions

The libraries we're using in this book, both the ones from the RSpec framework and other dependencies like Sinatra and Sequel, are designed to be backward-compatible across minor version upgrades. The code examples you see here should work just fine in future versions of these libraries—at least until their next *major* versions.

While we've tested this code on multiple Ruby versions as far back as Ruby 2.2, you'll have the best experience if you follow along with the exact same versions we call out in the text: Ruby 2.4, RSpec 3.6, and so on. With the same versions we use, you should get output that closely mirrors what we show in the book.

Online Resources

This book has a website.[5] There, you'll find links to source code, discussion forums, and errata. We've also set up GitHub repositories containing all the examples in the book, plus a version of the project you'll build in *Building an App With RSpec 3.*[6]

---

3.   https://learnrubythehardway.org
4.   http://exercism.io/languages/ruby/about
5.   https://pragprog.com/book/rspec3/effective-testing-with-rspec-3
6.   https://github.com/rspec-3-book

For more information about RSpec, you can turn to the official site and the full developer documentation.[7,8]

Myron Marston
Lead Maintainer of RSpec
myron.marston@gmail.com
Seattle, WA, August 2017

Ian Dees
Senior Software Engineer, New Relic
undees@gmail.com
Portland, OR, August 2017

---

7. http://rspec.info
8. http://rspec.info/documentation/

Part I

Getting Started

Welcome to RSpec! In this part of the book, you're going to get acquainted with the framework as you write your first few working tests.

First, you'll install RSpec and write your first few specs—RSpec's lingo for tests. RSpec's API is all about deciding how you want your code to behave and expressing that decision in your specs. Once you've got the basics down, we can't resist showing you a few of the things that make RSpec special.

In this chapter, you'll see:

- How to install RSpec and write your first spec
- How to organize your specifications using describe and it
- How to verify desired outcomes with expect
- How to interpret test failures
- How to keep your specs free of repeated setup code

CHAPTER 1

Getting Started With RSpec

RSpec 3 is a productive Ruby test framework. We say *productive* because everything about it—its style, API, libraries, and settings—are designed to support *you* as you write great software.

Writing effective tests helps you toward that goal of shipping your application. We have a specific definition of *effective* here: *does this test pay for the cost of writing and running it?* A good test will provide at least one of these benefits:

- Design guidance: helping you distill all those fantastic ideas in your head into running, maintainable code

- Safety net: finding errors in your code before your customers do

- Documentation: capturing the behavior of a working system to help its maintainers

As you follow along through the examples in this book, you'll practice several habits that will help you test effectively:

- When you describe precisely what you want your program to do, you avoid being too strict (and failing when an irrelevant detail changes) or too lax (and getting false confidence from incomplete tests).

- By writing your specs to report failure at the right level of detail, you give just enough information to find the cause of a problem—without drowning in excessive output.

- By clearly separating essential test code from noisy setup code, you communicate what's actually expected of the application—and you avoid repeating unnecessary detail.

- When you reorder, profile, and filter your specs, you unearth order dependencies, slow tests, and incomplete work.

Everything you'll write over the course of this book is going to serve one of these practices.

Installing RSpec

First, to use RSpec 3, you need a recent version of Ruby. We've tested our examples in this book with Ruby 2.4, and encourage you to use that version for the easiest path. You may get slightly different results on other versions of Ruby. If you're using something older, go to the Ruby download page and grab a newer one.[1]

RSpec is made of three independent Ruby gems:

- rspec-core is the overall test harness that runs your specs.

- rspec-expectations provides a readable, powerful syntax for checking properties of your code.

- rspec-mocks makes it easy to isolate the code you're testing from the rest of the system.

You can install these individually and mix them with other test frameworks, assertion libraries, and mocking tools. But they go great together, and so we'll be using them together in this book.

To install all of RSpec, just install the rspec gem:

```
$ gem install rspec -v 3.6.0
Successfully installed rspec-support-3.6.0
Successfully installed rspec-core-3.6.0
Successfully installed diff-lcs-1.3
Successfully installed rspec-expectations-3.6.0
Successfully installed rspec-mocks-3.6.0
Successfully installed rspec-3.6.0
6 gems installed
```

You can see the three gems listed here, plus a couple of supporting libraries and the rspec wrapper gem, for a total of six gems.

Now that RSpec is on your system, let's do a quick check to make sure it's ready:

```
$ rspec --version
RSpec 3.6
  - rspec-core 3.6.0
  - rspec-expectations 3.6.0
  - rspec-mocks 3.6.0
  - rspec-support 3.6.0
```

Perfect. Time to take it for a test drive.

---

1.   https://www.ruby-lang.org

Your First Spec

Rather than testing some intricate production system, let's imagine something a little more concrete: a sandwich. Yes, it's silly, but it'll keep the examples short—plus, we were hungry while writing this chapter.

What's the most important property of a sandwich? The bread? The condiments? No, the most important thing about a sandwich is that it should taste good. Let's say so using the language of RSpec.

RSpec uses the words describe and it to express concepts in a conversational format:

- "Describe an ideal sandwich"
- "First, it is delicious"

Create a new project directory, with a subdirectory called spec. Inside «your_project»/spec, create a file called sandwich_spec.rb with the following contents:

```
01-getting-started/01/spec/sandwich_spec.rb
RSpec.describe 'An ideal sandwich' do
  it 'is delicious' do
  end
end
```

Developers work this way with RSpec all the time; they start with an outline and fill it in as they go. Add the following highlighted lines to your outline:

```
01-getting-started/02/spec/sandwich_spec.rb
RSpec.describe 'An ideal sandwich' do
  it 'is delicious' do
➤    sandwich = Sandwich.new('delicious', [])
➤
➤    taste = sandwich.taste
➤
➤    expect(taste).to eq('delicious')
  end
end
```

Before you run this spec, let's break the code down a bit.

Groups, Examples, and Expectations

This file defines your tests, known in RSpec as your *specs*, short for *specifications* (because they *specify* the desired behavior of your code). The outer RSpec.describe block creates an *example group*. An example group defines what you're testing—in this case, a sandwich—and keeps related specs together.

The nested block—the one beginning with it 'is delicious'—is an *example* of the sandwich's use. (Other test frameworks might call this a *test case*.) As you write specs, you'll tend to keep each example focused on one particular slice of behavior you're testing.

Tests vs. Specs vs. Examples

What's the difference between tests, specs, and examples? They all refer to the code you write to check your program's behavior. The terms are semi-interchangeable, but each carries a different emphasis:

- A *test* validates that a bit of code is working properly.
- A *spec* describes the desired behavior of a bit of code.
- An *example* shows how a particular API is intended to be used.

We'll use all these terms in this book, depending on which aspect of testing we want to emphasize.

Inside the example, you follow the Arrange/Act/Assert pattern: set up an object, do something with it, and check that it behaved the way you wanted.[2] Here, you create a Sandwich, ask it for its taste, and verify that the result is delicious.

The line beginning with expect is an *expectation*. These are like assertions in other test frameworks, but (as we will see later) with a few more tricks up their sleeve.

Take one more look at the three RSpec methods we use in this snippet:

- RSpec.describe creates an example group (set of related tests).
- it creates an example (individual test).
- expect verifies an expected outcome (assertion).

These are the building blocks that you'll reach for again and again as you build your test suites.

Getting the Most Out of RSpec

The specs for your sandwich serve two purposes:

- Documenting what your sandwich should do
- Checking that the sandwich does what it's supposed to

We'd argue that this spec suits the first purpose pretty well. Even someone new to the project can read this code and see that sandwiches should be delicious.

---

2. http://xp123.com/articles/3a-arrange-act-assert/

Check out the expect line. It reads almost like its English equivalent: "We expect the sandwich's taste to be delicious." With a traditional test framework's assertions, you might write a line like the following one instead:

01-getting-started/02/sandwich_test.rb
```
assert_equal('delicious', taste, 'Sandwich is not delicious')
```

This code works fine, but in our opinion it is less clear than the RSpec version. Throughout this book we are going to be harping on keeping your specs readable.

Specs are also working code. You should be able to run them and check that the sandwich is really behaving as designed. In the next section, you'll do so.

Understanding Failure

To try your specs, run the rspec command from your project directory. RSpec will look inside the spec subdirectory for files named «something»_spec.rb and run them:

```
$ rspec
F

Failures:

  1) An ideal sandwich is delicious
     Failure/Error: sandwich = Sandwich.new('delicious', [])

     NameError:
       uninitialized constant Sandwich
     # ./spec/sandwich_spec.rb:4:in `block (2 levels) in <top (required)>'

Finished in 0.00076 seconds (files took 0.08517 seconds to load)
1 example, 1 failure

Failed examples:

rspec ./spec/sandwich_spec.rb:3 # An ideal sandwich is delicious
```

RSpec gives us a detailed report showing which spec failed, the line of code where the error occurred, and a description of the problem.

Additionally, the output is in color. RSpec uses color to emphasize different parts of the output:

- Passing specs are green.
- Failing specs, and failure details, are red.
- Example descriptions and structural text are black.
- Extra details such as stack traces are blue.
- Pending specs (which we'll see later in *Marking Work in Progress*, on page 26) are yellow.

It's a tremendous productivity boost to find what you're looking for in the output before you've even read it. In *From Writing Specs to Running Them*, we'll see how to view our spec output in different formats.

Starting with a failing spec, as you've done here, is the first step of the Red/Green/Refactor development practice essential to TDD and BDD.[3] With this workflow, you'll make sure each example catches failing or missing code before you implement the behavior you're testing.

The next step after writing a failing spec is to make it pass. For this example, all you have to do is add the following line at the top of the file:

01-getting-started/03/spec/sandwich_spec.rb
```
Sandwich = Struct.new(:taste, :toppings)
```

Here, you've defined a Sandwich struct with two fields, which is all your specs need in order to pass. Usually, you'd put this kind of implementation logic into a separate file, typically in the lib directory. For this simple example, it's fine to define it directly in the spec file.

Now, when you rerun your specs, they'll pass:

```
$ rspec
.

Finished in 0.00101 seconds (files took 0.08408 seconds to load)
1 example, 0 failures
```

The three methods you've used in your spec—describe, it, and expect—are the core APIs of RSpec. You can go a long way with RSpec using just these pieces without any other embellishment.

That said, we can't resist showing you a few more things.

Sharing Setup (But Not Sandwiches)

As you write more specs, you'll find yourself repeating setup code from example to example. This repetition clutters up your tests and makes changing the setup code harder.

Fortunately, RSpec provides ways to share common setup across several examples. Let's begin by adding a second example after the first it block:

01-getting-started/04/spec/sandwich_spec.rb
```
it 'lets me add toppings' do
  sandwich = Sandwich.new('delicious', [])
```

---

3.   https://webuild.envato.com/blog/making-the-most-of-bdd-part-1/

```
  sandwich.toppings << 'cheese'
  toppings = sandwich.toppings

  expect(toppings).not_to be_empty
end
```

The expectation for this example introduces two new twists. First, you can negate your expectation—that is, check for falsehood—by using not_to instead of to. Second, you can test that a collection such as an Array or Hash is empty using be_empty. You'll see more about how these constructs work in *Exploring RSpec Expectations*.

Now, run your new example:

```
$ rspec
..

Finished in 0.00201 seconds (files took 0.09252 seconds to load)
2 examples, 0 failures
```

This spec runs fine, but it's a little repetitive. We're copying the sandwich setup code in each example. This duplication makes it harder to change the common code later on. It also clouds up our examples with setup information.

Let's make a common sandwich available to all our tests. RSpec supports multiple ways to do so:

- RSpec *hooks* run automatically at specific times during testing.
- *Helper methods* are regular Ruby methods; you control when these run.
- RSpec's *let* construct initializes data on demand.

Each of these techniques has its advantages; you'll use them all as you follow along with the examples in the book. Let's take a look at each one in turn to see how you'd use them.

Hooks

The first thing we'll try is an RSpec *before hook*, which will run automatically before each example. Add the following highlighted line inside your example group, just inside the RSpec.describe block:

01-getting-started/05/spec/sandwich_spec.rb
```
RSpec.describe 'An ideal sandwich' do
➤   before { @sandwich = Sandwich.new('delicious', []) }
```

RSpec keeps track of all the hooks you've registered. Each time RSpec is about to start running one of your examples, it will run any before hooks that apply. The @sandwich instance variable will be set up and ready to use.

The setup code is shared across specs, but the individual Sandwich instance is not. Every example gets its own sandwich. That means you can add toppings (as you do in the second spec) with the confidence that the changes won't affect other examples.

Now that you've moved the setup code to a common place, you can remove the repeated code from your examples. You'll need to use @sandwich in place of sandwich:

01-getting-started/05/spec/sandwich_spec.rb
```ruby
it 'is delicious' do
  taste = @sandwich.taste

  expect(taste).to eq('delicious')
end

it 'lets me add toppings' do
  @sandwich.toppings << 'cheese'
  toppings = @sandwich.toppings

  expect(toppings).not_to be_empty
end
```

Once you've made the changes, run your new specs. They should all pass, as before.

Hooks are great for running common setup code that has real-world side effects. If you need to clear out a test database before each example, a hook is a great place to do so.

They also work fine for stashing your test objects in instance variables, as we've done here. However, instance variables have a few drawbacks.

First, if you misspell @sandwich, Ruby will silently return nil instead of aborting with a failure right away. The result is typically a confusing error message about code that's far away from the typo.

Second, to refactor your specs to use instance variables, you've had to go through the entire file and replace sandwich with @sandwich.

Finally, when you initialize an instance variable in a before hook, you pay the cost of that setup time for all the examples in the group, even if some of them never use the instance variable. That's inefficient and can be quite noticeable when setting up large or expensive objects.

Let's try a different approach. Undo the changes you made for the before hook so that your file looks like it did before:

01-getting-started/04/spec/sandwich_spec.rb
```ruby
Sandwich = Struct.new(:taste, :toppings)
```

```
RSpec.describe 'An ideal sandwich' do
  it 'is delicious' do
    sandwich = Sandwich.new('delicious', [])

    taste = sandwich.taste

    expect(taste).to eq('delicious')
  end

  it 'lets me add toppings' do
    sandwich = Sandwich.new('delicious', [])

    sandwich.toppings << 'cheese'
    toppings = sandwich.toppings

    expect(toppings).not_to be_empty
  end
end
```

Now, we'll look at a more traditional Ruby approach to reducing duplication.

Helper Methods

RSpec does a lot for us; it's easy to forget that it's just plain Ruby underneath. Each example group is a Ruby class, which means that we can define methods on it. Right after the describe line, add the following code:

01-getting-started/06/spec/sandwich_spec.rb
```
def sandwich
  Sandwich.new('delicious', [])
end
```

We've moved the common setup steps into a typical Ruby helper method, like you might do in one of your own classes. Now, you can remove the sandwich = ... lines from your examples.

This helper method isn't quite ready for prime time, though. Look at what happens when we rerun the specs:

```
$ rspec
.F

Failures:

  1) An ideal sandwich lets me add toppings
     Failure/Error: expect(toppings).not_to be_empty
       expected `[].empty?` to return false, got true
     # ./spec/sandwich_spec.rb:18:in `block (2 levels) in <top (required)>'

Finished in 0.0116 seconds (files took 0.08146 seconds to load)
2 examples, 1 failure

Failed examples:

rspec ./spec/sandwich_spec.rb:14 # An ideal sandwich lets me add toppings
```

In our toppings example, we call sandwich twice. Each call creates a new instance. So, the sandwich we added toppings to is a different one than the sandwich we're checking for toppings.

The traditional Ruby solution is a common technique called *memoization*, where we store the results of an operation (creating a sandwich) and refer to the stored copy from then on. For more on memoization, see Justin Weiss's article.[4]

A typical Ruby implementation might look something like the following code. Try this new definition for your sandwich method:

01-getting-started/07/spec/sandwich_spec.rb
```
def sandwich
  @sandwich ||= Sandwich.new('delicious', [])
end
```

Now, rerun your specs to make sure that your memoized method fixed the issue.

This pattern is pretty easy to find in Ruby code in the wild, but it's not without its pitfalls. The ||= operator works by seeing if @sandwich is "falsey"—that is, false or nil—before creating a new sandwich. That means it won't work if we're actually trying to store something falsey.

Consider how you'd test a Toaster class that lets you search for a specific toaster by its serial number. If no such toaster exists, the search will return nil. Here's a naïve approach to writing a helper method to cache this value:

01-getting-started/08/toaster.rb
```
def current_toaster
  @current_toaster ||= Toaster.find_by_serial('HHGG42')
end
```

If the search comes up empty, we'll store nil in the @current_toaster variable. On the next call to the helper method, we'll be doing the equivalent of the following code:

01-getting-started/08/toaster.rb
```
@current_toaster = nil || Toaster.find_by_serial('HHGG42')
```

We'll call the potentially slow find_by_serial() method every time; we're not actually memoizing anything. We could concoct a workaround to handle this edge case. But with RSpec, we don't need to.

---

4.   http://www.justinweiss.com/articles/4-simple-memoization-patterns-in-ruby-and-one-gem/

Sharing Objects With let

RSpec gives us an alternative construct, let, which handles this edge case. It gives us a nicer, less chatty syntax as well. Remove your sandwich method and replace it with the following code:

```
01-getting-started/09/spec/sandwich_spec.rb
let(:sandwich) { Sandwich.new('delicious', []) }
```

You can think of let as binding a name (sandwich) to the result of a computation (the block). Just as with a memoized helper method, RSpec will run the block the first time any example calls sandwich.

When you run your specs again with your let definition, they should still pass.

It's possible to go overboard in our quest to reduce duplication. We can end up with test suites that we can only read by bouncing back and forth endlessly between the examples and let declarations. Our recommendation is to use these code-sharing techniques where they improve maintainability, lessen noise, and increase clarity.

Your Turn

In this chapter, you installed RSpec and took it for a test drive. You wrote a few simple specs to get a feel for the major parts of the framework. You saw how to run your examples and interpret the output. Finally, you explored a few different ways to reduce duplication in your specs.

Now, it's time to put this knowledge to the test.

Exercises

1. We've shown you three primary ways to reduce duplication in RSpec: hooks, helper methods, and let declarations. Which way did you like best for this example? Why? Can you think of situations where the others might be a better option?

2. Run rspec --help and look at the available options. Try using a few of them to run your sandwich examples.

Ready to see some of our favorite ways to use RSpec? Take a quick sandwich break and then meet us in the next chapter.

In this chapter, you'll see:

- How to generate readable documentation from your specs
- How to identify the slowest examples in a suite
- How to run just the specs you care about at any given moment
- How to mark work in progress and come back to it later

CHAPTER 2

From Writing Specs to Running Them

You've installed RSpec and taken it for a test drive. You've written a few specs and gotten a feel for how they're different from test cases in traditional frameworks. You've also seen a few ways to trim repetition from your examples.

In the process, you've applied the following practices:

- Structuring your examples logically into groups
- Writing clear expectations that test at the right level of detail
- Sharing common setup code across specs

RSpec is designed around these habits, but you could learn to apply them to other test frameworks as well. You may be wondering if all that separates RSpec from the crowd is syntax.

In this chapter, we're going to show you that RSpec's usefulness isn't confined to how your specs *look*. It also applies to how they *run*. You're going to learn the following practices that will help you find problems in code more quickly:

- See your specs' output printed as documentation, to help your future self understand the intent of the code when something goes wrong

- Run a specific set of examples, to focus on one slice of your program at a time

- Fix a bug and rerun just the specs that failed last time

- Mark work in progress to remind you to finish something later

The tool that makes these activities possible—and even easy—is RSpec's *spec runner*. It decides which of your specs to run and when to run them. Let's take a look at how to make it sing.

Customizing Your Specs' Output

When you use RSpec on a real-world project, you'll build up a suite of dozens, hundreds, or even thousands of examples. Most test frameworks, including RSpec, are optimized for this kind of use. The default output format hides a lot of detail so that it can show your specs' progress.

The Progress Formatter

In this section, we're going to look at a different ways to view your specs' output. Create a new file called spec/coffee_spec.rb with the following contents:

```
02-running-specs/01/spec/coffee_spec.rb
RSpec.describe 'A cup of coffee' do
  let(:coffee) { Coffee.new }

  it 'costs $1' do
    expect(coffee.price).to eq(1.00)
  end

  context 'with milk' do
    before { coffee.add :milk }

    it 'costs $1.25' do
      expect(coffee.price).to eq(1.25)
    end
  end
end
```

This spec file uses the same techniques we saw in the previous chapter, with one new twist: the context block starting on the highlighted line. This method groups a set of examples and their setup code together with a common description—in this case "with milk." You can nest these example groups as deeply as you want.

There's nothing mysterious going on behind the scenes here: context is just an alias for describe. You could use them interchangeably, but we tend to use context for phrases that modify the object we're testing, the way "with milk" modifies "A cup of coffee."

This spec will need a Coffee class to test. In a full project, you'd put its definition in a separate file and use require in your specs. But for this simple example, it's fine just to put the class at the top of your spec file. Here's the start of an implementation that's not quite enough to pass the specs yet:

```
02-running-specs/01/spec/coffee_spec.rb
class Coffee
  def ingredients
    @ingredients ||= []
  end
```

```ruby
  def add(ingredient)
    ingredients << ingredient
  end

  def price
    1.00
  end
end
```

When you run your specs, you'll see one dot for each completed example, with failures and exceptions called out with letters:

```
$ rspec
.F

Failures:

  1) A cup of coffee with milk costs $1.25
     Failure/Error: expect(coffee.price).to eq(1.25)

       expected: 1.25
            got: 1.0

       (compared using ==)
     # ./spec/coffee_spec.rb:26:in `block (3 levels) in <top (required)>'

Finished in 0.01222 seconds (files took 0.08094 seconds to load)
2 examples, 1 failure

Failed examples:

rspec ./spec/coffee_spec.rb:25 # A cup of coffee with milk costs $1.25
```

Here, we see one dot for the passing example, and one F for the failure. This format is good for showing the progress of your specs as they execute. When you've got hundreds of examples, you'll see a row of dots marching across the screen.

On the other hand, this output doesn't give any indication of which example is currently running, or what the expected behavior is.

When you need more detail in your test report, or need a specific format such as HTML, RSpec's got you covered. By choosing a different *formatter*, you can tailor the output to your needs.

A formatter receives events from RSpec—such as when a test fails—and then reports the results. Under the hood, it's just a plain Ruby object. You can easily create your own, and in *How Formatters Work*, on page 153 you'll see how to do that. Formatters can write data in any format, and send the output anywhere (such as to the console, a file, or over a network). Let's take a look at another one of the formatters that ships with RSpec.

The Documentation Formatter

RSpec's built-in *documentation formatter* lists the specs' output in an outline format, using indentation to show grouping. If you've written example descriptions with legible output in mind, the result will read almost like project documentation. Let's give it a try.

To see the output in documentation format, pass --format documentation (or just -f d) to rspec:

```
$ rspec --format documentation

A cup of coffee
  costs $1
  with milk
    costs $1.25 (FAILED - 1)

Failures:

  1) A cup of coffee with milk costs $1.25
     Failure/Error: expect(coffee.price).to eq(1.25)

       expected: 1.25
            got: 1.0

       (compared using ==)
     # ./spec/coffee_spec.rb:26:in `block (3 levels) in <top (required)>'

Finished in 0.01073 seconds (files took 0.08736 seconds to load)
2 examples, 1 failure

Failed examples:

rspec ./spec/coffee_spec.rb:25 # A cup of coffee with milk costs $1.25
```

The test report is a list of the specifications of various cups of coffee that RSpec verified. There's a lot of information here, and RSpec uses spacing and capitalization to show you what's going on:

- An example group lists all of its examples indented underneath it.

- Contexts create additional nesting, the way the with milk example is indented further.

- Any failing examples show the text FAILED with a footnote number for looking up the details later on.

After the documentation at the top of the report, the Failures section shows the following details for each failure:

- The expectation that failed
- What result you expected versus what actually happened
- The file and line number of the failing expectation

This output is designed to help you find at a glance what went wrong and how. As we'll see next, RSpec can provide further cues through syntax highlighting.

Syntax Highlighting

We've seen how RSpec's color highlighting makes it *much* easier to scan the output for passing and failing specs. We can take it a step further by installing a code highlighter called CodeRay:[1]

```
$ gem install coderay -v 1.1.1
Successfully installed coderay-1.1.1
1 gem installed
```

When this gem is installed, the Ruby snippets in your specs' output will be color-coded just like they'd be in your text editor. For example:

```
$ rspec -fd

A cup of coffee
  costs $1
  with milk
    costs $1.25 (FAILED - 1)

Failures:

  1) A cup of coffee with milk costs $1.25
     Failure/Error: expect(coffee.price).to eq(1.25)

       expected: 1.25
            got: 1.0

       (compared using ==)
     # ./spec/coffee_spec.rb:26:in `block (3 levels) in <top (required)>'
Finished in 0.0102 seconds (files took 0.09104 seconds to load)
2 examples, 1 failure

Failed examples:

rspec ./spec/coffee_spec.rb:25 # A cup of coffee with milk costs $1.25
```

Now, the line expect(coffee.price).to eq(1.25) has Ruby syntax highlighting. Normal method calls like coffee and price aren't shaded, but other elements are. In particular, both the key RSpec expect method and the number 1.25 are highlighted in color. This syntax highlighting is even more helpful for complex Ruby expressions.

RSpec will automatically use CodeRay if it's available. For Bundler-based projects, drop it into your Gemfile and rerun bundle install. For non-Bundler projects, install it via gem install as we've done here.

---

1. https://github.com/rubychan/coderay

Identifying Slow Examples

Throughout this book, we're going to give you advice on how to keep your specs running quickly. To understand where the biggest bottlenecks are in your suite, you need to be able to identify the slowest examples.

RSpec's spec runner can help you do so. Consider the following group of examples that take too long to run:

02-running-specs/03/spec/slow_spec.rb
```ruby
RSpec.describe 'The sleep() method' do
  it('can sleep for 0.1 second') { sleep 0.1 }
  it('can sleep for 0.2 second') { sleep 0.2 }
  it('can sleep for 0.3 second') { sleep 0.3 }
  it('can sleep for 0.4 second') { sleep 0.4 }
  it('can sleep for 0.5 second') { sleep 0.5 }
end
```

We can ask RSpec to list the top time-wasters by passing the --profile option along with the number of offenders we'd like to see:

```
$ rspec --profile 2
.....

Top 2 slowest examples (0.90618 seconds, 59.9% of total time):
  The sleep() method can sleep for 0.5 second
    0.50118 seconds ./spec/slow_spec.rb:6
  The sleep() method can sleep for 0.4 second
    0.40501 seconds ./spec/slow_spec.rb:5

Finished in 1.51 seconds (files took 0.08911 seconds to load)
5 examples, 0 failures
```

Just two examples are taking over half our test time. Better get optimizing!

Running Just What You Need

In the examples in this chapter, we've always run all the specs together. On a real project, you don't necessarily want to load your entire test suite every time you invoke RSpec.

If you're diagnosing a specific failure, for instance, you'll want to run just that one example. If you're trying to get rapid feedback on your design, you can bypass slow or unrelated specs.

The easiest way to narrow down your test run is to pass a list of file or directory names to rspec:

```
$ rspec spec/unit                 # Load *_spec.rb in this dir and subdirs
$ rspec spec/unit/specific_spec.rb # Load just one spec file
```

```
$ rspec spec/unit spec/smoke        # Load more than one directory
$ rspec spec/unit spec/foo_spec.rb # Or mix and match files and directories
```

Not only can you load specific files or directories, you can also filter which of the loaded examples RSpec will actually run. Here, we'll explore a few different ways to run specific examples.

Running Examples by Name

Rather than running all the loaded specs, you can choose a specific example by name, using the --example or -e option plus a search term:

```
$ rspec -e milk -fd
Run options: include {:full_description=>/milk/}

A cup of coffee
  with milk
    costs $1.25 (FAILED - 1)

Failures:

  1) A cup of coffee with milk costs $1.25
     Failure/Error: expect(coffee.price).to eq(1.25)

       expected: 1.25
            got: 1.0

       (compared using ==)
     # ./spec/coffee_spec.rb:26:in `block (3 levels) in <top (required)>'
Finished in 0.01014 seconds (files took 0.08249 seconds to load)
1 example, 1 failure

Failed examples:

rspec ./spec/coffee_spec.rb:25 # A cup of coffee with milk costs $1.25
```

RSpec ran just the examples containing the word *milk* (in this case, just one example). When you use this option, RSpec searches the full description of each example; for instance, A cup of coffee with milk costs $1.25. These searches are case-sensitive.

Running Specific Failures

Often, what you really want to do is run just the most recent failing spec. RSpec gives us a handy shortcut here. If you pass a filename and line number separated by a colon, RSpec will run the example that starts on that line.

You don't even have to manually type in which file and line to rerun. Take a look at the end of the spec output:

```
$ rspec
.F
```

≪ truncated ≫

```
2 examples, 1 failure
```

```
Failed examples:
```

```
rspec ./spec/coffee_spec.rb:25 # A cup of coffee with milk costs $1.25
```

You can copy and paste the first part of that final line (before the hash) into your terminal to run just the failing spec. Let's do so now:

```
$ rspec ./spec/coffee_spec.rb:25
Run options: include {:locations=>{"./spec/coffee_spec.rb"=>[25]}}
F
```

≪ truncated ≫

```
1 example, 1 failure
```

```
Failed examples:
```

```
rspec ./spec/coffee_spec.rb:25 # A cup of coffee with milk costs $1.25
```

RSpec ran only the single example you specified. This focusing ability becomes even more powerful when you add a key binding for it to your text editor. Several IDEs and editor plugins provide this behavior for you, including the following:

- ThoughtBot's rspec.vim plugin[2]
- Peter Williams's RSpec Mode for Emacs[3]
- The RSpec package for Sublime Text[4]
- Felipe Coury's Atom RSpec Runner[5]
- The RubyMine IDE from JetBrains[6]

With good editor support, you can quickly run the example under your cursor with a single keystroke.

Use Editor Integration for a More Productive Experience

 Having to switch back and forth between your editor and a terminal window in order to run rspec really interrupts your workflow. We recommend taking the time to install an editor plugin so that running rspec is only a keystroke away.

---

2. https://github.com/thoughtbot/vim-rspec
3. https://www.emacswiki.org/emacs/RspecMode
4. https://github.com/SublimeText/RSpec
5. https://github.com/fcoury/atom-rspec
6. https://www.jetbrains.com/ruby/

Rerunning Everything That Failed

Using a line number works well when only one spec is failing. If you have more than one failure, you can run all of them with the --only-failures flag. This flag requires a little bit of configuration, but RSpec will coach you through the setup process:

```
$ rspec --only-failures
```

```
To use `--only-failures`, you must first set
`config.example_status_persistence_file_path`.
```

RSpec needs a place to store information about which examples are failing so that it knows what to rerun. You supply a filename through the RSpec.configure method, which is a catch-all for lots of different runtime options.

Add the following lines to your coffee_spec.rb file between the Coffee class definition and the specs:

```
02-running-specs/06/spec/coffee_spec.rb
RSpec.configure do |config|
  config.example_status_persistence_file_path = 'spec/examples.txt'
end
```

You'll need to rerun RSpec once without any flags (to record passing/failing status):

```
$ rspec
.F
```

```
≪ truncated ≫
```

```
2 examples, 1 failure
```

```
Failed examples:
```

```
rspec ./spec/coffee_spec.rb:29 # A cup of coffee with milk costs $1.25
```

Now, you can use the --only-failures option:

```
$ rspec --only-failures
Run options: include {:last_run_status=>"failed"}
F
```

```
≪ truncated ≫
```

```
1 example, 1 failure
```

```
Failed examples:
```

```
rspec ./spec/coffee_spec.rb:29 # A cup of coffee with milk costs $1.25
```

Let's see what happens when the behavior gets fixed and the specs pass. Take a swing at modifying the Coffee class to pass both examples. Here's one possible implementation:

02-running-specs/06/spec/coffee_spec.rb

```ruby
class Coffee
  def ingredients
    @ingredients ||= []
  end

  def add(ingredient)
    ingredients << ingredient
  end

  def price
    1.00 + ingredients.size * 0.25
  end
end
```

With your implementation in place, rerun RSpec with the --only-failures option:

```
$ rspec --only-failures
Run options: include {:last_run_status=>"failed"}
.

Finished in 0.00094 seconds (files took 0.09055 seconds to load)
1 example, 0 failures
```

RSpec reruns the formerly failing example and verifies that it passes. If we try this process once more, RSpec won't have any failing examples left to run:

```
$ rspec --only-failures
Run options: include {:last_run_status=>"failed"}

All examples were filtered out

Finished in 0.00031 seconds (files took 0.08117 seconds to load)
0 examples, 0 failures
```

Another command-line option, --next-failure, offers a twist on this idea. You'll get a chance to try it out in the exercise at the end of this chapter.

Passing options to the rspec command isn't the only way to run just a subset of your examples. Sometimes, it's more convenient to make temporary annotations to your specs instead.

Focusing Specific Examples

If you find yourself running the same subset of specs repeatedly, you can save time by marking them as *focused*. To do so, simply add an f to the beginning of the RSpec method name:

- context becomes fcontext
- it becomes fit
- describe becomes fdescribe

Let's see what that looks like with the "A cup of coffee with milk costs $1.25" example. In coffee_spec.rb, replace context with fcontext (think of it as shorthand for *focused context*):

```
02-running-specs/07/spec/coffee_spec.rb
fcontext 'with milk' do
```

Next, we need to configure RSpec to run just the focused examples. Edit the RSpec.configure block in this file and add the following highlighted line:

```
02-running-specs/07/spec/coffee_spec.rb
RSpec.configure do |config|
➤   config.filter_run_when_matching(focus: true)
    config.example_status_persistence_file_path = 'spec/examples.txt'
end
```

Now, when you run just rspec, it'll run only the example in the focused context:

```
$ rspec
Run options: include {:focus=>true}

.

Finished in 0.00093 seconds (files took 0.07915 seconds to load)
1 example, 0 failures
```

If you haven't marked any specs as focused, RSpec will run all of them.

We'd like to show you one more aspect of focused specs. Take a look at the first line of the output:

```
Run options: include {:focus=>true}
```

We saw something similar in the section on running only failed examples:

```
Run options: include {:last_run_status=>"failed"}
```

Although these two ways of slicing and dicing your specs feel very different, they're both built on the same simple abstraction.

Tag Filtering

Earlier, when you wrote the following line to focus on the with milk context:

```
02-running-specs/07/spec/coffee_spec.rb
fcontext 'with milk' do
```

...this code was really just shorthand for the following expression:

```
02-running-specs/08/spec/coffee_spec.rb
context 'with milk', focus: true do
```

Any time you define an example or group—that is, any time you use RSpec.describe, context, or it—you can add a hash like the focus: true tag you see here. This hash, known as *metadata*, can contain arbitrary keys and values.

Behind the scenes, RSpec will add metadata of its own, such as last_run_status to indicate whether each spec passed or failed the last time it ran.

You can filter examples directly from the command line using the --tag option. For example, if RSpec didn't already have an --only-failures command-line option, you could have gotten the same behavior like so:

```
$ rspec --tag last_run_status:failed
Run options: include {:last_run_status=>"failed"}
F
```

« *truncated* »

```
1 example, 1 failure
```

```
Failed examples:
```

```
rspec ./spec/coffee_spec.rb:29 # A cup of coffee with milk costs $1.25
```

Similarly, you could pass --tag focus to run just the focused specs, but instead we configured RSpec to do so by default.

Before continuing, don't forget to change fcontext back to context. The whole idea of focusing is to filter specs *temporarily*.

Marking Work in Progress

In BDD, you're typically working on getting just one spec at a time to pass. Trying to tackle too many features at once leads to the kinds of complicated, untestable designs that BDD seeks to avoid.

On the other hand, it can be extremely productive to *sketch out* several examples in a batch. You're thinking of all the things a software component needs to do, and you want to capture the ideas so you don't forget anything. RSpec supports this workflow really well, through *pending* examples.

Starting With the Description

While you were writing the coffee spec earlier, you may have been thinking ahead to other properties of coffee with milk: it's lighter in color, cooler, and so on. While these behaviors are on your mind, go ahead and add them inside the with milk context as empty examples:

02-running-specs/09/spec/coffee_spec.rb
```
it 'is light in color'
it 'is cooler than 200 degrees Fahrenheit'
```

There's no need to fill these in; just let them stand as they are while you're working on other specs. Here's what RSpec shows on the console when you have empty examples:

```
$ rspec
..**

Pending: (Failures listed here are expected and do not affect your suite's  ↩
status)

  1) A cup of coffee with milk is light in color
     # Not yet implemented
     # ./spec/coffee_spec.rb:34

  2) A cup of coffee with milk is cooler than 200 degrees Fahrenheit
     # Not yet implemented
     # ./spec/coffee_spec.rb:35

Finished in 0.00125 seconds (files took 0.07577 seconds to load)
4 examples, 0 failures, 2 pending
```

The two empty examples are marked with yellow asterisks on the progress bar and are listed as "Pending" in the output.

Marking Incomplete Work

When you're sketching out future work, you may actually have an idea of what you want the body of the spec to look like. It'd be nice to be able to mark some expectations as work in progress before you commit so that you're never committing a failing spec suite.

RSpec provides the pending method for this purpose. You can mark a spec as pending by adding the word pending anywhere inside the spec body, along with an explanation of why the test shouldn't pass yet. The location matters; any lines before the pending call will still be expected to pass. We typically add it at the top of the example:

```
02-running-specs/10/spec/coffee_spec.rb
it 'is light in color' do
  pending 'Color not implemented yet'
  expect(coffee.color).to be(:light)
end

it 'is cooler than 200 degrees Fahrenheit' do
  pending 'Temperature not implemented yet'
  expect(coffee.temperature).to be < 200.0
end
```

RSpec will run the body of the spec and print the failure so you can see it. But it won't mark the spec, or your overall suite, as failing:

```
$ rspec
..**

Pending: (Failures listed here are expected and do not affect your suite's  ↵
status)

  1) A cup of coffee with milk is light in color
     # Color not implemented yet
     Failure/Error: expect(coffee.color).to be(:light)

     NoMethodError:
       undefined method `color' for #<Coffee:0x007f83b1199a88        ↵
       @ingredients=[:milk]>
     # ./spec/coffee_spec.rb:36:in `block (3 levels) in <top (required)>'
  2) A cup of coffee with milk is cooler than 200 degrees Fahrenheit
     # Temperature not implemented yet
     Failure/Error: expect(coffee.temperature).to be < 200.0

     NoMethodError:
       undefined method `temperature' for #<Coffee:0x007f83b11984d0    ↵
       @ingredients=[:milk]>
     # ./spec/coffee_spec.rb:41:in `block (3 levels) in <top (required)>'
Finished in 0.00161 seconds (files took 0.07898 seconds to load)
4 examples, 0 failures, 2 pending
```

Of course, you could just comment out the examples instead of marking them as pending. But unlike commented-out code, pending examples still run and report their failures—which means you can use this information to drive your implementation.

Define an inspect Method for Clearer Test Output

Some failure messages—such as the NoMethodError exceptions printed for these pending coffee specs—include string representations of your objects. Ruby (and RSpec) generate this string by calling inspect on each object.

If a particular class doesn't define an inspect method, the resulting string will be something like #<Coffee:0x007f83b11984d0 @ingredients=[:milk]>. To make the output a little more programmer-friendly, we recommend defining this method to print a nice, readable string such as #<Coffee (with milk)>.

Completing Work in Progress

One of the nice things about marking examples as pending is that RSpec will let you know when they start passing.

Let's see what that looks like. Implement the missing color and temperature
methods inside the Coffee class:

02-running-specs/11/spec/coffee_spec.rb
```
def color
  ingredients.include?(:milk) ? :light : :dark
end

def temperature
  ingredients.include?(:milk) ? 190.0 : 205.0
end
```

Now, try rerunning your specs:

```
$ rspec
..FF

Failures:

  1) A cup of coffee with milk is light in color FIXED
     Expected pending 'Color not implemented yet' to fail. No error was
     raised.
     # ./spec/coffee_spec.rb:42

  2) A cup of coffee with milk is cooler than 200 degrees Fahrenheit FIXED
     Expected pending 'Temperature not implemented yet' to fail. No error
     was raised.
     # ./spec/coffee_spec.rb:47

Finished in 0.00293 seconds (files took 0.08214 seconds to load)
4 examples, 2 failures

Failed examples:

rspec ./spec/coffee_spec.rb:42 # A cup of coffee with milk is light in color
rspec ./spec/coffee_spec.rb:47 # A cup of coffee with milk is cooler than
200 degrees Fahrenheit
```

RSpec has marked the test suite as failing, because we have examples marked
as pending that are actually implemented now. When you remove the pending
bits, the entire suite will pass.

If you *really* don't want the body of the spec to run at all, you can use skip in
place of pending. Or you can use xit, which is a temporary annotation like fit
except that it skips the example instead of focusing it.

Use pending to Flag Errors in Third-Party Code

If your spec is failing because of a bug in a dependency, mark it
with pending and the ticket ID from their bug tracker; for example,
pending 'waiting for a fix for Hitchhiker's Guide bug #42'. When you later update
to a version containing the fix, RSpec will tell you.

Your Turn

In this chapter, you practiced several good testing habits related to running your specs. RSpec's support for these habits sets it apart from other test frameworks:

- Powerful formatters show your specs' output in a variety of ways.

- Filtering your examples lets you focus on a specific issue and run just the specs you need.

- The pending method helps you sketch out examples before implementing the behavior fully.

Now, you're going to experiment with these techniques a little further.

Exercise

In a new directory, create a file called spec/tea_spec.rb with the following contents:

```
02-running-specs/exercises/spec/tea_spec.rb
class Tea
end

RSpec.configure do |config|
  config.example_status_persistence_file_path = 'spec/examples.txt'
end

RSpec.describe Tea do
  let(:tea) { Tea.new }

  it 'tastes like Earl Grey' do
    expect(tea.flavor).to be :earl_grey
  end

  it 'is hot' do
    expect(tea.temperature).to be > 200.0
  end
end
```

Run bare rspec once so it can record the status of the examples; then run RSpec with the --next-failure flag and look at the output. How does it differ from that of the --only-failures technique we discussed in *Rerunning Everything That Failed*, on page 23?

Implement the Tea class's flavor method to make it pass the first example. Now, run RSpec again with the same --next-failure flag. What do you see?

Before finishing the implementation, try out the different formatters. Run rspec --help to see a list of built-in output formats. Try the ones we haven't covered in this chapter. When you get to HTML, open the page in your browser and see how RSpec renders passing and failing specs.

With the help of the --next-failure flag, implement the rest of the Tea class. Now, pour yourself a cup of your favorite hot beverage. You've earned it!

In this chapter, you'll see:

- How your specs can give you confidence in your code
- How a good test suite makes refactoring possible
- How to guide your design using your specs with behavior-driven development (BDD)

CHAPTER 3

The RSpec Way

Over the last couple of chapters, you've gotten to know RSpec. You've written your first few examples and organized them into groups. You've seen how to run just a filtered subset of your specs and how to customize output.

All these features of RSpec are designed to make certain habits easy:

- Writing examples that clearly spell out the expected behavior of the code
- Separating common setup code from the actual test logic
- Focusing on just what you need to do to make the next spec pass

None of these habits comes without a cost:

- Writing specs takes time.

- Running large suites takes time (or requires learning options to trim down the set).

- Reading heavily factored specs requires hopping between setup and test code.

We don't want anyone to take it for granted that the habits we're forming are good ones. We'd like to show you they're worth the cost. In this chapter, we're going to walk you through RSpec's approach to software development and what makes a good set of specs.

What Your Specs Are Doing for You

Writing specs isn't the goal of using RSpec—it's the benefits those specs provide. Let's talk about those benefits now; they're not all as obvious as "specs catch bugs."

Creating Confidence

Specs increase confidence in your project. We're not talking about the simplistic view that if your specs pass, your program is bug-free (we've been programming in the real world for far too long to believe that fairy tale).

When we say *confidence*, we mean that a well-written spec can provide evidence in favor of certain claims about your code. For instance:

- The "happy path" through a particular bit of code behaves the way you want it to.

- A method detects and reacts to an error condition you're anticipating.

- That last feature you added didn't break the existing ones.

- You're making measurable progress through the project.

None of these statements are absolutes. You're not going to prove them true by writing enough specs. But a well-crafted suite can give you enough confidence to know when you can move on to the next piece you're working on.

Eliminating Fear

Think back to a past project you've worked on that was downright *scary* to work on. What made it so frightening?

Here are some of the things we've encountered:

- A simple, innocuous change would break distant parts of the code that seemed unrelated.

- Developers felt paralyzed by fear, unable to safely make any changes to the code at all.

Working on a project with a good set of specs is a refreshing change from this situation. With broad test coverage, developers find out early if new code is breaking existing features. When your specs have your back, you can fearlessly refactor tricky bits of code, ensuring your code base does not stagnate. Speaking of refactoring....

Enabling Refactoring

Truth is rarely permanent in software projects. Your understanding of the problem domain will improve as you discover new facts. Your startup may pivot. Old assumptions embedded into the code may make implementing new features difficult.

To deal with these sorts of changes, you'll need to refactor code. Without a good set of specs, refactoring is a daunting task. It's impossible to predict how much code you'll need to rework for any given change.

Our challenge as developers is to structure our projects so that big changes are easy and predictable. As Kent Beck says, "for each desired change, make the change easy (warning: this may be hard), then make the easy change."[1]

Your specs will help you toward this goal. They provide a safety net and guard against regressions. They also point out places where the code is too tightly coupled—where you'll need to work harder to "make the change easy."

Guiding Design

If you write your specs before your implementation, you'll be your own first client. You'll get a feel for what it's like to use the interfaces you're building. A good suite of examples will guide the initial design and will support the refactoring as your design evolves.

As counterintuitive as it may sound, one of the purposes of writing specs is to cause pain—or rather, to make poorly designed code painful. By surfacing the pain of a design problem early, specs allow you to fix it while it's cheap and easy to do so.

If you find yourself wrestling a bunch of ungainly objects into place just to test a single method, what are the odds your team is going to be able to use that method correctly every time?

Sustainability

When you drive your code with RSpec, it may take a little extra time to build your first feature. With each new feature you add, however, you'll gain consistent productivity.

Without RSpec or a similar tool in your arsenal, later features tend to take much longer than the first. You're constantly fighting with existing code to make sure it continues working.

This benefit doesn't apply to all projects. If you're writing a throwaway project, or an app with a tiny, frozen feature set, testing extensively at every layer might be overkill.

---

1. https://twitter.com/kentbeck/status/250733358307500032

Documenting Behavior

Well-written specs document how your system is intended to behave. Unlike a static documentation file, your specs are *executable*. You'll find out when they've grown stale, because you'll start seeing failures in the output. That means they're much easier to keep up to date than other forms of documentation.

RSpec encourages you to write examples that make great documentation. Its API favors plain-spoken descriptions of behavior, as in An ideal sandwich is delicious. Its rich expectation library helps you make it clear what the code you're testing is supposed to do. Its output formatters can even organize your specs' output into a coherent HTML document.

Transforming Your Workflow

Consider a world without test frameworks or BDD. Each feature you wrote would be a gamble. You'd fire up the app and poke around in the hopes of uncovering any obvious problems.

Driving your design from your specs completely transforms your workflow. Now, each run of your suite is an *experiment* you've designed in order to validate (or refute) a hypothesis about how the code behaves. You get fast, frequent feedback when something doesn't work, and you can change course immediately.

It's Fun!

Finally, driving your design from your specs is fun! Tackling a big problem all at once is hard and tends to give us a bad case of "programmer's block." TDD encourages us to break things down into small, achievable steps.

It's almost like a game: First, we come up with an example exposing a behavior the code doesn't yet implement. Then, we implement the behavior to make the specs pass. It's a constant stream of satisfaction.

Comparing Costs and Benefits

We hope you're convinced that BDD and RSpec can help you build good designs, and build them quickly. It's important to acknowledge the costs of what we do, whether we're talking about the minutiae of a single example or an entire approach to software development.

Writing Specs

Every spec takes time to write. That's why so many of the habits you've been practicing—outlining several examples at once, or creating reusable helper code, for instance—revolve around saving time.

Running the Entire Suite

Over the lifetime of a BDD project, your specs will run often, perhaps even thousands or tens of thousands of times. The time it takes to run the suite of specs will be multiplied by that huge number.

Consider the difference between a test suite taking 12 seconds and one taking 10 minutes. After 1,000 runs, the former has taken 3 hours and 20 minutes. The latter has cumulatively taken nearly 7 days. Team velocity takes a nosedive when they have to wait forever to find out if their changes broke anything. Throughout this book, we'll show you practices for keeping your specs snappy.

Getting Feedback from a Single Example

There's a huge difference between waiting less than a second for an example to run and waiting for several seconds or even multiple minutes. It's not just a quantitative shift. Once you've seen specs that give you near-instant feedback as you type, anything slower will feel like an unbearable interruption to your train of thought.

Gary Bernhardt makes effective use of this rapid-feedback development style, which he demonstrates in his *Destroy All Software* screencasts and blog posts:

> These tests are fast enough that I can hit enter (my test-running keystroke) and have a response before I have time to think. It means that the flow of my thoughts never breaks.[2]

Dealing with Failure

Failure is a good thing—really, it is. A failing spec points to the behavior that your recent change broke. However, it does cost time and energy to track down the source of the failure.

Much worse are failures caused by *brittle specs*—that is, specs that fail (perhaps intermittently) when the code is actually working. By writing precise RSpec expectations that describe exactly the behavior you're looking for—and no more—you keep your specs from becoming brittle.

Don't Overdo It!

Historically, developers have complained that their projects have lacked sufficient test suites. Now that TDD has become more mainstream, we're witnessing the opposite problem: projects that suffer from *overtesting*.

---

2.   https://www.destroyallsoftware.com/blog/2014/tdd-straw-men-and-rhetoric

In overtested projects, even the simplest change takes too long to complete. Either seemingly unrelated tests start failing, or the test suite takes too long to run for developers to be productive.

Not all tests are worth the effort it takes to write and maintain them. In fact, some tests have *negative value*. Kent Beck's Stack Overflow answer on this topic is instructive here:

> I get paid for code that works, not for tests, so my philosophy is to test as little as possible to reach a given level of confidence....[3]

We recommend periodically taking stock of long-running projects. Are basic logic bugs making it into production? Consider shoring up those areas of your test suite. Are bogus failures getting in the way of code changes? Try modifying your specs to be less brittle, or even deleting some of them.

As your architecture changes, tests can become superfluous. Deleting a test doesn't mean any of the effort writing it was wasted or misspent. It simply means it's overstayed its welcome. A test that can't pay for itself shouldn't be in your suite any more.

Deciding What *Not* to Test

Every behavior you specify in a test is another point of coupling between your tests and your project code. That means you'll have one more thing you'll have to fix if you ever need to change your implementation's behavior.

Sometimes, it's better to decide intentionally *not* to test certain things. For instance, user interfaces can change rapidly. If you couple your automated tests tightly to incidental details of your UI, you increase the cost of change. You may get more mileage out of manual exploratory testing—see Elisabeth Hendrickson's *Explore It! [Hen13]* for more information on this topic.

If you do need to drive a UI from automated tests, try to test in terms of your problem domain ("log in as an administrator") rather than implementation details ("type admin@example.com into the third text field").

Another key place to show restraint is the level of detail in your test assertions. Rather than asserting that an error message exactly matches a particular string ("Could not find user with ID 123"), consider using substrings to match just the key parts ("Could not find user"). Likewise, don't specify the exact order of a collection unless the order is important.

---

3. https://stackoverflow.com/questions/153234/how-deep-are-your-unit-tests/153565#153565

Different Types of Specs

Our goal as developers is to write specs that maximize the values we've listed here—guiding the design, building confidence, and so on—while minimizing the time lost to writing, running, and fixing them.

Every spec has a job to do. These jobs fall into different categories: catching regressions in an application, guiding the design of a single class or method, and so on.

The software development community continually argues about how many of these categories there are, and their exact definitions. While these endless arguments and subcategories are fun to ponder, we recommend focusing on just a few different, well-defined types of specs. That way, you'll end up *intentionally* picking what to write at any given moment, based on the benefit you're pursuing.

For this book, we are going to consider three types of specs described by Steve Freeman and Nat Pryce in *Growing Object-Oriented Software, Guided by Tests [FP09]*:

- *Acceptance:* Does the whole system work?
- *Unit:* Do our objects do the right thing, are they convenient to work with?
- *Integration:* Does our code work against code we can't change?

Let's look at each of these types of specs one by one.

Acceptance Specs

Acceptance specs describe a feature in an end-to-end, black-box style that exercises the entire system. These specs are hard to write, comparatively brittle, and slow. But they also provide a great deal of confidence that the parts of the system are working together as a whole. They're also supremely useful for large-scale refactoring.

Unit Specs

At the other end of the spectrum, unit specs focus on individual units of code—often as small as a single object or method. They check the behavior of a piece of code *relative to the environment you construct for it.*

Well-written unit specs tend to run extremely quickly (often in a few milliseconds or less!), and thus tend to cost less than other kinds of specs. Their isolated, focused nature provides immediately useful design feedback. Their independent nature makes them less likely to interfere with one another in a large suite.

On the other hand, unit specs are typically too low-level to be of much use during large-scale refactoring. In fact, you may even need to throw some unit specs away during such a refactoring. Since they're meant to be cheap to write and run, that shouldn't feel like a big sacrifice.

Integration Specs

Integration specs sit somewhere between these two extremes. Code that interacts with an external service—such as a database or third-party REST API—should have an integration spec.

There's a fine line to draw here. Any nontrivial software project will depend on other libraries. A strict interpretation of these definitions would require you to separate your unit and integration specs as follows:

- Your unit specs would have to isolate your code from *any* third-party dependency.

- Your (comparatively slow) integration specs would be allowed to hit third-party code indirectly.

We recommend applying common sense here. If your Ruby class depends on small, stable, fast libraries that don't hit the network and don't have side effects, it's probably okay to call them as is from your unit specs.

Integration specs are often an order of magnitude slower than unit specs. Consequently, you most likely won't run them constantly, the way you might with unit specs. We do, however, recommend running integration specs when you modify the code they cover, or at the very least before you commit your changes.

Moreover, integration specs require more care to avoid interference. When your code writes a database record, its spec will need to delete the record (or roll back the database transaction) so as not to affect the subsequent examples. These sorts of dependency issues make integration specs more difficult to run in parallel (something that can save you a lot of time) than unit specs.

We recommend putting as little branching logic as possible in the sections of your code that deal with dependencies. The simpler these parts of your system are, the fewer expensive integration specs you'll need to check them thoroughly.

Guidelines

With these definitions in mind, we've adopted a set of guidelines for the projects in this book. They're an adaptation of principles that have served us well in real-world situations. That said, they may not be applicable for every project. Our goal is to give you the tools and context to decide what's best for your own situation.

Integration specs are harder to write than unit specs, and they run more slowly. Therefore, we prefer to write fewer integration specs and more unit specs.

To make this arrangement possible, we need to keep our interfaces to external resources small and well defined. That way, we only have to write a few integration specs for these interfaces. Our faster unit specs can easily substitute fake versions of the interfaces.

Unfortunately, the general advice to favor unit specs isn't always easy to carry out in the real world. For many projects, the highest-value specs are also the ones that cost the most.

For instance, the ability to refactor your application logic is extremely valuable. End-to-end acceptance specs provide the best refactoring support. Because they only use your code's public interfaces, they don't depend on implementation details.

Of course, unit specs help with low-level refactoring such as reimplementing a specific method. But they won't support larger refactoring efforts such as removing a class entirely and distributing its logic elsewhere.

Acceptance specs' refactoring support comes at a price. They are more difficult to write, more brittle, and slower than other specs. But they provide so much confidence that it's important to have them—we just write very few of them, focus on the happy path, and don't use them for exhaustive coverage of conditional branches.

In the next part of this book, you're going to write an app from scratch, using all three of these types of specs along the way. As you reach each stage of the project, think about your goal for the spec you're about to write. That will guide you naturally toward which type to use.

Part II

Building an App With RSpec 3

How do we build software that does what our users want? And how do we keep it working well while we're writing it?

With outside-in development, you sketch the app at its outermost layer—the user interface or network protocol—and work your way inward to the classes and methods that contain the logic behind the interface. This approach helps you make sure you're using everything you build.

RSpec 3 makes it easy to do outside-in development. This part of the book is going to transform you into a testing powerhouse. By building an app and testing it with RSpec, you'll add several tools to your toolbox that will make you more effective.

In this chapter, you'll see:

- An overview of the project you'll be building
- Setting up RSpec for a real project
- How to get started writing acceptance specs
- How to mark work in progress

## CHAPTER 4

Starting On the Outside: Acceptance Specs

You've seen the basic parts of RSpec: example groups, examples, and expectations. Now, you're going to put those pieces together as you build and test a real application.

In this chapter, we'll pick a problem to solve and sketch out the major pieces of the solution. As you follow along, you'll create a new project and start testing it with RSpec. You'll start with *acceptance specs*, which check the behavior of the application as a whole. By the end of the chapter, you'll have the skeleton of a live app and a spec to test it—plus some clues on where to start filling in the details.

First Steps

Before we get started, we need to decide what kind of app we're going to build: an embedded system, a search engine, a Twitter clone, or what have you. We'll need to sketch out just enough pieces to decide what technologies we're going to use. Then, we can set up RSpec in our new project directory. Over the course of the project, you'll see how outside-in development helps you build a better system.

The Project: An Expense Tracker

We'll need a project big enough to contain some real-world problems, but small enough to work on over a few chapters. How about a web service for tracking expenses? Customers will use some kind of client software—a command-line app, a GUI, or even a web app—to track and report their daily expenses.

Here are the major parts of the app:

- A web application written in Sinatra that will receive incoming HTTP requests (to add new expenses or search for existing ones)[1]

- A database layer using Sequel to store expenses between requests[2]

- A set of Ruby objects to represent expenses and glue the other pieces together

The following diagram shows how the pieces fit together:

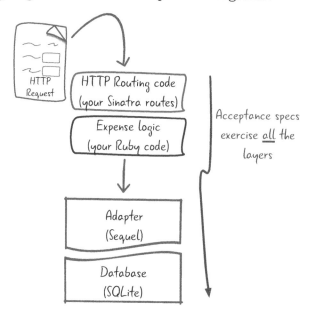

We need to test all of these in different ways. We begin with acceptance specs that drive the entire app from the outermost layer, the HTTP request/response cycle.

Why Not Rails?

We could have used Rails to build this project. However, Rails has a lot of features we don't need here, such as mailers, user-facing views, an asset pipeline, and a job queueing system. Also, Rails sets up a test harness for you. That's useful for real-world projects but gets in the way when you're learning how to configure your own tests.

On the other hand, small JSON APIs like the one we're building here are right in Sinatra's sweet spot. And it's simple enough that you can easily connect it to RSpec on your own. Everything you learn in this book will still apply to Rails projects.

Getting Started

You've already installed RSpec for a few stand-alone experiments. But this project has more dependencies than just RSpec. Customers deploying our app will want to use the exact same versions of Ruby gems we've tested with.

For this app, we'll use Bundler to catalog and install all the libraries we depend on.[3] If you've never used Bundler, don't worry; while we won't be explaining it in depth, you won't need any prior experience with it to follow along.

Create a new directory called expense_tracker. From there, install Bundler the same way you'd install any Ruby gem, and then run bundle init to set your project up to use Bundler:

```
$ gem install bundler
Successfully installed bundler-1.15.3
1 gem installed
$ bundle init
Writing new Gemfile to ~/code/expense_tracker/Gemfile
```

We'll need four Ruby libraries to get started:

- RSpec to test our project
- Coderay for easy-to-read, syntax-highlighted failure output
- Rack::Test to provide an API for driving web services from tests
- Sinatra to implement the web application; its light footprint and simple API are a good fit for this project

To bring these dependencies into the project, add the following lines to the end of the newly generated Gemfile:

```
04-acceptance-specs/01/expense_tracker/Gemfile
gem 'rspec',     '3.6.0'
gem 'coderay',   '1.1.1'
gem 'rack-test', '0.7.0'
gem 'sinatra',   '2.0.0'
```

Then, tell Bundler to install the required libraries and their dependencies:

```
$ bundle install
Fetching gem metadata from https://rubygems.org/.........
Fetching version metadata from https://rubygems.org/..
Resolving dependencies...
Using bundler 1.15.3
Using coderay 1.1.1
Using diff-lcs 1.3
Fetching mustermann 1.0.0
```

---

3. http://bundler.io

```
Installing mustermann 1.0.0
Fetching rack 2.0.3
Installing rack 2.0.3
Using rspec-support 3.6.0
Fetching tilt 2.0.7
Installing tilt 2.0.7
Fetching rack-protection 2.0.0
Installing rack-protection 2.0.0
Fetching rack-test 0.7.0
Installing rack-test 0.7.0
Using rspec-core 3.6.0
Using rspec-expectations 3.6.0
Using rspec-mocks 3.6.0
Fetching sinatra 2.0.0
Installing sinatra 2.0.0
Using rspec 3.6.0
Bundle complete! 4 Gemfile dependencies, 14 gems now installed.
Use `bundle info [gemname]` to see where a bundled gem is installed.
```

Now, set up the project to use RSpec. For now, we'll always run rspec using bundle exec, to make sure we're using the exact library versions we're expecting. In *Bundler*, on page 293, we'll talk about another, quicker way to run our specs.

```
$ bundle exec rspec --init
  create   .rspec
  create   spec/spec_helper.rb
```

This command will generate two files:

- .rspec, which contains default command-line flags
- spec/spec_helper.rb, which contains configuration options

The default flags in .rspec will cause RSpec to load spec_helper.rb for us before loading and running our spec files.

You'll need to add one line to the top of spec/spec_helper.rb:

04-acceptance-specs/01/expense_tracker/spec/spec_helper.rb
```
ENV['RACK_ENV'] = 'test'
```

Now that all the pieces are in place, we can write our first example.

Use the Right Rack Environment

Setting the RACK_ENV environment variable to test switches on test-friendly behavior in your web framework. Sinatra normally swallows exceptions and renders a "500 Internal Server Error" response. With this variable set, Sinatra will instead allow errors to bubble up to your test framework.

Deciding What to Test First

Even this simple app has several pieces. It's easy to feel overwhelmed as we're deciding what to test first. Where do we start?

To drive the first example, ask yourself: what's the core of the project? What's the one thing we agree our API should do? It should faithfully save the expenses we record.

Let's encode the first part of that desired behavior in a spec, and then implement the behavior. Place the following code in spec/acceptance/expense_tracker_api_spec.rb:

`04-acceptance-specs/01/expense_tracker/spec/acceptance/expense_tracker_api_spec.rb`
```ruby
require 'rack/test'
require 'json'

module ExpenseTracker
  RSpec.describe 'Expense Tracker API' do
    include Rack::Test::Methods

    it 'records submitted expenses' do
      coffee = {
        'payee'  => 'Starbucks',
        'amount' => 5.75,
        'date'   => '2017-06-10'
      }

      post '/expenses', JSON.generate(coffee)
    end
  end
end
```

Note that we can nest RSpec contexts inside modules. In our codebase, we'll enclose both our app and our specs inside the ExpenseTracker module so that we have easy access to all the classes defined by our app.

Use a Precise Data Type to Represent Currency

To simplify our code examples so you can focus on learning RSpec, we're using regular Ruby floating-point numbers to represent expense amounts—even though floating-point arithmetic isn't precise enough to handle money.[4]

On a real project, we'd either use the BigDecimal class built into Ruby or a dedicated currency library like the Money gem.[5,6]

---

4. https://spin.atomicobject.com/2014/08/14/currency-rounding-errors/
5. https://ruby-doc.org/stdlib-2.4.1/libdoc/bigdecimal/rdoc/BigDecimal.html
6. http://rubymoney.github.io/money/

We don't need to design the entire API up front. Let's assume we'll be POSTing some key-value pairs to the /expenses endpoint. As many web APIs do, we'll support sending and receiving data in JSON format.[7] Because JSON objects convert to Ruby hashes with string keys, our example data will also have string keys. For example, we'll say { 'payee' => 'Starbucks' } instead of { payee: 'Starbucks' }.

A Quick Look at HTTP APIs

Our expense tracker API is built on Hypertext Transfer Protocol (HTTP). This is the same protocol that your web browser uses to connect to websites, but in our case the requests won't necessarily be coming from a browser. A command-line program, a desktop GUI, or a set of RSpec examples may generate these requests.

We're only going to use two of the most basic features of HTTP in these examples:

- A GET request reads data from the app.
- A POST request modifies data.

There's a lot more to HTTP than just this. For more information, see one of the many tutorials available.[a]

_____

a.   https://code.tutsplus.com/tutorials/a-beginners-guide-to-http-and-rest--net-16340

To get the data into and out of our app, we'll use several different helper methods from Rack::Test::Methods. As you can see, you can include Ruby modules into an RSpec context, just like you're used to doing inside Ruby classes.

The first Rack::Test helper we'll use is post. This will simulate an HTTP POST request, but will do so by calling our app directly rather than generating and parsing HTTP packets.

We don't have an app yet, but let's go ahead and run our specs anyway. This will give us a hint on what to implement next:

```
$ bundle exec rspec
F

Failures:

  1) Expense Tracker API records submitted expenses
     Failure/Error: post '/expenses', JSON.generate(coffee)

     NameError:
       undefined local variable or method `app' for                    ↩
       #<RSpec::ExampleGroups::ExpenseTrackerAPI:0x007fef0404f560>
```

《 truncated 》

_____

7.   http://json.org

This error message, and the Rack::Test documentation, tell us that our test suite needs to define an app method that returns an object representing our web app.[8]

We haven't built this object yet. Let's assume it will be a class called API in the ExpenseTracker module. Add the following code inside your context, just above the it line:

04-acceptance-specs/02/expense_tracker/spec/acceptance/expense_tracker_api_spec.rb
```
def app
  ExpenseTracker::API.new
end
```

RSpec contexts are just Ruby classes, which means you can define helper methods like app, and they'll be available inside all your examples.

The Code You Wish You Had

Does it seem like we're getting ahead of ourselves by instantiating a nonexistent class? This technique can help flesh out your design.

First, you write the code you wish you had. Then, you fill in the implementation. Designing things from the caller's perspective helps you write an easy-to-use API.

Run your specs again to see where they fail:

```
$ bundle exec rspec
F

Failures:

  1) Expense Tracker API records submitted expenses
     Failure/Error: ExpenseTracker::API.new

     NameError:
       uninitialized constant ExpenseTracker::API

« truncated »
```

We haven't defined this class yet. Let's do so.

Unlike Ruby on Rails, Sinatra doesn't have an established directory naming convention. Let's follow the Rails convention and put our application code in a folder called app. Place the following code in app/api.rb:

04-acceptance-specs/02/expense_tracker/app/api.rb
```
require 'sinatra/base'
require 'json'
```

---

8. https://github.com/rack-test/rack-test#examples

```
module ExpenseTracker
  class API < Sinatra::Base
  end
end
```

This class defines the barest skeleton of a Sinatra app. Now, our tests need to load it. Back in your spec, add the following line to the require section at the top:

04-acceptance-specs/02/expense_tracker/spec/acceptance/expense_tracker_api_spec.rb
```
require_relative '../../app/api'
```

Now, your specs are passing. You may be wondering, "Did we actually test anything? Shouldn't we expect or assert something?"

We'll get to that. Right now, we're verifying only that the POST request completes without crashing the app. Next, we'll actually check that we got a valid response back from the app.

Checking the Response

Rack::Test provides the last_response method for checking HTTP responses. Add the following line inside your spec, right after the post request:

04-acceptance-specs/03/expense_tracker/spec/acceptance/expense_tracker_api_spec.rb
```
expect(last_response.status).to eq(200)
```

You've encountered code like this before, in *Your First Spec*, on page 5. It's an *expectation* fulfilling the role an assertion method would play in other test frameworks.

Together, expect() and to() check a result in order to signal success or failure. They compare a value—in this case, the HTTP status code returned by last_response.status—using a *matcher*. Here, we create a matcher using the eq method, which indicates whether or not the value wrapped by expect equals the provided argument of 200. When we pass the matcher from eq(200) as an argument to the to() method, we'll get a passing or failing result.

This may seem like a lot of moving parts compared to a traditional assertion-style method like assert_equal. Matchers are, however, more powerful and more composable than traditional assertions. We'll see more about them in *Exploring RSpec Expectations*.

Let's look at what happens when we run this code:

```
$ bundle exec rspec
F
```

Failures:

  1) Expense Tracker API records submitted expenses

```
Failure/Error: expect(last_response.status).to eq(200)

  expected: 200
       got: 404

  (compared using ==)
```

« truncated »

Our app is returning a 404 (Not Found) status code. That's not surprising; we haven't added any routes to the Sinatra code yet. Go ahead and do so now:

04-acceptance-specs/03/expense_tracker/app/api.rb
```
post '/expenses' do
end
```

When you rerun your specs, you should see a passing result.

Filling In the Response Body

Think about what you'd like the response data to look like. It'd be nice to get back a unique ID for the expense we just recorded so that we can refer to it later. Let's return a JSON object that looks something like this:

```
{ "expense_id": 42 }
```

Ruby's JSON library can safely parse simple a record like this into a Ruby hash:

```
>> require 'json'
=> true
>> JSON.parse('{ "expense_id": 42 }')
=> {"expense_id"=>42}
```

At this point, we don't really care what the specific ID is, just that the data has this general structure. RSpec's matchers make it easy to express this idea. Add the following highlighted lines inside your spec, just after the HTTP response check:

04-acceptance-specs/04/expense_tracker/spec/acceptance/expense_tracker_api_spec.rb
```
it 'records submitted expenses' do
  coffee = {
    'payee'  => 'Starbucks',
    'amount' => 5.75,
    'date'   => '2017-06-10'
  }

  post '/expenses', JSON.generate(coffee)
  expect(last_response.status).to eq(200)

➤ parsed = JSON.parse(last_response.body)
➤ expect(parsed).to include('expense_id' => a_kind_of(Integer))
end
```

The include and a_kind_of matchers let us spell out in general terms what we want: a hash containing a key of 'expense_id' and an integer value. By passing one matcher into another, we've *composed* them to create a new one that specifies just the right level of detail. We'll talk more about composable matchers in *Composing Matchers*, on page 176.

When we run our updated spec, we get another failure:

```
$ bundle exec rspec
F

Failures:

  1) Expense Tracker API records submitted expenses
     Failure/Error: parsed = JSON.parse(last_response.body)

     JSON::ParserError:
       743: unexpected token at ''
```

« *truncated* »

Our empty post block just sends an empty string back to the client. We need to send some JSON-formatted text instead. Add the following line to your Sinatra app:

04-acceptance-specs/04/expense_tracker/app/api.rb
```
post '/expenses' do
➤   JSON.generate('expense_id' => 42)
end
```

Once we're generating text that matches our expected pattern, our specs will be back to passing. Of course, this passing example isn't telling us much. We've managed to fool it by returning some canned data. This practice of hard-coding return values just to satisfy an expectation—known as *sliming the test*—allows us to flesh out the spec end-to-end and then come back later to implement the behavior properly.[9]

Querying the Data

Saving expenses is all fine and good, but it'd be nice to retrieve them. We want to allow users to fetch expenses by date, so let's post a few expenses with different dates and then request the expenses for one of those dates. We expect the app to respond with just the expenses recorded on that date.

Posting one expense after another will get really old if we have to keep repeating all that code. Let's extract that helper logic into a post_expense helper method inside the RSpec.describe block:

---

9.   https://www.youtube.com/watch?v=PhiXo5CWjYU

04-acceptance-specs/05/expense_tracker/spec/acceptance/expense_tracker_api_spec.rb

```ruby
def post_expense(expense)
  post '/expenses', JSON.generate(expense)
  expect(last_response.status).to eq(200)

  parsed = JSON.parse(last_response.body)
  expect(parsed).to include('expense_id' => a_kind_of(Integer))
  expense.merge('id' => parsed['expense_id'])
end
```

This is basically the same code as before, except we've added a call to merge at the end. This line just adds an id key to the hash, containing whatever ID gets auto-assigned from the database. Doing so will make writing expectations easier later on; we'll be able to compare for exact equality.

Now, change the coffee expense to the following, shorter code:

04-acceptance-specs/05/expense_tracker/spec/acceptance/expense_tracker_api_spec.rb

```ruby
coffee = post_expense(
  'payee'  => 'Starbucks',
  'amount' => 5.75,
  'date'   => '2017-06-10'
)
```

Using the same helper, let's post one expense on the same date and one on a different date:

04-acceptance-specs/05/expense_tracker/spec/acceptance/expense_tracker_api_spec.rb

```ruby
zoo = post_expense(
  'payee'  => 'Zoo',
  'amount' => 15.25,
  'date'   => '2017-06-10'
)

groceries = post_expense(
  'payee'  => 'Whole Foods',
  'amount' => 95.20,
  'date'   => '2017-06-11'
)
```

Finally, you can query all the expenses for June 10th, and make sure the results contain only the values from that date. Add the following highlighted lines inside the same spec we've been working in, right after the zoo and groceries expenses:

04-acceptance-specs/05/expense_tracker/spec/acceptance/expense_tracker_api_spec.rb

```ruby
it 'records submitted expenses' do
  # POST coffee, zoo, and groceries expenses here
➤ get '/expenses/2017-06-10'
➤ expect(last_response.status).to eq(200)
➤
```

```
➤    expenses = JSON.parse(last_response.body)
➤    expect(expenses).to contain_exactly(coffee, zoo)
     end
```

We're using the same techniques from before: driving the app, grabbing the last_response from Rack::Test, and looking at the results. There are lots of ways to compare collections in RSpec. Here, we want to check that the array contains the two expenses we want—and only those two—without regard to the order. The contain_exactly matcher captures this requirement.

If we had a specific business requirement that the expenses be in a certain sequence, we could compare the collections with eq instead, as in eq [coffee, zoo]. Here, we don't care about the order. Using a matcher more flexible than eq makes our spec more resilient, giving us the latitude to change the ordering in the future without fighting a broken test.

Go ahead and run the latest version of your spec:

```
$ bundle exec rspec
F

Failures:

  1) Expense Tracker API records submitted expenses
     Failure/Error: expect(last_response.status).to eq(200)

       expected: 200
            got: 404

       (compared using ==)
```

« truncated »

Since we haven't defined a way for clients to read back data yet, we're getting another 404 status code. Let's add a route to the Sinatra app that returns an empty JSON array:

04-acceptance-specs/05/expense_tracker/app/api.rb
```
get '/expenses/:date' do
  JSON.generate([])
end
```

Now, when we rerun our specs, we get an incorrect response, rather than an HTTP error:

```
$ bundle exec rspec
F

Failures:

  1) Expense Tracker API records submitted expenses
     Failure/Error: expect(expenses).to contain_exactly(coffee, zoo)
```

```
expected collection contained:  [{"payee"=>"Starbucks",            ↩
"amount"=>5.75, "date"=>"2017-06-10", "id"=>42}, {"payee"=>"Zoo",  ↩
"amount"=>15.25, "date"=>"2017-06-10", "id"=>42}]
actual collection contained:    []
the missing elements were:      [{"payee"=>"Starbucks",            ↩
"amount"=>5.75, "date"=>"2017-06-10", "id"=>42}, {"payee"=>"Zoo",  ↩
"amount"=>15.25, "date"=>"2017-06-10", "id"=>42}]
```

≪ *truncated* ≫

There's not much point in putting off the inevitable. We're going to have to write some code to save and load expenses.

Saving Your Progress: Pending Specs

Before veering off into low-level implementation, it's a good idea to save your work so far. We don't recommend leaving specs in a failing state, though. So let's mark this one as in progress. Add the following highlighted line at the top of your spec:

04-acceptance-specs/06/expense_tracker/spec/acceptance/expense_tracker_api_spec.rb

```
it 'records submitted expenses' do
➤   pending 'Need to persist expenses'
```

Now, when you run your specs, you will get a reminder of what you were working on:

```
$ bundle exec rspec
*

Pending: (Failures listed here are expected and do not affect your suite's  ↩
status)

  1) Expense Tracker API records submitted expenses
     # Need to persist expenses
     Failure/Error: expect(expenses).to contain_exactly(coffee, zoo)

       expected collection contained:  [{"payee"=>"Starbucks",            ↩
       "amount"=>5.75, "date"=>"2017-06-10", "id"=>42}, {"payee"=>"Zoo",  ↩
       "amount"=>15.25, "date"=>"2017-06-10", "id"=>42}]
       actual collection contained:    []
       the missing elements were:      [{"payee"=>"Starbucks",            ↩
       "amount"=>5.75, "date"=>"2017-06-10", "id"=>42}, {"payee"=>"Zoo",  ↩
       "amount"=>15.25, "date"=>"2017-06-10", "id"=>42}]
     # ./spec/acceptance/expense_tracker_api_spec.rb:46:in `block (2       ↩
     levels) in <module:ExpenseTracker>'

Finished in 0.03437 seconds (files took 0.1271 seconds to load)
1 example, 0 failures, 1 pending
```

Once you implement that behavior, you'll take out the pending line. RSpec will fail your specs if you forget—in effect, it's saying, "Hey, you said this wasn't working yet!"

Before moving on, let's hook our application up to a web server so we can actually see it working. Rack, the HTTP toolkit that Sinatra is built on top of, ships with a tool named rackup that makes it easy to run any Rack application (including apps built using Sinatra). We just need to define a rackup config file named config.ru with the following contents:

04-acceptance-specs/06/expense_tracker/config.ru
```
require_relative 'app/api'
run ExpenseTracker::API.new
```

Simple enough. We're just loading our application and telling Rack to run it. With that in place, we can boot our application by running rackup:

```
$ bundle exec rackup
[2017-06-13 13:34:10] INFO  WEBrick 1.3.1
[2017-06-13 13:34:10] INFO  ruby 2.4.1 (2017-03-22) [x86_64-darwin15]
[2017-06-13 13:34:10] INFO  WEBrick::HTTPServer#start: pid=45203 port=9292
```

While that's running, we can use a command-line tool like curl in another terminal window to send requests to our application.[10] The port=9292 bit from that last line tells us what port our application is running on, so let's send a request to localhost:9292:

```
$ curl localhost:9292/expenses/2017-06-10 -w "\n"
[]
```

It works! As expected, our application is responding with an empty JSON array.

Before moving on, commit the code into your favorite revision control system. That way, you'll easily be able to pick up where you left off. Grab a cup of coffee, try a couple of the exercises, and meet us in the next chapter.

Your Turn

In this chapter, we went over the major pieces of the software we're building. You used Bundler to manage all of your project's dependencies, including RSpec. You wrote your first spec to drive the app from its outermost layer, the HTTP interface, then wrote just enough Ruby code to get an idea of what the business logic needs to look like.

---

10. https://curl.haxx.se/

Next, we'll narrow our focus to the HTTP routing logic, and test it in isolation from the rest of the system.

Exercises

1. Skim through the introductory Sinatra documentation to get a feel for how apps are structured.[11]

2. Read "Testing Sinatra with Rack::Test" to learn the testing approach favored by the Sinatra team.[12]

3. Remember the spec_helper.rb file that RSpec generated for you? Read through a few of the comments and try enabling some of the commented-out settings.

11. http://www.sinatrarb.com/intro.html
12. http://www.sinatrarb.com/testing.html

In this chapter, you'll see:

- The difference between acceptance specs and unit specs
- How to use dependency injection to write flexible, testable code
- The use of test doubles / mock objects to stand in for real ones
- How to refactor your specs to keep them clean and readable

CHAPTER 5

Testing in Isolation: Unit Specs

You finished off the last chapter with a working acceptance spec. This spec is (correctly) reporting that the underlying logic isn't implemented yet. You're going to start filling in the application skeleton with a working implementation now, picking up where you left off: the HTTP routing layer.

Since you'll be testing the routing logic in isolation (without a live application server or a real database), you're going to use *unit specs* to drive the behavior at this layer:

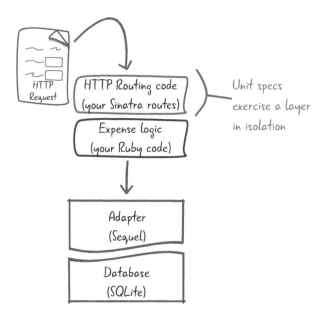

When you finish this chapter and the exercises, you'll have a complete set of passing unit specs for your HTTP layer.

From Acceptance Specs to Unit Specs

We should take a moment to revisit what we mean by "unit specs." The common term *unit testing* means different things to different people—or even to the same person on different projects. Unit tests typically involve isolating a class or method from the rest of the code. The result is faster tests and easier-to-find errors.

Where unit testing approaches differ is the *degree* of isolation; that is, whether to remove every possible dependency or to test a related group of collaborating objects together. In this book, we'll use *unit spec* to refer to the fastest, most isolated set of tests for a particular project. For more information, see Martin Fowler's article on the subject.[1]

With the unit tests in this chapter, you won't be calling methods on the API class directly. Instead, you'll still be simulating HTTP requests through the Rack::Test interface. Typically, you test a class through its public interface, and this one is no exception. The HTTP interface *is* the public interface.

Drive Each Layer's Public API

 Your tests for any particular layer—from customer-facing code down to low-level model classes—should drive that layer's public API. You'll find yourself making more careful decisions about what does or doesn't go into the API. Moreover, your tests will be less brittle and will give you greater latitude for refactoring your code.

You will, however, be isolating the public-facing API from the underlying storage engine. In effect, you're testing one layer of the app at a time. In this chapter, that means driving the behavior of the API class that routes incoming requests to the storage engine. In the next chapter, you'll test and design the storage engine itself.

For more on the nuances among different kinds of specs, see Xavier Shay's article, "How I Test Rails Applications."[2]

A Better Testing Experience

Before jumping into the tests, let's take a moment to configure RSpec for the task at hand. The default RSpec setup is minimal by design. But the framework offers a number of suggested settings that are easy to turn on.

---

1. https://martinfowler.com/bliki/UnitTest.html
2. https://rhnh.net/2012/12/20/how-i-test-rails-applications/

Here are a few things RSpec's suggested settings will do for you:

- Run RSpec without any changes to Ruby core classes (zero monkey-patch mode)

- Use the more verbose documentation formatter when you're running just one spec file

- Run your specs in random order

When you start a project with the rspec --init command (as we did in *First Steps*, on page 45), RSpec adds these suggestions to spec/spec_helper.rb but leaves them commented out. To enable them, find and delete the two lines marked =begin and =end.

Although all of these recommended settings are useful, we've actually turned two of them off to generate slightly shorter output for this book. The first one is the warnings setting for extra diagnostic info—great when you're writing a gem, but a little chatty when you're using a gem like Sequel that generates a lot of Ruby warnings.

05-unit-specs/01/expense_tracker/spec/spec_helper.rb
```
# config.warnings = true
```

We've also turned off profile_examples, a feature you already encountered in *Identifying Slow Examples*, on page 20:

05-unit-specs/01/expense_tracker/spec/spec_helper.rb
```
# config.profile_examples = 10
```

Getting a list of slow examples is helpful for large test suites, but we're not quite there with this project yet.

While we're in this file, add the following line inside the RSpec.configure block:

05-unit-specs/01/expense_tracker/spec/spec_helper.rb
```
RSpec.configure do |config|
➤   config.filter_gems_from_backtrace 'rack', 'rack-test', 'sequel', 'sinatra'
```

When a spec fails, the printed backtrace can contain dozens of lines of framework code, obscuring the application code you're looking for. RSpec already filters out its own code from the backtrace, and you can easily filter out other gems as well.[3] You'll have less to read, and you'll find errors more quickly.

---

3. http://rspec.info/documentation/3.6/rspec-core/RSpec/Core/Configuration.html#filter_gems_from_backtrace-instance_method

If you ever need to see the full backtrace, you still can; just pass the --backtrace or -b flag to RSpec.

Take some time to read through the comments inside spec_helper.rb. They explain how the new configuration options will affect your tests. Once you're done, you'll be ready to write some unit tests.

Sketching the Behavior

The behavior you're testing breaks down into a couple of broad categories. You'll want to see what happens when an API call succeeds and when it fails.

Use Unit Specs for Edge Cases

 Unit tests' speed and simplicity make them the perfect place to test all your conditional branches and edge cases. Exhaustively covering all the cases in a slower integration or acceptance test tends to be too inefficient.

Start by sketching out the success case. Create a new file called spec/unit/app/api_spec.rb with the following contents:

```
05-unit-specs/02/expense_tracker/spec/unit/app/api_spec.rb
require_relative '../../../app/api'

module ExpenseTracker
  RSpec.describe API do
    describe 'POST /expenses' do
      context 'when the expense is successfully recorded' do
        it 'returns the expense id'
        it 'responds with a 200 (OK)'
      end

      # ... next context will go here...
    end
  end
end
```

The context block groups these two success-related specs together and allows you to share common setup code between them.

Now, add a second context. This one will handle the failure case:

```
05-unit-specs/02/expense_tracker/spec/unit/app/api_spec.rb
context 'when the expense fails validation' do
  it 'returns an error message'
  it 'responds with a 422 (Unprocessable entity)'
end
```

This is enough content to get started. Run your suite now, and RSpec will report these test cases as pending:

```
$ bundle exec rspec spec/unit/app/api_spec.rb
```

Randomized with seed 34086

ExpenseTracker::API
  POST /expenses
    when the expense fails validation
      returns an error message (PENDING: Not yet implemented)
      responds with a 422 (Unprocessable entity) (PENDING: Not yet   ↵
      implemented)
    when the expense is successfully recorded
      responds with a 200 (OK) (PENDING: Not yet implemented)
      returns the expense id (PENDING: Not yet implemented)

≪ truncated ≫

Finished in 0.00107 seconds (files took 0.15832 seconds to load)
4 examples, 0 failures, 4 pending

Randomized with seed 34086

It's time to fill in the behavior.

Filling In the First Spec

You don't have any classes or methods yet for indicating whether recording an expense succeeded or failed. Let's take a moment to sketch out what that code would look like.

Connecting to Storage

First, you'll need some kind of storage engine that keeps the expense history; call it a Ledger. The simplest approach would be for the API class to create a Ledger instance directly:

05-unit-specs/03/expense_tracker/api_snippets.rb
```ruby
class API < Sinatra::Base
  def initialize
    @ledger = Ledger.new
    super() # rest of initialization from Sinatra
  end
end

# Later, callers do this:
app = API.new
```

But this style limits the code's flexibility and testability, as it doesn't allow you to use a substitute ledger for custom behavior. Instead, consider structuring the code so that callers pass an object filling the Ledger role into the API initializer:

```
05-unit-specs/03/expense_tracker/api_snippets.rb
class API < Sinatra::Base
  def initialize(ledger:)
    @ledger = ledger
    super()
  end
end

# Later, callers do this:
app = API.new(ledger: Ledger.new)
```

This technique—passing in collaborating objects instead of hard-coding them—is known as *dependency injection* (*DI* for short). This phrase conjures up nightmares of verbose Java frameworks and incomprehensible XML files for some folks. But as the previous snippet shows, DI in Ruby is as simple as passing an argument to a method. And with it, you get several advantages:

- Explicit dependencies: they're documented right there in the signature of initialize

- Code that's easier to reason about (no global state)

- Libraries that are easier to drop into another project

- More testable code

One disadvantage of the way we've sketched the code here is that callers *always* have to pass in an object to record expenses. We'd like callers to be able just to say API.new in the common case. Fortunately, we can have our cake and eat it too. All we have to do is give the parameter a default value. Add the following code to app/api.rb, just inside your API class:

```
05-unit-specs/03/expense_tracker/app/api.rb
def initialize(ledger: Ledger.new)
  @ledger = ledger
  super()
end
```

When the HTTP POST request arrives, the API class will tell the Ledger to record() the expense. The return value of record() should indicate status and error information:

```
05-unit-specs/03/expense_tracker/api_snippets.rb
# Pseudocode for what happens inside the API class:
#
result = @ledger.record({ 'some' => 'data' })
result.success?      # => a Boolean
result.expense_id    # => a number
result.error_message # => a string or nil
```

It's not time to write the Ledger class yet. You're not testing its behavior here; you're testing the API class. Instead, you'll need something to stand in for a Ledger instance. Specifically, you'll need a *test double*.

Test Doubles: Mocks, Stubs, and Others

A test double is an object that stands in for another one during a test. Testers tend to refer to them as *mocks*, *stubs*, *fakes*, or *spies*, depending on how they are used. RSpec supports all of these uses under the umbrella term of *doubles*. We'll explain the differences in *Understanding Test Doubles*, or you can read Martin Fowler's article "Test Doubles" for a quick summary.[4]

To create a stand-in for an instance of a particular class, you'll use RSpec's instance_double method, and pass it the name of the class you're imitating (this class need not actually exist yet). Since you'll need to access this phony Ledger instance from all of your specs, you'll define it using a let construct, just like you did with the sandwich object in the first chapter.

There are a couple of other additions to make to your spec, which we've highlighted for you. Alter api_spec.rb to the following structure:

```
05-unit-specs/03/expense_tracker/spec/unit/app/api_spec.rb
require_relative '../../../app/api'
➤ require 'rack/test'

module ExpenseTracker
➤   RecordResult = Struct.new(:success?, :expense_id, :error_message)

    RSpec.describe API do
➤     include Rack::Test::Methods
➤
➤     def app
➤       API.new(ledger: ledger)
➤     end
➤
➤     let(:ledger) { instance_double('ExpenseTracker::Ledger') }

      describe 'POST /expenses' do
        context 'when the expense is successfully recorded' do
          # ... specs go here ...
        end

        context 'when the expense fails validation' do
          # ... specs go here ...
        end
      end
    end
end
```

---

4. https://martinfowler.com/bliki/TestDouble.html

As with the acceptance specs, you'll be using Rack::Test to route HTTP requests to the API class. The other big change is packaging up the status information in a simple RecordResult class. Eventually, we'll move this definition into the application code. But that can wait until we've defined Ledger.

Use Value Objects at Layer Boundaries

 The seam between layers is where integration bugs hide. Using a simple value object like a RecordResult or Struct between layers makes it easier to isolate code and trust your tests. See Gary Bernhardt's excellent "Boundaries" talk for more details.[5]

Now, you're ready to fill in the body of the first example. Inside the first context, find the empty 'returns the expense id' spec that you sketched out earlier. Change it to the following code:

```
05-unit-specs/03/expense_tracker/spec/unit/app/api_spec.rb
it 'returns the expense id' do
  expense = { 'some' => 'data' }

➤ allow(ledger).to receive(:record)
➤   .with(expense)
➤   .and_return(RecordResult.new(true, 417, nil))

  post '/expenses', JSON.generate(expense)

  parsed = JSON.parse(last_response.body)
  expect(parsed).to include('expense_id' => 417)
end
```

On the highlighted lines, we're calling the allow method from rspec-mocks. This method configures the test double's behavior: when the caller (the API class) invokes record, the double will return a new RecordResult instance indicating a successful posting.

Another thing to note: The expense hash we're passing doesn't look anything like valid data. In the live app, the incoming data will look more like { 'payee' => ..., 'amount' => ..., 'date' => ... }. This is okay; the whole point of the Ledger test double is that it will return a canned success or failure response, no matter the input.

Having data that looks obviously fake can actually be a big help. You'll never mistake it for the real thing in your test output and waste time wondering, "How did *this* expense result in *that* report?"

Run your specs; they should fail, because the API behavior is not implemented yet:

---

5. https://www.destroyallsoftware.com/talks/boundaries

```
$ bundle exec rspec spec/unit/app/api_spec.rb
« truncated »
```

Failures:

```
  1) ExpenseTracker::API POST /expenses when the expense is successfully     ↩
  recorded returns the expense id
     Failure/Error: expect(parsed).to include('expense_id' => 417)

       expected {"expense_id" => 42} to include {"expense_id" => 417}
       Diff:
       @@ -1,2 +1,2 @@
       -"expense_id" => 417,
       +"expense_id" => 42,

     # ./spec/unit/app/api_spec.rb:30:in `block (4 levels) in              ↩
     <module:ExpenseTracker>'
```

```
Finished in 0.03784 seconds (files took 0.16365 seconds to load)
4 examples, 1 failure, 3 pending
```

Failed examples:

```
rspec ./spec/unit/app/api_spec.rb:20 # ExpenseTracker::API POST /expenses     ↩
when the expense is successfully recorded returns the expense id
```

Randomized with seed 56373

Once you have a failing spec, it's time to fill in the implementation.

Handling Success

To pass this spec, the /expenses route of our API needs to do three things:

- Parse an expense from the request body

- Use its Ledger (either a real database-based one or a fake one for testing) to record the expense

- Return a JSON document containing the resulting expense ID

Change your /expenses route inside app/api.rb to the following code:

05-unit-specs/03/expense_tracker/app/api.rb
```
post '/expenses' do
  expense = JSON.parse(request.body.read)
  result = @ledger.record(expense)
  JSON.generate('expense_id' => result.expense_id)
end
```

Now, rerun the specs:

```
$ bundle exec rspec spec/unit/app/api_spec.rb
« truncated »
```

```
Finished in 0.02645 seconds (files took 0.14491 seconds to load)
4 examples, 0 failures, 3 pending
```

Randomized with seed 23924

The API is now correctly recording the expense and returning the result we expect.

Now that we know the app is returning the expense ID correctly, let's move on to the next bit of behavior: rendering the correct HTTP status code. Fill in the body of the 'responds with a 200 (OK)' spec as follows:

05-unit-specs/04/expense_tracker/spec/unit/app/api_spec.rb
```ruby
it 'responds with a 200 (OK)' do
  expense = { 'some' => 'data' }

  allow(ledger).to receive(:record)
    .with(expense)
    .and_return(RecordResult.new(true, 417, nil))

  post '/expenses', JSON.generate(expense)
  expect(last_response.status).to eq(200)
end
```

Go ahead and run this spec file:

```
$ bundle exec rspec spec/unit/app/api_spec.rb
```

Randomized with seed 55289

```
ExpenseTracker::API
  POST /expenses
    when the expense is successfully recorded
      returns the expense id
      responds with a 200 (OK)
    when the expense fails validation
      responds with a 422 (Unprocessable entity) (PENDING: Not yet    ↩
      implemented)
      returns an error message (PENDING: Not yet implemented)
```

≪ truncated ≫

```
Finished in 0.02565 seconds (files took 0.12232 seconds to load)
4 examples, 0 failures, 2 pending
```

Randomized with seed 55289

It passes, because Sinatra returns a 200 HTTP status code unless an error occurs or you explicitly set one. That should make you wonder whether or not the test actually works. Let's temporarily break the app code to make sure the test will catch it:

Always See Your Specs Fail

Tests, like implementation code, can contain bugs, but we don't have tests for our tests! So, check each test by making it go red, confirming it fails the way you expect, and making it pass.

05-unit-specs/04/expense_tracker/app/api.rb

```ruby
post '/expenses' do
  status 404

  expense = JSON.parse(request.body.read)
  result = @ledger.record(expense)
  JSON.generate('expense_id' => result.expense_id)
end
```

Now, rerunning the spec fails as expected:

```
$ bundle exec rspec spec/unit/app/api_spec.rb
« truncated »

Failures:

  1) ExpenseTracker::API POST /expenses when the expense is successfully    ↩
  recorded responds with a 200 (OK)
     Failure/Error: expect(last_response.status).to eq(200)

       expected: 200
            got: 404

       (compared using ==)
     # ./spec/unit/app/api_spec.rb:41:in `block (4 levels) in              ↩
     <module:ExpenseTracker>'

Finished in 0.03479 seconds (files took 0.14115 seconds to load)
4 examples, 1 failure, 2 pending

Failed examples:

rspec ./spec/unit/app/api_spec.rb:33 # ExpenseTracker::API POST /expenses    ↩
when the expense is successfully recorded responds with a 200 (OK)

Randomized with seed 32399
```

Make sure you un-break the app before continuing. Once you do that, you'll be back to two passing specs. Now, we can turn our attention to test maintainability. There's a lot of duplicated code in these two test cases. Before moving on to the next section, consider how you might make the code a little less repetitive.

Refactor While Green

It's tempting to start factoring out duplicate code while you're still writing your specs. Avoid that temptation: get your specs passing first, and *then* refactor. That way, you can use your specs to check your refactoring.

Refactoring

Both test cases have identical expressions setting up the ledger test double. You can remove the duplication by moving these into a common before hook. Place the following code just inside the first context block:

05-unit-specs/05/expense_tracker/spec/unit/app/api_spec.rb
```ruby
let(:expense) { { 'some' => 'data' } }

before do
  allow(ledger).to receive(:record)
    .with(expense)
    .and_return(RecordResult.new(true, 417, nil))
end
```

Now, remove the setup code from both examples:

05-unit-specs/05/expense_tracker/spec/unit/app/api_spec.rb
```ruby
it 'returns the expense id' do
  post '/expenses', JSON.generate(expense)

  parsed = JSON.parse(last_response.body)
  expect(parsed).to include('expense_id' => 417)
end

it 'responds with a 200 (OK)' do
  post '/expenses', JSON.generate(expense)
  expect(last_response.status).to eq(200)
end
```

These refactored specs report "just the facts" of the expected behavior. When a POST request arrives, the body should contain the expense ID returned by our ledger and the response code should be 200.

The examples are a little more DRY now ("Don't Repeat Yourself," an approach explained in the book *The Pragmatic Programmer [HT00]*). It may be tempting to DRY them up even further by also moving the post '/expenses' ... lines into the before hook. Such a move would be overkill, though.

Putting the post in the before hook will likely get in the way of future specs for this context. For instance, adding support for XML clients would require a different HTTP header. If you send the HTTP request from your setup code, you won't be able to tweak the headers for just your XML examples.

Keep Setup and Test Code Separate

Consider the traditional three steps of testing: *arrange*, *act*, and *assert*. Moving just the arrange (setup) step into a before hook makes it clear what is and isn't part of the behavior you're testing. You still retain the flexibility to add additional setup code for individual specs that need it.

Handling Failure

Now that your specs are testing the "happy path" of a successful expense, let's turn our attention to the failure case. You can apply the hard-won knowledge from the previous sections, and start with an already-factored before hook. Here, the setup code will fill the RecordResult value object with a false success status and an error message:

05-unit-specs/06/expense_tracker/spec/unit/app/api_spec.rb
```
context 'when the expense fails validation' do
  let(:expense) { { 'some' => 'data' } }

  before do
    allow(ledger).to receive(:record)
      .with(expense)
      .and_return(RecordResult.new(false, 417, 'Expense incomplete'))
  end

  it 'returns an error message' do
    post '/expenses', JSON.generate(expense)

    parsed = JSON.parse(last_response.body)
    expect(parsed).to include('error' => 'Expense incomplete')
  end

  it 'responds with a 422 (Unprocessable entity)' do
    post '/expenses', JSON.generate(expense)
    expect(last_response.status).to eq(422)
  end
end
end
```

The expectations in the examples are different, too; they're checking for an error message in the body and an HTTP error code.

These new specs will fail when you run them, as the behavior isn't implemented yet:

```
$ bundle exec rspec spec/unit/app/api_spec.rb
« truncated »

Failures:

  1) ExpenseTracker::API POST /expenses when the expense fails validation    ↵
  returns an error message
```

```
      Failure/Error: expect(parsed).to include('error' => 'Expense    ↩
      incomplete')

        expected {"expense_id" => 417} to include {"error" => "Expense    ↩
        incomplete"}
        Diff:
        @@ -1,2 +1,2 @@
        -"error" => "Expense incomplete",
        +"expense_id" => 417,

      # ./spec/unit/app/api_spec.rb:52:in `block (4 levels) in    ↩
      <module:ExpenseTracker>'

  2) ExpenseTracker::API POST /expenses when the expense fails validation    ↩
  responds with a 422 (Unprocessable entity)
      Failure/Error: expect(last_response.status).to eq(422)

        expected: 422
            got: 200

        (compared using ==)
      # ./spec/unit/app/api_spec.rb:57:in `block (4 levels) in    ↩
      <module:ExpenseTracker>'

Finished in 0.03552 seconds (files took 0.13746 seconds to load)
4 examples, 2 failures

Failed examples:

rspec ./spec/unit/app/api_spec.rb:48 # ExpenseTracker::API POST /expenses    ↩
when the expense fails validation returns an error message
rspec ./spec/unit/app/api_spec.rb:55 # ExpenseTracker::API POST /expenses    ↩
when the expense fails validation responds with a 422 (Unprocessable entity)

Randomized with seed 8222
```

The POST route needs to check the success? flag of the RecordResult and set the HTTP status and body accordingly. Open up app/api.rb and change the post '/expenses' route to the following:

05-unit-specs/07/expense_tracker/app/api.rb
```ruby
post '/expenses' do
  expense = JSON.parse(request.body.read)
  result = @ledger.record(expense)

  if result.success?
    JSON.generate('expense_id' => result.expense_id)
  else
    status 422
    JSON.generate('error' => result.error_message)
  end
end
```

Rerun your specs, and make sure they pass. Then, go back and take a peek at the latest iteration of your unit specs. Notice how the test doubles define the interface that the Ledger class needs to provide. Before we finish off this chapter, let's sketch out the Ledger class.

Defining the Ledger

We'll start with an empty Ledger class. In your project directory, create a new file called app/ledger.rb with the following contents:

05-unit-specs/08/expense_tracker/app/ledger.rb
```
module ExpenseTracker
  RecordResult = Struct.new(:success?, :expense_id, :error_message)

  class Ledger
  end
end
```

Notice we've also moved the temporary RecordResult struct definition from earlier into its permanent home here. Don't forget to delete the old version of RecordResult from spec/unit/app/api_spec.rb.

You'll need to require this new file from app/api.rb:

05-unit-specs/08/expense_tracker/app/api.rb
```
require_relative 'ledger'
```

The specs you have so far are still using the fake ledger. They passed without a real Ledger class defined, so you might expect them to keep passing now that we have one. Go ahead and try it:

```
$ bundle exec rspec spec/unit/app/api_spec.rb
« truncated »

Failures:

  1) ExpenseTracker::API POST /expenses when the expense is successfully    ↩
  recorded returns the expense id
     Failure/Error:
       allow(ledger).to receive(:record)
         .with(expense)
         .and_return(RecordResult.new(true, 417, nil))

       the ExpenseTracker::Ledger class does not implement the instance      ↩
       method: record
     # ./spec/unit/app/api_spec.rb:19:in `block (4 levels) in              ↩
     <module:ExpenseTracker>'

« truncated »

Finished in 0.00783 seconds (files took 0.13142 seconds to load)
4 examples, 4 failures
```

```
Failed examples:
```

```
rspec ./spec/unit/app/api_spec.rb:24 # ExpenseTracker::API POST /expenses    ↵
when the expense is successfully recorded returns the expense id
rspec ./spec/unit/app/api_spec.rb:31 # ExpenseTracker::API POST /expenses    ↵
when the expense is successfully recorded responds with a 200 (OK)
rspec ./spec/unit/app/api_spec.rb:53 # ExpenseTracker::API POST /expenses    ↵
when the expense fails validation responds with a 422 (Unprocessable entity)
rspec ./spec/unit/app/api_spec.rb:46 # ExpenseTracker::API POST /expenses    ↵
when the expense fails validation returns an error message
```

```
Randomized with seed 40684
```

Notice the complaint: the ExpenseTracker::Ledger class does not implement the instance method: record. The specs are failing because the real Ledger class doesn't act enough like the fake one.

You've just encountered a feature of RSpec called *verifying doubles*. They help prevent *fragile mocks*, a problem where specs pass when they should be failing.

Recall that test doubles mimic the interface of a real object. When the real object's method names or parameters change, a traditional test double will still respond to the old methods. It's easy to forget to update your specs when this happens.

RSpec's verifying doubles actually inspect the real object they're standing in for and fail the test if the method signatures don't match. You'll learn more about them in *Verifying Doubles*, on page 243.

Let's follow the guidance of the error message and add an empty record method to Ledger:

```
05-unit-specs/09/expense_tracker/app/ledger.rb
def record
end
```

Now, rerun the spec:

```
$ bundle exec rspec spec/unit/app/api_spec.rb
« truncated »
```

```
Failures:
```

```
  1) ExpenseTracker::API POST /expenses when the expense is successfully    ↵
  recorded responds with a 200 (OK)
     Failure/Error:
       allow(ledger).to receive(:record)
         .with(expense)
         .and_return(RecordResult.new(true, 417, nil))

     Wrong number of arguments. Expected 0, got 1.
     # ./spec/unit/app/api_spec.rb:19:in `block (4 levels) in    ↵
     <module:ExpenseTracker>'
```

《 *truncated* 》

Finished in 0.00762 seconds (files took 0.12669 seconds to load)
4 examples, 4 failures

Failed examples:

rspec ./spec/unit/app/api_spec.rb:31 # ExpenseTracker::API POST /expenses ↵
when the expense is successfully recorded responds with a 200 (OK)
rspec ./spec/unit/app/api_spec.rb:24 # ExpenseTracker::API POST /expenses ↵
when the expense is successfully recorded returns the expense id
rspec ./spec/unit/app/api_spec.rb:53 # ExpenseTracker::API POST /expenses ↵
when the expense fails validation responds with a 422 (Unprocessable entity)
rspec ./spec/unit/app/api_spec.rb:46 # ExpenseTracker::API POST /expenses ↵
when the expense fails validation returns an error message

Randomized with seed 8060

The error message has changed to Wrong number of arguments. Expected 0, got 1.
RSpec sees the new record method, but points out that it doesn't take an
argument like the test double does.

Make the method signatures match by adding a parameter:

05-unit-specs/10/expense_tracker/app/ledger.rb
```
def record(expense)
end
```

When you run the specs again, they should pass.

```
$ bundle exec rspec spec/unit/app/api_spec.rb
```
《 *truncated* 》

Finished in 0.0266 seconds (files took 0.13459 seconds to load)
4 examples, 0 failures

Randomized with seed 13686

A mock object guiding the interface for a real one—how's that for life imitating
art? Now that you've got green specs, commit your work and take a well-
deserved break. In the next chapter, you'll fill in the behavior behind the
interface.

Your Turn

In this chapter, you've clarified exactly how your API is supposed to behave.
You've spelled out what happens when storing an expense record succeeds
or fails, using a test double to stand in for the unwritten persistence layer.
You've refactored your specs so that they spell out exactly what behavior
you're testing. Finally, you've used the design suggested by your tests to guide
the interface of a real object.

Now, it's time to put these new skills to the test. *Don't skip this one;* you're going to build on this work in the next chapter.

Exercises

In these exercises, you're going to implement another key piece of your application at the routing layer. Along the way, you'll be looking for opportunities to share code.

Reducing Duplication

Search through your unit specs for JSON.parse; you will see several snippets that look like this:

05-unit-specs/11/expense_tracker/spec/unit/api_example_spec.rb
```
parsed = JSON.parse(last_response.body)
expect(parsed).to do_something
```

We're repeatedly grabbing the last_response from Rack::Test, and then parsing it from JSON. Find a way to reduce this duplicated logic.

Implementing the GET Route

Through this chapter, we built a spec for the POST route together. Now, it's time to build one for the GET route and make it pass. This will be much easier than the POST version; all the pieces are already in place.

The goal is to be able to hit a URL containing a date:

```
get '/expenses/2017-06-12'
```

...and get back JSON data containing whatever expenses were recorded on that day.

First, add the following outline to spec/unit/app/api_spec.rb, *inside* the RSpec.describe API block:

05-unit-specs/11/expense_tracker/spec/unit/app/api_spec.rb
```
describe 'GET /expenses/:date' do
  context 'when expenses exist on the given date' do
    it 'returns the expense records as JSON'
    it 'responds with a 200 (OK)'
  end

  context 'when there are no expenses on the given date' do
    it 'returns an empty array as JSON'
    it 'responds with a 200 (OK)'
  end
end
```

Fill in the body of each example one by one. You'll need to consider the following questions:

- What test doubles or other objects will you need to set up?

- What will the expected JSON look like when there are expenses recorded on the given date?

- What underlying data will your test doubles need to supply in order for you to return the correct JSON?

- How do the answers to the two previous questions change when there are no expenses in the ledger for that date?

Hint: Your Ledger class will need a method that returns expenses on a specific date. We suggest the name expenses_on for this method; the examples in the next chapter will use that name. (You won't need to fill in the body of expenses_on until the next chapter.)

Look to the work you've already done in this chapter for ideas on how to structure your setup code and expectations. If you get stuck, have a look at the source code for this chapter. But do your best to finish this exercise. The next chapter will build on the implementation of the GET route that you write for this exercise.

In this chapter, you'll see:

- How to set up a database for testing, without damaging your real data
- Techniques for organizing shared and global setup code
- How to use metadata to control how RSpec runs certain specs
- How to diagnose an ordering dependency between your specs

## CHAPTER 6

Getting Real: Integration Specs

By now, you've got a solid HTTP routing layer designed with the help of unit specs. To write these unit specs, you isolated the code under test. Your specs assumed that the underlying dependencies would eventually be implemented, and provided *test doubles*—fake versions for the test.

Now, it's time to write those dependencies for real. In this chapter, you're going to implement the Ledger class as the bottom layer of the app. You'll write code to store expense records into a database. You'll create powerful *integration specs* to make sure the data's really getting stored:

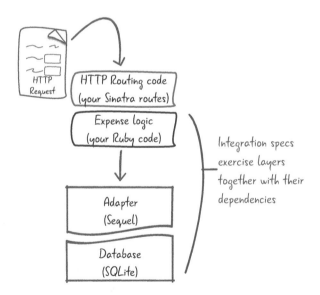

By the end of the chapter, not only will your integration specs work, but so will the end-to-end acceptance specs you began this project with.

Hooking Up the Database

We've put off implementing the database layer for as long as we could. But with the rest of the surrounding layers defined, it's all that's left.

Getting to Know Sequel

For this exercise, you're going to use a Ruby database library called Sequel. Sequel allows you to create tables, add data, and so on, without tying your code to any specific database product. You'll still need to *choose* a database, though, and for this project the low-maintenance SQLite library will do fine.[1]

Go ahead and add the following two lines to your Gemfile:

06-integration-specs/01/expense_tracker/Gemfile
```
gem 'sequel',    '4.48.0'
gem 'sqlite3',   '1.3.13'
```

Now, rerun Bundler to install the new libraries:

```
$ bundle install
Fetching gem metadata from https://rubygems.org/.........
Fetching version metadata from https://rubygems.org/..
Resolving dependencies...
Using bundler 1.15.3
Using coderay 1.1.1
Using diff-lcs 1.3
Using mustermann 1.0.0
Using rack 2.0.3
Using rspec-support 3.6.0
Fetching sequel 4.48.0
Installing sequel 4.48.0
Using tilt 2.0.7
Fetching sqlite3 1.3.13
Installing sqlite3 1.3.13 with native extensions
Using rack-protection 2.0.0
Using rack-test 0.7.0
Using rspec-core 3.6.0
Using rspec-expectations 3.6.0
Using rspec-mocks 3.6.0
Using sinatra 2.0.0
Using rspec 3.6.0
Bundle complete! 6 Gemfile dependencies, 16 gems now installed.
Use `bundle info [gemname]` to see where a bundled gem is installed.
```

Once Sequel and SQLite are installed, you're ready to use them. In our application, you'll eventually do the following:

---

1.   https://sqlite.org

- Load the Sequel library
- Create a database connection
- Create an expenses table so we have a place to store our records
- Insert records into the expenses table
- Query records from the expenses table

That's quite a task list, but the APIs to perform these steps are simple. In fact, the first example from the Sequel homepage provides a short code snippet that shows how to do all of these![2] If you're following along, we encourage you to launch an IRB session and try all these steps based on the example:

```
>> require 'sequel'
=> true
>> DB = Sequel.sqlite
=> #<Sequel::SQLite::Database: {:adapter=>:sqlite}>
>> DB.create_table(:gems) { String :name }
=> nil
>> DB[:gems].insert(name: 'rspec')
=> 1
>> DB[:gems].insert(name: 'sinatra')
=> 2
>> DB[:gems].all
=> [{:name=>"rspec"}, {:name=>"sinatra"}]
```

Now that you're familiar with the APIs, you're ready to create some databases.

Creating a Database

You'll want to create separate SQLite databases for testing, development, and production (so that you don't clobber your real data during testing).

An environment variable is the easiest way to configure separate databases for this app. In *Getting Started*, on page 47, you used the RACK_ENV variable to indicate which environment the code was running in. Let's piggyback off that work. Create a new file called config/sequel.rb with the following code:

```
06-integration-specs/03/expense_tracker/config/sequel.rb
require 'sequel'
DB = Sequel.sqlite("./db/#{ENV.fetch('RACK_ENV', 'development')}.db")
```

This configuration will create a database file such as db/test.db or db/production.db depending on the RACK_ENV environment variable. Note that you're assigning the database connection to a top-level DB constant; this is the Sequel convention when there's just one global database.[3]

---

2.   http://sequel.jeremyevans.net
3.   http://sequel.jeremyevans.net/rdoc/files/doc/opening_databases_rdoc.html

With this configuration in place, you don't have to worry about accidentally overwriting your production data during testing.

Now, it's time to think about the structure of your data. Each expense item will need several pieces of information:

- A unique ID
- Name of the payee
- Amount
- Date

You'll use a Sequel *migration* to create the table structure that holds this information.[4] You can put migration files anywhere, but a common convention is to keep them in db/migrations. Add the following code to db/migrations/0001_create_expenses.rb:

```
06-integration-specs/03/expense_tracker/db/migrations/0001_create_expenses.rb
Sequel.migration do
  change do
    create_table :expenses do
      primary_key :id
      String :payee
      Float :amount
      Date :date
    end
  end
end
```

To apply this migration to your database, you'll need to tell Sequel to run it. In a minute, you'll configure RSpec to do so automatically every time you run your integration tests. For now, try running this migration against the development database. To do so, you can use the sequel command that ships with the Sequel library:

```
$ bundle exec sequel -m ./db/migrations sqlite://db/development.db --echo
« truncated »

I, [2017-06-13T13:34:25.536511 #14630]  INFO -- : Finished applying        ↩
migration version 1, direction: up, took 0.001514 seconds
```

Now that you've configured Sequel, it's time to write some specs.

Testing Ledger Behavior

We've seen how to run Sequel migrations manually from the command line. You'll need to configure RSpec to run them automatically, so that the database structure is in place before your first integration spec runs.

---

4.   http://sequel.jeremyevans.net/rdoc/files/doc/migration_rdoc.html

The following code will make sure the database structure is set up and empty, ready for your specs to add data to it:

```
Sequel.extension :migration
Sequel::Migrator.run(DB, 'db/migrations')
DB[:expenses].truncate
```

First, we run all the migration files in to make sure that all the database tables exist with their current schema. Then, we remove any leftover test data from the table using the truncate method. That way, each run of the spec suite starts with a clean database—no matter what happened before.

The only problem is that it's not obvious where to put these lines. Up to this point, you've tended to keep setup routines like this in one of two places:

- The top of a single spec file
- The global spec_helper.rb file

Database migrations sit somewhere in between these two extremes. We want to load them for any spec that touches the database, but not for unit specs—those need to stay snappy, even as our database migrations grow over the lifetime of the application.

The RSpec convention for this kind of "partially shared" code is to put it in a folder called spec/support; then we can load it from whatever spec files need it. Create a new file called spec/support/db.rb with the following content:

```
06-integration-specs/03/expense_tracker/spec/support/db.rb
RSpec.configure do |c|
  c.before(:suite) do
    Sequel.extension :migration
    Sequel::Migrator.run(DB, 'db/migrations')
    DB[:expenses].truncate
  end
end
```

This snippet defines a *suite-level hook*. We first encountered before hooks in *Hooks*, on page 9. A typical hook will run before each example. This one will run just once: after all the specs have been *loaded*, but before the first one actually *runs*. That's what before(:suite) hooks are for.

Bootstrap Your Environment for Easy Testing

 Your spec suite should set up the test database for you, rather than requiring you to run a separate setup task. People testing your code (including you!) can easily forget to run the extra step, or might not even know they need to.

Now that we have defined our hook, we are ready to define our spec and load the support file. Create a file called spec/integration/app/ledger_spec.rb with the following code:

06-integration-specs/03/expense_tracker/spec/integration/app/ledger_spec.rb
```ruby
require_relative '../../../app/ledger'
require_relative '../../../config/sequel'
require_relative '../../support/db'

module ExpenseTracker
  RSpec.describe Ledger do
    let(:ledger) { Ledger.new }
    let(:expense) do
      {
        'payee'  => 'Starbucks',
        'amount' => 5.75,
        'date'   => '2017-06-10'
      }
    end

    describe '#record' do
      # ... contexts go here ...
    end
  end
end
```

The :ledger and :expense setup will be the same for each example, so we've used let to initialize this data.

Now, it's time to spell out the behavior we want in the first example. We want to tell the ledger to save the expense, and then actually read the database from disk and make sure the expense really got saved:

06-integration-specs/03/expense_tracker/spec/integration/app/ledger_spec.rb
```ruby
context 'with a valid expense' do
  it 'successfully saves the expense in the DB' do
    result = ledger.record(expense)

    expect(result).to be_success
    expect(DB[:expenses].all).to match [a_hash_including(
      id: result.expense_id,
      payee: 'Starbucks',
      amount: 5.75,
      date: Date.iso8601('2017-06-10')
    )]
  end
end
```

We're using a couple of new matchers here. The first, be_success, simply checks that result.success? is true. This matcher is built into RSpec; you'll learn more about it in *Dynamic Predicates*, on page 194.

The second matcher, match [a_hash_including(...)], expects our app to return data matching a certain structure; in this case, a one-element array of hashes with certain keys and values. This expression is another use of RSpec's *composable matchers*; here, you're passing the a_hash_including matcher into the match one.

We're deviating a bit from general TDD practice in this snippet. Normally, each example would only have one expectation in it—otherwise, one failure can mask another. Here, we've got two expectations in the same example.

There's a bit of a trade-off to consider here. Any spec that touches the database is going to be slower, particularly in its setup and teardown steps. If we follow "one expectation per example" too rigorously, we're going to be repeating that setup and teardown many times. By judiciously combining a couple of assertions, we're keeping our suite speedy.

Let's see what we're giving up to get this performance boost. Go ahead and run your specs:

```
$ bundle exec rspec spec/integration/app/ledger_spec.rb
« truncated »
```

```
Failures:

  1) ExpenseTracker::Ledger#record with a valid expense successfully saves ↵
  the expense in the DB
     Failure/Error: expect(result).to be_success
       expected nil to respond to `success?`
     # ./spec/integration/app/ledger_spec.rb:23:in `block (4 levels) in ↵
     <module:ExpenseTracker>'

Finished in 0.02211 seconds (files took 0.15418 seconds to load)
1 example, 1 failure
```

```
Failed examples:

rspec ./spec/integration/app/ledger_spec.rb:20 #                         ↵
ExpenseTracker::Ledger#record with a valid expense successfully saves the ↵
expense in the DB
```

```
Randomized with seed 27984
```

As you'd expect, the spec failed on the first assertion. We never even see the second assertion, because by default, RSpec aborts the test on the first failure.

It would be nice to record the first failure, but continue to try the second expectation. Good news! The :aggregate_failures tag does just that. Change your example declaration to the following:

06-integration-specs/04/expense_tracker/spec/integration/app/ledger_spec.rb
```
it 'successfully saves the expense in the DB', :aggregate_failures do
```

Now, RSpec's output shows both failures underneath a description of the example:

```
$ bundle exec rspec spec/integration/app/ledger_spec.rb
« truncated »
```

Failures:

```
  1) ExpenseTracker::Ledger#record with a valid expense successfully saves  ↵
  the expense in the DB
     Got 1 failure and 1 other error:

    1.1) Failure/Error: expect(result).to be_success
           expected nil to respond to `success?`
         # ./spec/integration/app/ledger_spec.rb:23:in `block (4 levels)   ↵
         in <module:ExpenseTracker>'

    1.2) Failure/Error: id: result.expense_id,

         NoMethodError:
           undefined method `expense_id' for nil:NilClass
         # ./spec/integration/app/ledger_spec.rb:25:in `block (4 levels)   ↵
         in <module:ExpenseTracker>'
```

```
Finished in 0.02142 seconds (files took 0.15952 seconds to load)
1 example, 1 failure
```

Failed examples:

```
rspec ./spec/integration/app/ledger_spec.rb:20 #                          ↵
ExpenseTracker::Ledger#record with a valid expense successfully saves the  ↵
expense in the DB
```

```
Randomized with seed 41929
```

We're likely to want our other integration tests to get this benefit. Move the :aggregate_failures property up one level from the example to the group:

06-integration-specs/05/expense_tracker/spec/integration/app/ledger_spec.rb
```
RSpec.describe Ledger, :aggregate_failures do
```

RSpec refers to these properties of specs as *metadata*. When you define metadata—arbitrary symbols or hashes—on an example group, all the examples in that group inherit it, as do any nested groups. We previously saw an example of metadata being specified as a hash in *Tag Filtering*, on page 25. Here we are defining our metadata using just a symbol as a shortcut. Internally, RSpec expands this into a hash like { aggregate_failures: true }.

Now, it's time to fill in the behavior. The Ledger class's record method needs to store the expense in the database, then return a RecordResult indicating what happened:

06-integration-specs/06/expense_tracker/app/ledger.rb
```
def record(expense)
```

```
  DB[:expenses].insert(expense)
  id = DB[:expenses].max(:id)
  RecordResult.new(true, id, nil)
end
```

When you rerun RSpec, your integration spec should pass now.

Testing the Invalid Case

So far, our integration spec checks only the "happy path" of saving a valid expense. Let's add a second spec that tries an expense missing a payee:

06-integration-specs/07/expense_tracker/spec/integration/app/ledger_spec.rb
```
context 'when the expense lacks a payee' do
  it 'rejects the expense as invalid' do
    expense.delete('payee')

    result = ledger.record(expense)

    expect(result).not_to be_success
    expect(result.expense_id).to eq(nil)
    expect(result.error_message).to include('`payee` is required')

    expect(DB[:expenses].count).to eq(0)
  end
end
```

Here, the Ledger instance should return the correct failure status and message, and the database should have no expenses in it.

Since this behavior isn't implemented, we want this new spec to fail:

```
$ bundle exec rspec spec/integration/app/ledger_spec.rb
« truncated »

Failures:

  1) ExpenseTracker::Ledger#record when the expense lacks a payee rejects    ↵
  the expense as invalid

« truncated »

  2) ExpenseTracker::Ledger#record with a valid expense successfully saves    ↵
  the expense in the DB

« truncated »

Finished in 0.02597 seconds (files took 0.18213 seconds to load)
2 examples, 2 failures

Failed examples:

rspec ./spec/integration/app/ledger_spec.rb:34 #                             ↵
ExpenseTracker::Ledger#record when the expense lacks a payee rejects the     ↵
expense as invalid
```

```
rspec ./spec/integration/app/ledger_spec.rb:20 #                        ↵
ExpenseTracker::Ledger#record with a valid expense successfully saves the ↵
expense in the DB
```

Randomized with seed 57045

That's strange. *Both* specs failed. Did we break any other specs outside the two we're running here? Try rerunning the entire suite a few times. Your exact output will differ from ours—you might see two failures or just one. Here's a test run with two failures:

```
$ bundle exec rspec
« truncated »

Finished in 0.06926 seconds (files took 0.21812 seconds to load)
11 examples, 2 failures, 1 pending
```

Failed examples:

```
rspec ./spec/integration/app/ledger_spec.rb:20 #                        ↵
ExpenseTracker::Ledger#record with a valid expense successfully saves the ↵
expense in the DB
rspec ./spec/integration/app/ledger_spec.rb:34 #                        ↵
ExpenseTracker::Ledger#record when the expense lacks a payee rejects the ↵
expense as invalid
```

Randomized with seed 32043

The output is slightly different each time you run it, because RSpec is running the specs in random order. This technique—enabled via the config.order = :random line in spec_helper.rb—is useful for finding *order dependencies*; that is, specs whose behavior depends on which one runs first.

Test in Random Order to Find Order Dependencies

 If your specs run in the same order every time, you may have one that's only passing because an earlier, broken one left some state behind. Use your test suite's random ordering option to surface these dependencies.

A *random seed* gives you a specific, repeatable test order. You can replay any such sequence by passing the --seed option to RSpec along with the seed number reported in the output.

For example, RSpec's output tells us that the previous run was using seed 32043. You can replay that specific test order any time you want:

```
$ bundle exec rspec --seed 32043
« truncated »

Finished in 0.05941 seconds (files took 0.22746 seconds to load)
11 examples, 2 failures, 1 pending
```

Failed examples:

```
rspec ./spec/integration/app/ledger_spec.rb:20 #                          ↵
ExpenseTracker::Ledger#record with a valid expense successfully saves the  ↵
expense in the DB
rspec ./spec/integration/app/ledger_spec.rb:34 #                          ↵
ExpenseTracker::Ledger#record when the expense lacks a payee rejects the  ↵
expense as invalid

Randomized with seed 32043
```

While RSpec isn't able to tell you *why* the ordering dependency is happening, it can certainly help you identify *which* specs you need to run to reproduce it.

With the --bisect option, RSpec will systematically run different portions of your suite until it finds the smallest set that triggers a failure:

```
$ bundle exec rspec --bisect --seed 32043
Bisect started using options: "--seed 32043"
Running suite to find failures... (0.45293 seconds)
Starting bisect with 2 failing examples and 9 non-failing examples.
Checking that failure(s) are order-dependent... failure appears to be  ↵
order-dependent

Round 1: bisecting over non-failing examples 1-9 . ignoring examples 1-5  ↵
(0.45132 seconds)
Round 2: bisecting over non-failing examples 6-9 . ignoring examples 6-7  ↵
(0.43739 seconds)
Round 3: bisecting over non-failing examples 8-9 . ignoring example 8  ↵
(0.43102 seconds)
Bisect complete! Reduced necessary non-failing examples from 9 to 1 in 1.64 ↵
seconds.

The minimal reproduction command is:
  rspec './spec/acceptance/expense_tracker_api_spec.rb[1:1]'            ↵
  './spec/integration/app/ledger_spec.rb[1:1:1:1,1:1:2:1]' --seed 32043
```

RSpec has given us a minimal set of specs we can run any time to see the failure:

```
$ bundle exec rspec './spec/acceptance/expense_tracker_api_spec.rb[1:1]'  ↵
'./spec/integration/app/ledger_spec.rb[1:1:1:1,1:1:2:1]' --seed 32043
Run options: include                                                      ↵
{:ids=>{"./spec/acceptance/expense_tracker_api_spec.rb"=>["1:1"],         ↵
"./spec/integration/app/ledger_spec.rb"=>["1:1:1:1", "1:1:2:1"]}}

Randomized with seed 32043
*FF

« truncated »

Finished in 0.0485 seconds (files took 0.21859 seconds to load)
3 examples, 2 failures, 1 pending
```

```
Failed examples:

rspec ./spec/integration/app/ledger_spec.rb:20 #                          ↩
ExpenseTracker::Ledger#record with a valid expense successfully saves the  ↩
expense in the DB
rspec ./spec/integration/app/ledger_spec.rb:34 #                          ↩
ExpenseTracker::Ledger#record when the expense lacks a payee rejects the   ↩
expense as invalid

Randomized with seed 32043
```

The numbers in square brackets are called *example IDs*; they indicate each example's position in its file, relative to other examples and nested groups. For example, some_spec.rb[2:3] would mean "the third example inside the second group in some_spec.rb." You can paste these values into your terminal just as you did with line numbers in *Running Specific Failures*, on page 21.

With this set of specs, we can see that the new spec causes the prior spec to fail if the new one runs first. Our database writes are leaking between tests.

Watch for Test Interaction in Integration Specs

Your integration specs interact with external resources: the file system, the database, the network, and so on. Because these resources are shared, you have to take extra care to restore the system to a clean slate after each spec.

Isolating Your Specs Using Database Transactions

To solve this issue, we're going to wrap each spec in a database transaction. After each example runs, we want RSpec to *roll back* the transaction, canceling any writes that happened and leaving the database in a clean state. Sequel provides a test-friendly method for wrapping code in transactions.[5]

An RSpec around hook would be perfect for this task. You already have a spec/support/db.rb file for database support code, so add it there, inside the RSpec.configure block:

```
06-integration-specs/07/expense_tracker/spec/support/db.rb
c.around(:example, :db) do |example|
  DB.transaction(rollback: :always) { example.run }
end
```

The sequence of calls in the new hook is a bit twisty, so bear with us for a second. For each example marked as requiring the database (via the :db tag; you'll see how to use this in a moment), the following events happen:

---

5.   http://sequel.jeremyevans.net/rdoc/files/doc/testing_rdoc.html

1. RSpec calls our around hook, passing it the example we're running.

2. Inside the hook, we tell Sequel to start a new database transaction.

3. Sequel calls the inner block, in which we tell RSpec to run the example.

4. The body of the example finishes running.

5. Sequel rolls back the transaction, wiping out any changes we made to the database.

6. The around hook finishes, and RSpec moves on to the next example.

We only want to spend time setting up the database when we actually use it. Although starting and rolling back a transaction takes less than a tenth of a second, that dwarfs the runtime of our fast, focused unit specs.

This is where the notion of *tagging* comes in. A tag is a piece of metadata—custom information—attached to an example or group. Here, you'll use a new symbol, :db, to indicate that an example touches the database:

06-integration-specs/07/expense_tracker/spec/integration/an_integration_spec.rb
```
require_relative '../support/db'

RSpec.describe 'An integration spec', :db do
  # ...
end
```

Notice that we've had to do two things to make sure this spec runs inside a database transaction:

- Explicitly load the setup code from support/db
- Tag the example group with :db

If you have several spec files that touch the database, it's easy to forget to do one or the other of these things. The result can be specs that pass or fail inconsistently (depending on when and how you run them).

It'd be nice to be able to tag the database-related example groups with :db and trust that the support code will be loaded as needed. Luckily, RSpec has an option that supports exactly this usage. In your spec_helper.rb, add the following snippet inside the RSpec.configure block:

06-integration-specs/07/expense_tracker/spec/spec_helper.rb
```
RSpec.configure do |config|
➤   config.when_first_matching_example_defined(:db) do
➤     require_relative 'support/db'
➤   end
```

With that hook in place, RSpec will *conditionally* load spec/support/db.rb if (and only if) any examples are loaded that have a :db tag.

Now, you'll need to go add the tag to your specs. Both your acceptance and integration specs need it at the end of the RSpec.describe line, just before the do keyword. First, spec/acceptance/expense_tracker_api_spec.rb:

06-integration-specs/08/expense_tracker/spec/acceptance/expense_tracker_api_spec.rb
```
RSpec.describe 'Expense Tracker API', :db do
```

Next, spec/integration/app/ledger_spec.rb:

06-integration-specs/08/expense_tracker/spec/integration/app/ledger_spec.rb
```
RSpec.describe Ledger, :aggregate_failures, :db do
```

While you're at it, you can also remove the require_relative '../../support/db' line from ledger_spec.rb.

At last, you can run RSpec with the same random seed and get just the single failure we were expecting:

```
$ bundle exec rspec --seed 32043
« truncated »

Finished in 0.05786 seconds (files took 0.22818 seconds to load)
11 examples, 1 failure, 1 pending
```

```
Failed examples:
```

```
rspec ./spec/integration/app/ledger_spec.rb:33 #                        ↵
ExpenseTracker::Ledger#record when the expense lacks a payee rejects the ↵
expense as invalid
```

```
Randomized with seed 32043
```

We're back down to just one spec failing predictably. It's time to continue the Red/Green/Refactor cycle by adding just enough behavior to your object to make the spec pass.

Filling In the Behavior

The failing spec is expecting the Ledger class's record method to return error information if we pass in an invalid expense (one with no payee defined). Add the following highlighted lines to the record definition in app/ledger.rb:

06-integration-specs/08/expense_tracker/app/ledger.rb
```
module ExpenseTracker
  RecordResult = Struct.new(:success?, :expense_id, :error_message)

  class Ledger
    def record(expense)
➤     unless expense.key?('payee')
➤       message = 'Invalid expense: `payee` is required'
```

➤   `return RecordResult.new(false, nil, message)`
➤   `end`

```
      DB[:expenses].insert(expense)
      id = DB[:expenses].max(:id)
      RecordResult.new(true, id, nil)
    end

    def expenses_on(date)
    end
  end
end
```

Rerun your specs; they should all pass. Well done! You've implemented saving a single expense at all layers of the app, from top to bottom.

```
$ bundle exec rspec spec/integration/app/ledger_spec.rb
« truncated »

Finished in 0.01205 seconds (files took 0.15597 seconds to load)
2 examples, 0 failures

Randomized with seed 38450
```

Now that you've got the hang of the process, and have put in all the data and routing infrastructure, the next bit of Ledger behavior will be much easier to implement.

Querying Expenses

Let's turn our attention to the final piece of the puzzle: querying expenses back from the database. First, you'll need a failing spec that records a few expenses into the ledger, with some of the expenses on the same date. Querying for that date should return only the matching expenses.

Add the following specs inside the RSpec.describe block in spec/integration/app/ ledger_spec.rb:

06-integration-specs/09/expense_tracker/spec/integration/app/ledger_spec.rb
```
describe '#expenses_on' do
  it 'returns all expenses for the provided date' do
    result_1 = ledger.record(expense.merge('date' => '2017-06-10'))
    result_2 = ledger.record(expense.merge('date' => '2017-06-10'))
    result_3 = ledger.record(expense.merge('date' => '2017-06-11'))

    expect(ledger.expenses_on('2017-06-10')).to contain_exactly(
      a_hash_including(id: result_1.expense_id),
      a_hash_including(id: result_2.expense_id)
    )
  end
```

```
  it 'returns a blank array when there are no matching expenses' do
    expect(ledger.expenses_on('2017-06-10')).to eq([])
  end
end
```

The overall flow—adding three expenses and then searching for two of them by date—looks similar to what we did in the acceptance spec in *Querying the Data*, on page 54. Here, you're testing at the level of the individual Ledger object, rather than the entire app.

We're using another composable matcher here to combine two matchers you've used before—contain_exactly and a_hash_including—into a new matcher that describes a nested data structure.

Run the spec file to make sure both specs fail:

```
$ bundle exec rspec spec/integration/app/ledger_spec.rb

Randomized with seed 3824

ExpenseTracker::Ledger
  #record
    with a valid expense
      successfully saves the expense in the DB
    when the expense lacks a payee
      rejects the expense as invalid
  #expenses_on
    returns a blank array when there are no matching expenses (FAILED - 1)
    returns all expenses for the provided date (FAILED - 2)

Failures:

  1) ExpenseTracker::Ledger#expenses_on returns a blank array when there     ↵
  are no matching expenses
     Failure/Error: expect(ledger.expenses_on('2017-06-10')).to eq([])

       expected: []
            got: nil

       (compared using ==)
       # ./spec/integration/app/ledger_spec.rb:59:in `block (3 levels) in    ↵
       <module:ExpenseTracker>'
       # ./spec/support/db.rb:9:in `block (3 levels) in <top (required)>'
       # ./spec/support/db.rb:9:in `block (2 levels) in <top (required)>'

  2) ExpenseTracker::Ledger#expenses_on returns all expenses for the         ↵
  provided date
     Failure/Error:
       expect(ledger.expenses_on('2017-06-10')).to contain_exactly(
         a_hash_including(id: result_1.expense_id),
         a_hash_including(id: result_2.expense_id)
       )
```

```
        expected a collection that can be converted to an array with    ↵
          `#to_ary` or `#to_a`, but got nil
      # ./spec/integration/app/ledger_spec.rb:52:in `block (3 levels) in   ↵
      <module:ExpenseTracker>'
      # ./spec/support/db.rb:9:in `block (3 levels) in <top (required)>'
      # ./spec/support/db.rb:9:in `block (2 levels) in <top (required)>'
```

```
Finished in 0.02766 seconds (files took 0.16616 seconds to load)
4 examples, 2 failures
```

```
Failed examples:
```

```
rspec ./spec/integration/app/ledger_spec.rb:58 #                   ↵
ExpenseTracker::Ledger#expenses_on returns a blank array when there are no  ↵
matching expenses
rspec ./spec/integration/app/ledger_spec.rb:47 #                   ↵
ExpenseTracker::Ledger#expenses_on returns all expenses for the provided date
```

```
Randomized with seed 3824
```

Now, you're ready to implement the logic to make the spec pass. The Ledger class will need to query the database's expenses table for rows that have a matching date. You can use Sequel's where method to filter by the date field.

In the exercises at the end of the previous chapter, you defined an empty expenses_on method for the Ledger class. Fill in its body with the following code:

06-integration-specs/09/expense_tracker/app/ledger.rb
```ruby
def expenses_on(date)
  DB[:expenses].where(date: date).all
end
```

Your integration specs should pass now:

```
$ bundle exec rspec spec/integration/app/ledger_spec.rb
```

```
Randomized with seed 22267
```

```
ExpenseTracker::Ledger
  #record
    with a valid expense
      successfully saves the expense in the DB
    when the expense lacks a payee
      rejects the expense as invalid
  #expenses_on
    returns all expenses for the provided date
    returns a blank array when there are no matching expenses
```

```
Finished in 0.01832 seconds (files took 0.16797 seconds to load)
4 examples, 0 failures
```

```
Randomized with seed 22267
```

At this point, all the logic and specs are implemented at every layer of the app. It's time to see if our outermost acceptance spec passes yet. Let's run the entire suite:

```
$ bundle exec rspec
```

Randomized with seed 21580
F............

Failures:

  1) Expense Tracker API records submitted expenses FIXED
     Expected pending 'Need to persist expenses' to fail. No error was   ↵
     raised.
     # ./spec/acceptance/expense_tracker_api_spec.rb:22

Finished in 0.04844 seconds (files took 0.22185 seconds to load)
13 examples, 1 failure

Failed examples:

rspec ./spec/acceptance/expense_tracker_api_spec.rb:22 # Expense Tracker   ↵
API records submitted expenses

Randomized with seed 21580

RSpec is listing one failure, but says the spec has been fixed. Back in *Saving Your Progress: Pending Specs*, on page 57, you marked the acceptance spec as pending because it wasn't yet passing. That means it'll pass as soon as you remove the pending line.

Search inside spec/acceptance/expense_tracker_api_spec.rb for the line containing the word pending, and delete the whole line. Once that's done, your acceptance specs will pass, too:

```
$ bundle exec rspec
```

Randomized with seed 14629
....

Finished in 0.04986 seconds (files took 0.21623 seconds to load)
13 examples, 0 failures

Randomized with seed 14629

Nice! Over the span of just a few chapters, you've implemented a working JSON API to track expenses. At every step of the process, you've used RSpec to guide your design, catch regressions, and build your app with confidence.

Ensuring the Application Works for Real

There's one last thing to try before we call it a day. Your specs provide *evidence* that the application works, but they certainly don't provide *proof*. Let's try running the app by hand (as we did at the end of *Saving Your Progress: Pending Specs*) to see for ourselves whether or not it really works. First, boot up the app using the `rackup` command:

```
$ bundle exec rackup
[2017-06-13 13:34:47] INFO  WEBrick 1.3.1
[2017-06-13 13:34:47] INFO  ruby 2.4.1 (2017-03-22) [x86_64-darwin15]
[2017-06-13 13:34:47] INFO  WEBrick::HTTPServer#start: pid=45899 port=9292
```

With your API server running, try hitting the application's HTTP endpoint from another terminal:

```
$ curl localhost:9292/expenses/2017-06-10 -w "\n"
NameError: uninitialized constant ExpenseTracker::Ledger::DB
    ~/code/expense_tracker/app/ledger.rb:17:in `expenses_on'
    ~/code/expense_tracker/app/api.rb:25:in `block in <class:API>'

« truncated »
```

Oh, no—a failure! The DB constant is undefined. When you were first setting up the database, you kept the configuration—including the definition of DB—in config/sequel.rb. You can use a text search tool like grep to find where this file is being loaded in the application.[6] The following command will search the current directory (.) recursively (-r) for the text config/sequel:

```
$ grep config/sequel -r . --exclude-dir=.git
./spec/integration/app/ledger_spec.rb:require_relative '../../../config    ↵
/sequel'
```

Right now, the only code that loads this file is the Ledger integration spec. Anything that tries to use the database will only work when this spec file is loaded. That's causing the failure we see when we try to use the app for real. It will also prevent us from successfully running the acceptance specs in spec/acceptance/expense_tracker_spec.rb by themselves.

Being able to run any spec file in isolation is important. You'll often need to do so when you're debugging spec failures, or when you're jumping between writing a class and working with its unit specs.

You can use a little command-line magic to try running each of your spec files individually. Here's an example using bash, the default shell on most Unix-like systems (including the Cygwin and MinGW tools available for Windows):

```
$ (for f in `find spec -iname '*_spec.rb'`; do                              ↵
    echo "$f:"                                                              ↵
    bundle exec rspec $f -fp || exit 1                                      ↵
  done)
```

---

6. https://en.wikipedia.org/wiki/Grep

```
spec/acceptance/expense_tracker_api_spec.rb:

Randomized with seed 24954

An error occurred in a `before(:suite)` hook.
Failure/Error: Sequel.extension :migration

NameError:
  uninitialized constant Sequel
# ./spec/support/db.rb:3:in `block (2 levels) in <top (required)>'

Finished in 0.01902 seconds (files took 0.16858 seconds to load)
0 examples, 0 failures, 1 error occurred outside of examples

Randomized with seed 24954
```

We need to find a better place to load config/sequel.rb. In general, it's a good idea to load dependencies right where they are used. In this case, ledger.rb has a direct dependency on your Sequel configuration. Let's load the config from the top of that file:

06-integration-specs/09/expense_tracker/app/ledger.rb
```
require_relative '../config/sequel'
```

With that line in place, you can remove the require_relative call from spec/integration/app/ledger_spec.rb. Now, each of your spec files will pass when you run it individually:

```
$ (for f in `find spec -iname '*_spec.rb'`; do          ↩
    echo "$f:"                                          ↩
    bundle exec rspec $f -fp || exit 1                  ↩
  done)
spec/acceptance/expense_tracker_api_spec.rb:

Randomized with seed 64689

.

Finished in 0.02758 seconds (files took 0.20933 seconds to load)
1 example, 0 failures

Randomized with seed 64689

spec/integration/app/ledger_spec.rb:

Randomized with seed 7247

....

Finished in 0.01689 seconds (files took 0.15956 seconds to load)
4 examples, 0 failures

Randomized with seed 7247

spec/unit/app/api_spec.rb:

Randomized with seed 21495

........
```

```
Finished in 0.02619 seconds (files took 0.21264 seconds to load)
8 examples, 0 failures

Randomized with seed 21495
```

Try booting the app with rackup again, and use curl to make a few requests:

```
$ curl localhost:9292/expenses --data '{"payee":"Zoo", "amount":10,        ↵
"date":"2017-06-10"}' -w "\n"
{"expense_id":1}
$ curl localhost:9292/expenses --data '{"payee":"Starbucks", "amount":7.5,  ↵
"date":"2017-06-10"}' -w "\n"
{"expense_id":2}
$ curl localhost:9292/expenses/2017-06-10 -w "\n"
[{"id":1,"payee":"Zoo","amount":10.0,"date":"2017-06-10"},{"id":2,"payee":"St
arbucks","amount":7.5,"date":"2017-06-10"}]
```

It works! Buy yourself a glass of your favorite beverage, commit your work, and then let's wrap up in the next section. Just don't forget to record the expense.

Your Turn

In this chapter, you implemented the final piece of the app: the storage layer that writes to a real database. You wrote *integration specs* to test this layer. Because these specs made changes to the same global state (the database), they could interfere with one another. You used RSpec's random test ordering and --bisect ability to unearth these dependencies. You fixed them with a clean around hook, and kept noisy database transaction code out of your integration specs.

Once your integration specs were passing, you found that your end-to-end specs were also green. You've completed the first major piece of a real app.

During this project, you've come to know RSpec quite well. You've learned how to test individual methods using expectations and test doubles. You've created example groups and shared test data to keep your specs laser-focused on what the code is supposed to be doing. You've used RSpec's spec runner to unearth and fix problems in your test code.

Over the next few parts of the book, we're going to take a deep dive into each of these aspects of RSpec. But first, try your hand at an exercise or two.

Exercises

In these exercises, you're going to flesh out your specs so that they check your code's behavior more closely. Then, you'll use outside-in development to add a new feature (specifically, support for a new data format) to your expense tracker.

More Validations

So far, the Ledger class only validates one property of incoming expenses: that they have a payee. What are some other things the record method should check before saving an expense? Write integration specs for these checks, and implement the behavior.

Data Format

The current version of the app assumes all input is JSON. You could post XML, and the code would still try to parse it as JSON:

```
$ curl --data 'some xml here' \
       --header "Content-Type: text/xml" \
       http://localhost:9292/expenses
```

For this exercise, you'll add the ability for the expense tracker to read and write XML in addition to JSON. First, you'd need to decide on an XML format. If you use something like the Ox library, you'll get a format, reader, and writer for free.[7]

The next thing to consider is how callers will select the data format. Luckily, HTTP provides a means to do this with headers, which many HTTP clients and servers already understand:[8]

- The expenses POST endpoint would look at the HTTP Content-Type header for the standard MIME types for these formats, application/json or text/xml, to know how to parse the incoming data.[9]

- The expenses/:date GET endpoint would read the Accept header, similar to Content-Type, and decide how to format the outbound data.

Along the way, you'll end up deciding what to do when the caller asks for an unsupported format, or when the incoming data doesn't match the format advertised. The unit specs for your routing layer are a good place to check for all these edge cases.

Rack::Test and Sinatra provide helper methods for you to read and write the various HTTP headers:

- In Rack::Test, call header to set up your request headers before calling get or post.[10]

---

7.   http://www.ohler.com/ox/
8.   https://en.wikipedia.org/wiki/Content_negotiation
9.   https://en.wikipedia.org/wiki/MIME#Content-Type
10. http://www.rubydoc.info/gems/rack-test/0.6.3/Rack/Test/Session#get-instance_method

- In Sinatra, call request.accept or request.media_type to read the particular headers needed for this exercise.[11]

- Also in Sinatra, write your response headers into the headers hash before returning from your routing code.[12]

Jump down into your routing layer, then spec out and implement the logic to read and write XML—including any edge cases for invalid input you thought of while planning this feature.

What's Next?

You're now armed with the tools to build a major app feature from acceptance spec all the way down to implementation. We could walk you through one more major feature (or you could build one on your own). Doing so would be good practice, but wouldn't show off all the ways RSpec can help you test more effectively.

Instead, we'll take a close look at each aspect of how you'll use RSpec in your daily life. We'll start with core RSpec components like the command-line interface.

---

11. http://www.sinatrarb.com/intro.html#Accessing%20the%20Request%20Object
12. http://www.sinatrarb.com/intro.html#Setting%20Body,%20Status%20Code%20and%20Headers

Part III

RSpec Core

RSpec 3 provides a lot of useful ways to help you test your code, but it's not an all-or-nothing deal. You can pick and choose which aspects of RSpec will work best for your project.

In this part, we'll look at rspec-core, which runs your specs. You'll see how to organize your specs, how to share code effectively, how to apply features to arbitrary sets of examples, and how to configure RSpec 3's more commonly used options.

In this chapter, you'll see:

- How to arrange your specs into meaningful groups
- How to "get the words right" with names for your groups
- Where to put shared setup and teardown code

CHAPTER 7

Structuring Code Examples

Now that you've used RSpec to design and build the beginnings of an application, you've got a mental model of "where things go." You've written short, clear examples that explain exactly what the expected behavior of the code is. You've laid these examples out in logical groups—not only to share setup code, but to keep related specs together.

By the end of this chapter, you'll be an organizational expert—for RSpec examples, at least. You'll use RSpec's flexible language to communicate your intent clearly when you organize your specs into groups. You'll also know the various places you can put shared setup code, and what the trade-offs are.

We're not asking you to memorize every possible RSpec API for code organization. We certainly haven't! But when you're deep in a big project and looking to make the tests easier to read and maintain, we hope you'll think, "Aha! I could use one of those techniques," and refer back to this chapter.

Well-structured specs are about more than just tidiness. Sometimes, you need to attach special behavior to certain examples or groups, such as setting up a database or adding custom error handling. The mechanism for this behavior—metadata—relies on good grouping, so let's talk about example groups first.

Getting the Words Right

Specs can't exist on their own. From the first spec you wrote while reading this book, every spec has been part of an example group. The example group fulfills the role of a *test case class* in other test frameworks. It has multiple purposes:

- Gives a logical structure for understanding how individual examples relate to one another

- Describes the context—such as a particular class, method, or situation—of what you're testing

- Provides a Ruby class to act as a scope for your shared logic, such as hooks, let definitions, and helper methods

- Runs common setup and teardown code shared by several examples

Let's look at a few different ways to create these groups.

The Basics

We saw the basic ways to organize specs in *Groups, Examples, and Expectations*, on page 5:

- describe creates an example group.
- it creates a single example.

Before we move on to other ways to organize specs, let's discuss the finer points of these building blocks.

describe

All of the different variations on describe amount to the same thing: you say what it is you're testing. The description can be a string:

07-structuring-code-examples/01/getting_the_words_right.rb
```
RSpec.describe 'My awesome gardening API' do
end
```

...or any Ruby class, module, or object:

07-structuring-code-examples/01/getting_the_words_right.rb
```
RSpec.describe Perennials::Rhubarb do
end

RSpec.describe Perennials do
end

RSpec.describe my_favorite_broccoli do
end
```

You can combine these two approaches, and pass in a Ruby class/module/object followed by a string:

07-structuring-code-examples/01/getting_the_words_right.rb
```
RSpec.describe Garden, 'in winter' do
end
```

The differences may seem subtle, but passing a class name has some advantages. It requires the class to exist and to be spelled correctly—which will help you catch mistakes. It also allows RSpec extension authors to provide conveniences for you. For example, the rspec-rails library can tell from your specs which controller you're testing.[1]

All of these variants work just fine with metadata, which you used in *Tag Filtering*, on page 25 to tag examples with extra information:

```
07-structuring-code-examples/01/getting_the_words_right.rb
RSpec.describe WeatherStation, 'radar updates', uses_network: true do
end
```

We'll talk more about metadata in *Slicing and Dicing Specs with Metadata.*

it

Within an example group, it creates one example. You pass a description of the behavior you're specifying. As with describe, you can also pass custom metadata to help RSpec run specific examples differently. Here's how you might indicate the specs for a computer-controlled lawn sprinkler need access to a serial bus:

```
07-structuring-code-examples/01/getting_the_words_right.rb
RSpec.describe Sprinkler do
  it 'waters the garden', uses_serial_bus: true
end
```

These two building blocks are enough to get a great start with BDD. But a crucial part of BDD is "getting the words right." Some concepts don't fit well into phrases with describe and it. Fortunately, RSpec provides different ways to word your specs.

Other Ways to Get the Words Right

Using describe makes the most sense when the examples in a group are all describing a single class, method, or module. Not everything fits into such a pat template of "subject does action," though.

context Instead of describe

Sometimes, you want to group examples together because they're related to a shared situation or condition. You could do so using describe:

```
07-structuring-code-examples/01/getting_the_words_right.rb
RSpec.describe 'A kettle of water' do
  describe 'when boiling' do
    it 'can make tea'
    it 'can make coffee'
  end
end
```

---

1. https://relishapp.com/rspec/rspec-rails/v/3-6/docs/controller-specs

See how awkwardly that inner block reads, though? "Describe when boiling?" For groups like these, RSpec provides context, an alias for describe.

07-structuring-code-examples/01/getting_the_words_right.rb
```
RSpec.describe 'A kettle of water' do
➤   context 'when boiling' do
      it 'can make tea'
      it 'can make coffee'
    end
end
```

It may seem picky to fuss over wording, but readable specs are crucial for communicating your ideas and for long-term maintainability. They show the intent behind the code.

example Instead of it

RSpec's it method, too, has helpful aliases. Most of the time, the thing you're describing is the subject of a sentence, such as "A kettle of water can make tea." Here, the pronoun it makes a lot of sense, as it's standing in for the subject.

At other times, you're providing several data examples rather than several sentences about a subject. For instance, you might be designing a telephone number parser and want to demonstrate that it works with multiple phone number formats:

07-structuring-code-examples/01/getting_the_words_right.rb
```
RSpec.describe PhoneNumberParser, 'parses phone numbers' do
  it 'in xxx-xxx-xxxx form'
  it 'in (xxx) xxx-xxxx form'
end
```

Here, it doesn't make sense to phrase each example as a sentence beginning with it. Instead, you can use example, which works just like it but reads much more clearly:

07-structuring-code-examples/01/getting_the_words_right.rb
```
RSpec.describe PhoneNumberParser, 'parses phone numbers' do
➤   example 'in xxx-xxx-xxxx form'
➤   example 'in (xxx) xxx-xxxx form'
end
```

This fixes the awkward wording, without our having to repeat the phrase parses phone numbers for each it line.

specify Instead of it

As a catch-all for times when neither it nor example reads well, RSpec provides the specify alias:

```
07-structuring-code-examples/01/getting_the_words_right.rb
RSpec.describe 'Deprecations' do
  specify 'MyGem.config is deprecated in favor of MyGem.configure'
  specify 'MyGem.run is deprecated in favor of MyGem.start'
end
```

We've grouped these examples along a cross-cutting concern—library deprecations—instead of a common subject. specify works well for cases like these,
where each example has its own subject.

Defining Your Own Names

You're not limited to these aliases. RSpec allows you to define your own names
for describe and it.

For instance, suppose you're hunting a bug related to the database, and you
want to pause execution after each example in a group to inspect the data.
The Pry gem supports this style of debugging.[2] With Pry loaded, you can pause
execution by calling binding.pry inside each it block.

It'd be easier and less error-prone, though, to have a method that acts like
describe but adds the Pry behavior for you. Remember the x and f prefixes from
Chapter 2, *From Writing Specs to Running Them*, on page 15? These let you
skip or focus an example or group. Let's use the same technique to define
new aliases, pdescribe and pit. Here's how you'd change one of your expense
tracker examples from it to pit:

```
07-structuring-code-examples/02/expense_tracker/spec/integration/app/ledger_spec.rb
➤ pit 'successfully saves the expense in the DB' do
    result = ledger.record(expense)

    expect(result).to be_success
    expect(DB[:expenses].all).to match [a_hash_including(
      id: result.expense_id,
      payee: 'Starbucks',
      amount: 5.75,
      date: Date.iso8601('2017-06-10')
    )]
  end
```

To define both of these aliases, you'd add the following code to an RSpec.configure
block:

```
07-structuring-code-examples/02/expense_tracker/spec/spec_helper.rb
RSpec.configure do |rspec|
  rspec.alias_example_group_to :pdescribe, pry: true
  rspec.alias_example_to :pit, pry: true
```

---

2.   http://pryrepl.org

```
  rspec.after(:example, pry: true) do |ex|
    require 'pry'
    binding.pry
  end
end
```

Each of these aliases will add the pry: true metadata to its respective example group or single example. The after hook then calls binding.pry only after examples that have the :pry metatada defined.

Now, you can quickly toggle the Pry behavior on or off by adding or removing a p at the beginning of describe or it.

Every technique you've seen in this section has been about *clarity*—specifically, about organizing your examples so that they read logically. We're going to continue this theme of clarity in the next section. You'll see how to keep common setup routines from cluttering up the content of your specs.

Sharing Common Logic

Over the past several chapters, you've used several different techniques to share common setup logic.

The main three organization tools are let definitions, hooks, and helper methods. Here's a snippet that contains all three of these items side by side. It's a stripped-down version of the API specs you wrote for *Testing in Isolation: Unit Specs*, including a minor refactoring from the exercises.

07-structuring-code-examples/03/expense_tracker/spec/api_spec.rb
```
RSpec.describe 'POST a successful expense' do
  # let definitions
  let(:ledger)  { instance_double('ExpenseTracker::Ledger') }
  let(:expense) { { 'some' => 'data' } }

  # hook
  before do
    allow(ledger).to receive(:record)
      .with(expense)
      .and_return(RecordResult.new(true, 417, nil))
  end

  # helper method
  def parsed_last_response
    JSON.parse(last_response.body)
  end
end
```

As you've worked through the examples in this book, you've used let definitions several times in your specs. They're great for setting up anything that can be initialized in a line or two of code, and they give you lazy evaluation for free (RSpec never runs the block until it's actually needed).

You've seen all there is to let. But we'd like to show you a little more about the other two techniques.

Hooks

Hooks are for situations where a let block just won't cut it. For instance, your shared setup code may need to have side effects such as modifying global configuration or writing to a file. Or you may be implementing cross-cutting concerns like database transactions.

Writing a hook involves two concepts. The *type* of hook controls *when* it runs relative to your examples. The *scope* controls *how often* your hook runs.

Let's look at both of these concepts in turn.

Type

There are three types of hooks in RSpec, named after when they run:

- before
- after
- around

The before and after hooks are related, so let's dive into those first.

before and after

As the name implies, your before hooks will run before your examples.

after hooks are *guaranteed* to run after your examples—even if the example fails or the before hook raises an exception. These hooks are intended to clean up after your setup logic and specs.

Here's an example that stashes the ENV hash containing your app's environment variables (so that your specs can safely modify them without affecting other specs), then restores the hash afterward:

07-structuring-code-examples/04/before_and_after_hooks_spec.rb
```ruby
RSpec.describe MyApp::Configuration do
  before(:example) do
    @original_env = ENV.to_hash
  end

  after(:example) do
    ENV.replace(@original_env)
  end
end
```

This style of hook is easy to read, but it does split the setup and teardown logic into two halves that we have to keep track of. If you want to keep all this related code together, you can use an around hook instead.

Favor before over after for Data Cleanup

When your database cleanup logic doesn't fit neatly into a transactional around hook, you'll want to consider either a before hook or an after hook. In these situations, we recommend using a before hook for the following reasons:

- If you forget to add the before hook to a particular spec, the failure will happen in *that* example rather than a later one.

- When you run a single example to diagnose a failure, the records will stick around in the database so that you can investigate them.

---

around

around hooks are bit more complex than what we've seen so far: they sandwich your spec code inside your hook, so part of the hook runs before the example and part runs after. Here's the setup and teardown logic from the previous snippet, wrapped in an around hook instead:

```
07-structuring-code-examples/04/around_hooks_spec.rb
RSpec.describe MyApp::Configuration do
  around(:example) do |ex|
    original_env = ENV.to_hash
    ex.run
    ENV.replace(original_env)
  end
end
```

The behavior of these two snippets is the same; it's just a question of which reads better for your application.

Before we move on to the concept of *scope*, let's take a quick look at one of the finer points of writing hooks: where to put the code.

Config Hooks

So far in this chapter, we've put our before, after, and around hooks inside example groups. If you only need your hooks to run for one set of examples, then this approach works fine. But if you need your hooks to run for multiple groups, you're going to get tired of copying and pasting all that code into each group.

In these situations, you can define the hooks once for your entire suite, in an RSpec.configure block (typically in spec/spec_helper.rb or somewhere in spec/support):

```
07-structuring-code-examples/04/spec/spec_helper.rb
RSpec.configure do |config|
  config.around(:example) do |ex|
    original_env = ENV.to_hash
    ex.run
    ENV.replace(original_env)
  end
end
```

You've defined these *config hooks* in one place, but they'll run for *every* example in your test suite. Note the trade-offs here:

- Global hooks reduce duplication, but can lead to surprising "action at a distance" effects in your specs.[3]

- Hooks inside example groups are easier to follow, but it's easy to leave out an important hook by mistake when you're creating a new spec file.

Use Config Hooks for Incidental Details

 We recommend you only use config hooks for things that aren't essential for understanding how your specs work. The bits of logic that isolate each example—such as database transactions or environment sandboxing—are prime candidates.

We prefer to keep things simple and run our hooks unconditionally. If, however, our config hooks are only needed by a subset of examples—and particularly if they are slow—we'll use metadata to make sure they run only for the subset that need them. You've already used this technique in *Isolating Your Specs Using Database Transactions*, on page 92.

Scope

Most of the hooks you've written are meant to run once per example. After all, you want to make sure your examples can run in any order and that any individual example can run on its own. Since this behavior is the norm, RSpec sets the scope to :example if you do not provide one.

Sometimes, though, a hook needs to do a really time-intensive operation like creating a bunch of database tables or launching a live web browser. Running the hook once per spec would be cost-prohibitive.

---

3. https://en.wikipedia.org/wiki/Action_at_a_distance_(computer_programming)

For these cases, you can run the hook just once for the entire suite of specs or once per example group. Hooks take a :suite or :context argument to modify the scope.

In the following snippet, we use a before(:context) hook to launch a web browser just once for an example group:

07-structuring-code-examples/04/before_and_after_hooks_spec.rb
```
RSpec.describe 'Web interface to my thermostat' do
  before(:context) do
    WebBrowser.launch
  end

  after(:context) do
    WebBrowser.shutdown
  end
end
```

Use :context Hooks Cautiously

We only consider using :context hooks for side effects—such as launching a web browser—that satisfy both of the following two conditions:

- Does not interact with things that have a per-example lifecycle
- Is noticeably slow to run

 When you use a :context hook, you're responsible for cleaning up any resulting state—otherwise, it can cause other specs to pass or fail incorrectly.

This is a particularly common problem with database code. Any records created in a before(:context) hook will not run in your per-example database transactions. The records will stick around after the example group completes, potentially affecting later specs.

Sometimes, you need a way to run a piece of setup code just once, before the first example begins. That's what :suite hooks are for:

07-structuring-code-examples/04/spec/spec_helper.rb
```
require 'fileutils'

RSpec.configure do |config|
  config.before(:suite) do
    # Remove leftover temporary files
    FileUtils.rm_rf('tmp')
  end
end
```

Note that we've written this code as a config hook. In fact, RSpec.configure is the *only* place :suite hooks are allowed, because they exist independently of any examples or groups.

You can use before and after hooks with any of the three scopes. As we write this chapter, around hooks only support :example scope.

What about before(:each) and before(:all)?

You may occasionally run across some specs that define their hooks using :each and :all for the scope argument. These are the terms RSpec originally used instead of :example and :context. However, we found that :all was confusing when used to define config hooks:

```
RSpec.configure do |config|
  config.before(:all) do
    # ...
  end
end
```

In this configuration file, the word "all" suggests the hook will run before *all* the examples in the entire suite—but that's not the case. This hook will run once per top-level *example group*. To run once for the suite, you'd use before(:suite) instead.

RSpec 3 fixed the confusing wording by renaming :each to :example and :all to :context. The old names :each and :all are still there for backward compatibility with existing specs, but we recommend using only the newer terms.

One last thing to note about hooks: If you have one example group nested inside another, your hooks will run in the following order:

- before hooks run from the outside in.
- after hooks run from the inside out.

around hooks behave similarly. The beginning of each around hook—the bits before the call to example.run—will run outside-in, just like a before hook. The end of each around hook will run from the inside out.

When to Use Hooks

The hooks you've written have had two purposes:

- Removing duplicated or incidental details that would distract readers from the point of your example

- Expressing the English descriptions of your example groups as executable code

The database transaction code you added in *Isolating Your Specs Using Database Transactions*, on page 92 is an example of the first situation:

07-structuring-code-examples/05/expense_tracker/spec/support/db.rb
```
RSpec.configure do |c|
  # ...

  c.around(:example, :db) do |example|
    DB.transaction(rollback: :always) { example.run }
  end
end
```

By putting your transaction rollback in an around hook, you avoided littering each database-dependent spec with this transaction logic.

In *Handling Failure*, on page 73, you wrote the second kind of hook:

07-structuring-code-examples/05/expense_tracker/spec/unit/app/api_spec.rb
```
context 'when the expense fails validation' do
  # ...

  before do
    allow(ledger).to receive(:record)
      .with(expense)
      .and_return(RecordResult.new(false, 417, 'Expense incomplete'))
  end

  # ...
end
```

Your before hook translates the description 'when the expense fails validation' into Ruby code. Inside your hook, you configure the ledger test double to *fail* to record the expense. In doing so, you ensure that the description holds true for all the examples inside the context. You also make it easy for a reader to see what the English description means in terms of your domain model.

A hook should make it easier to follow your examples. Abusing RSpec hooks will make you skip all over your spec directory to trace the program flow.

In the next section, we'll show you how to recognize a bad hook and deal with it using another organizational tool: helper methods.

Helper Methods

Sometimes, we can get too clever for our own good and misuse these constructs in an effort to remove every last bit of repetition from our specs. Have a look at the following spec. It's quite complex, so we'll go through it in detail afterward.

07-structuring-code-examples/06/transit/spec/berlin_transit_ticket_spec.rb
```
Line 1  RSpec.describe BerlinTransitTicket do
```

```
-     let(:ticket) { BerlinTransitTicket.new }
-
-     before do
5       # These values depend on `let` definitions
-       # defined in the nested contexts below!
-       #
-       ticket.starting_station = starting_station
-       ticket.ending_station   = ending_station
10    end
-
-     let(:fare) { ticket.fare }
-
-     context 'when starting in zone A' do
15      let(:starting_station) { 'Bundestag' }
-
-       context 'and ending in zone B' do
-         let(:ending_station) { 'Leopoldplatz' }
-
20        it 'costs €2.70' do
-           expect(fare).to eq 2.7
-         end
25      end
-
-       context 'and ending in zone C' do
-         let(:ending_station) { 'Birkenwerder' }
-
30        it 'costs €3.30' do
-           expect(fare).to eq 3.3
-         end
35      end
-     end
- end
```

Let's trace through what happens when RSpec runs the first example:

1. The before hook on line 4 begins to run.

2. We refer to ticket on line 8, which jumps us to the let definition on line 2 to create that object.

3. We reference starting_station on line 8, which jumps to the let definition on line 15 and back.

4. On line 9, we reference ending_station, which jumps to the inner let definition on line 18 and back.

5. The before hook completes, so now we start running the example on line 20.

6. The example references fare, which jumps to the let definition on line 12 and back.

7. The expectation runs, and the example completes.

And that's just for the first example! Now, imagine that this spec file has grown a number of additional examples over time. Some of these definitions are not even going to be visible on your screen when you are looking at a failing example.

Consider the person who has to read through this code in six months when something breaks (it might be you!). The reader's first reaction at seeing those highlighted one-liner specs is, "What happened? What behavior are we testing here?" The TDD community calls this separation of cause and effect a *mystery guest*.[4]

The fare calculation is the core thing we're testing. It should be front and center in the specs.

That doesn't mean we need to repeat all that setup code, though. Recall that an RSpec example group is just a Ruby class. That means we can define helper methods on it, just as we would for any other class:

07-structuring-code-examples/06/transit/spec/berlin_transit_ticket_refactored_spec.rb
```ruby
RSpec.describe BerlinTransitTicket do
  def fare_for(starting_station, ending_station)
    ticket = BerlinTransitTicket.new
    ticket.starting_station = starting_station
    ticket.ending_station   = ending_station
    ticket.fare
  end

  context 'when starting in zone A and ending in zone B' do
    it 'costs €2.70' do
      expect(fare_for('Bundestag', 'Leopoldplatz')).to eq 2.7
    end
  end

  context 'when starting in zone A and ending in zone C' do
    it 'costs €3.30' do
      expect(fare_for('Bundestag', 'Birkenwerder')).to eq 3.3
    end
  end
end
```

Now, it's explicit exactly what behavior we're testing, without our needing to repeat the details of the ticketing API. Someone reading your spec won't need to guess at implicit behavior; they'll see everything spelled out in black and white.

Moreover, we've gained a little flexibility. With the before hook, all our specs were required to run the hook just as it was written. With a helper method, we control the timing and content of the setup.

---

4. https://robots.thoughtbot.com/mystery-guest

Putting Your Helpers in a Module

As with any other Ruby class, you can also define helper methods in a separate module and include them in your example groups. For instance, here's the outline of the acceptance specs you wrote in *Starting On the Outside: Acceptance Specs*:

07-structuring-code-examples/07/expense_tracker/spec/acceptance/expense_tracker_api_spec.rb
```ruby
RSpec.describe 'Expense Tracker API', :db do
  include Rack::Test::Methods

  def app
    ExpenseTracker::API.new
  end

  # ...
end
```

As you define specs in new files that drive the API, you'll find yourself using rack-test in multiple places. If you put this bit of glue code in a module, you can easily include it into all your acceptance specs:

07-structuring-code-examples/08/expense_tracker/spec/acceptance/expense_tracker_api_spec.rb
```ruby
module APIHelpers
  include Rack::Test::Methods

  def app
    ExpenseTracker::API.new
  end
end

RSpec.describe 'Expense Tracker API', :db do
  include APIHelpers

  # ...
end
```

Because of the added layer of indirection, we recommend using a module only if you need to use the same helper methods in more than one example group.

Including Modules Automatically

Even a one-liner like include APIHelpers is easy to forget. If you need to include the same helper module into many or all of your specs, you can call config.include in an RSpec.configure block:

07-structuring-code-examples/08/expense_tracker/spec/acceptance/expense_tracker_api_spec.rb
```ruby
RSpec.configure do |config|
  config.include APIHelpers
end
```

This example will include the APIHelpers module into *every* example group. Most of the time, you probably want to load this module into just the groups that need it. In *Sharing Code Conditionally*, on page 140, we'll show you how.

As with all global settings that are buried away in a support file, take care not to hide important details behind a call to config.include.

Sharing Example Groups

As we've seen, plain old Ruby modules work really nicely for sharing helper methods across example groups. But that's all they can share. If you want to reuse an example, a let construct or a hook, you'll need to reach for another tool: *shared example groups*.

Just like its non-shared counterpart, a shared example group can contain examples, helper methods, let declarations, and hooks. The only difference is the way they're used. A shared example group exists *only* to be shared.

In order to help you "get the words right," RSpec provides multiple ways to create and use shared example groups. These come in pairs, with one method for *defining* a shared group and another for *using* it:

- shared_context and include_context are for reusing *common setup* and *helper logic*.

- shared_examples and include_examples are for reusing *examples*.

The choice between the ..._context and ..._examples wording is purely a matter of communicating your intent. Behind the scenes, they behave identically.

There's one more way to share behavior that *is* different, though. it_behaves_like creates a new, *nested* example group to hold the shared code. The difference lies in how isolated the shared behavior is from the rest of your examples. In the coming sections, we'll talk about when you'd want to use each approach.

Sharing Contexts

Earlier in this chapter, we saw that you can group common helper methods into a module:

07-structuring-code-examples/08/expense_tracker/spec/acceptance/expense_tracker_api_spec.rb
```
module APIHelpers
  include Rack::Test::Methods

  def app
    ExpenseTracker::API.new
  end
end
```

This technique works fine as long as you're only dealing with helper methods. Sooner or later, though, you'll find that you want to share some let declarations or hooks instead.

For example, you may want to add authentication to your API. After you've done so, you'll need to modify your existing specs to log in before they make their requests. Since being logged in is an extraneous detail for most of your specs, a before hook would be the perfect place to put this new behavior:

07-structuring-code-examples/09/expense_tracker/spec/acceptance/expense_tracker_api_spec.rb
```
before do
  basic_authorize 'test_user', 'test_password'
end
```

Here, we're using the basic_authorize method from Rack::Test to treat the HTTP request as coming from a logged-in test user.

This hook can't go into your APIHelpers module, though. Plain Ruby modules aren't aware of RSpec constructs such as hooks. Instead, you can convert your module to a shared context:

07-structuring-code-examples/09/expense_tracker/spec/acceptance/expense_tracker_api_spec.rb
```
RSpec.shared_context 'API helpers' do
  include Rack::Test::Methods

  def app
    ExpenseTracker::API.new
  end

  before do
    basic_authorize 'test_user', 'test_password'
  end
end
```

To use this shared context, you'd just call include_context from any example group that needs to make API calls:

07-structuring-code-examples/09/expense_tracker/spec/acceptance/expense_tracker_api_spec.rb
```
RSpec.describe 'Expense Tracker API', :db do
  include_context 'API helpers'

  # ...
end
```

With include_context, RSpec evaluates your shared group block inside this group, causing it to add the hook, helper method, and module inclusion here. As with include, you can also use it in an RSpec.configure block for those rare situations where you want to include the shared group in *all* example groups:

07-structuring-code-examples/09/expense_tracker/spec/acceptance/expense_tracker_api_spec.rb
```ruby
RSpec.configure do |config|
  config.include_context 'API helpers'
end
```

Next, let's turn to the other common use case for shared example groups: sharing *examples* instead of *context*.

Sharing Examples

One of the most powerful ideas in software is defining a single interface with multiple implementations. For example, your web app might need to cache data in a key-value store.[5] There are many implementations of this idea, each with its own advantages over the others. Because they all implement the same basic functionality of kv_store.store(key, value) and kv_store.fetch(key), you can choose the implementation that best fits your needs.

You don't even have to pick just one implementation. You might use one key-value store for production and a different one for testing. In production, you're likely to want a *persistent* store that keeps data around between requests. For testing, you can save time and complexity by using an in-memory key-value store.

If you're using more than one key-value store, it's important to have some confidence that they have the same behavior. You can write specs to test this behavior, and organize them using shared examples.

Without shared examples, you might start with the following spec for an in-memory HashKVStore:

07-structuring-code-examples/10/shared_examples/spec/hash_kv_store_spec.rb
```ruby
require 'hash_kv_store'

RSpec.describe HashKVStore do
  let(:kv_store) { HashKVStore.new }

  it 'allows you to fetch previously stored values' do
    kv_store.store(:language, 'Ruby')
    kv_store.store(:os, 'linux')

    expect(kv_store.fetch(:language)).to eq 'Ruby'
    expect(kv_store.fetch(:os)).to eq 'linux'
  end

  it 'raises a KeyError when you fetch an unknown key' do
    expect { kv_store.fetch(:foo) }.to raise_error(KeyError)
  end
end
```

---

5. https://en.wikipedia.org/wiki/Key-value_database

To test a second implementation of this interface—such as a disk-backed FileKVStore—you could copy and paste the entire spec and replace all occurrences of HashKVStore with FileKVStore. But then you'd have to add any new common behavior to both spec files. We'd have to manually keep the two spec files in sync.

This is exactly the kind of duplication that shared example groups can help you fix. To make the switch, move your describe block into its own file in spec/support, change it to a shared_examples block taking an argument, and use that argument in the let(:kv_store) declaration:

07-structuring-code-examples/11/shared_examples/spec/support/kv_store_shared_examples.rb
```ruby
➤ RSpec.shared_examples 'KV store' do |kv_store_class|
➤   let(:kv_store) { kv_store_class.new }

    it 'allows you to fetch previously stored values' do
      kv_store.store(:language, 'Ruby')
      kv_store.store(:os, 'linux')

      expect(kv_store.fetch(:language)).to eq 'Ruby'
      expect(kv_store.fetch(:os)).to eq 'linux'
    end

    it 'raises a KeyError when you fetch an unknown key' do
      expect { kv_store.fetch(:foo) }.to raise_error(KeyError)
    end
  end
```

By convention, shared examples go in spec/support; we've named this file kv_store_shared_examples.rb after the common interface we're testing.

The block argument, kv_store_class, will come from the calling code (which we'll see in a moment). Here, it represents the class we're testing.

Conventions Are There for a Reason

 When we suggest names and locations for support files, we're not just being fussy. Choosing the right name can help you avoid errors. We've seen people name their support files something like shared_spec.rb—which RSpec will attempt to load as a regular spec file, resulting in warning messages.

Now, you can replace your original spec file with a much simpler one:

07-structuring-code-examples/11/shared_examples/spec/hash_kv_store_spec.rb
```ruby
require 'hash_kv_store'
require 'support/kv_store_shared_examples'

RSpec.describe HashKVStore do
  it_behaves_like 'KV store', HashKVStore
end
```

We're explicitly passing the HashKVStore implementation class when we bring in the shared examples with it_behaves_like. The shared_examples block from the previous snippet uses this class in its let(:kv_store) declaration.

Nesting

In the introduction to this section, we mentioned that you can include shared examples with either include_examples or it_behaves_like call. So far, we've just used it_behaves_like. Let's talk about the difference between the two calls. Here's a version of the snippet with include_examples instead:

07-structuring-code-examples/11/shared_examples/spec/include_examples_spec.rb
```
RSpec.describe HashKVStore do
  include_examples 'KV store', HashKVStore
end
```

The spec would behave just fine, but problems creep in if we add a second call to include_examples:

07-structuring-code-examples/11/shared_examples/spec/include_examples_twice_spec.rb
```
RSpec.describe 'Key-value stores' do
  include_examples 'KV store', HashKVStore
  include_examples 'KV store', FileKVStore
end
```

Calling include_examples is like pasting everything in the shared example group directly into this describe block. In particular, you'd get two let declarations for :kv_store: one for HashKVStore and one for FileKVStore. One would overwrite the other. The documentation output shows how they are stepping on each other's toes:

```
$ rspec spec/include_examples_twice_spec.rb --format documentation

Key-value stores
  allows you to fetch previously stored values
  raises a KeyError when you fetch an unknown key
  allows you to fetch previously stored values
  raises a KeyError when you fetch an unknown key

Finished in 0.00355 seconds (files took 0.10257 seconds to load)
4 examples, 0 failures
```

Using it_behaves_like avoids this issue:

07-structuring-code-examples/11/shared_examples/spec/it_behaves_like_twice_spec.rb
```
RSpec.describe 'Key-value stores' do
  it_behaves_like 'KV store', HashKVStore
  it_behaves_like 'KV store', FileKVStore
end
```

Here, each example group gets nested into its own context. You can see the difference when you run with the --format documentation option to RSpec:

```
$ rspec spec/it_behaves_like_twice_spec.rb --format documentation
```

```
Key-value stores
  behaves like KV store
    allows you to fetch previously stored values
    raises a KeyError when you fetch an unknown key
  behaves like KV store
    allows you to fetch previously stored values
    raises a KeyError when you fetch an unknown key

Finished in 0.00337 seconds (files took 0.09726 seconds to load)
4 examples, 0 failures
```

Because each use of the shared example group gets its own nested context, the two let declarations don't interfere with each other.

When in Doubt, Choose it_behaves_like

Wondering about which method to use to include your shared examples? it_behaves_like is almost always the one you want. It ensures that the contents of the shared group don't "leak" into the surrounding context and interact with your other examples in surprising ways.

We recommend using include_examples only when you're sure the shared group's context won't conflict with anything in the surrounding group, *and* you have a specific reason to use it. One such reason is clarity: sometimes, your spec output (using the documentation formatter) will read more legibly without the extra nesting.

Customizing Shared Groups With Blocks

As these examples have shown, you can customize your shared example groups' behavior by passing an argument into the it_behaves_like block. This technique works fine when all you need to do is pass in a static argument. Sometimes, though, you need more flexiblity than that.

In our examples so far, we've passed the class we're testing—HashKVStore or FileKVStore—as a static argument when we include the group. The shared code just calls new on the passed-in class to create a new store.

If these classes require arguments for instantiation, passing an argument is not going to work. For example, a file-based key-value store may require you to pass in a filename as an argument.

Fortunately, you have one more trick up your sleeve: you can pass a block (instead of just an argument) to your it_behaves_like call:

07-structuring-code-examples/11/shared_examples/spec/pass_block_spec.rb

```ruby
require 'tempfile'

RSpec.describe FileKVStore do
  it_behaves_like 'KV store' do
    let(:tempfile) { Tempfile.new('kv.store') }
    let(:kv_store) { FileKVStore.new(tempfile.path) }
  end
end
```

With this technique, your block can contain whatever RSpec constructs you need. Here, we've used a let definition, but you can also also add helper methods and hooks inside the same kind of block.

To make this technique work, you'd need to change the definition of the KV store shared example group.

07-structuring-code-examples/11/shared_examples/spec/pass_block_spec.rb

```ruby
➤ RSpec.shared_examples 'KV store' do
    it 'allows you to fetch previously stored values' do
      kv_store.store(:language, 'Ruby')
      kv_store.store(:os, 'linux')

      expect(kv_store.fetch(:language)).to eq 'Ruby'
      expect(kv_store.fetch(:os)).to eq 'linux'
    end

    # remainder of examples...
  end
```

The shared group no longer needs to take a block argument or define let(:kv_store). It just uses kv_store normally inside each example, trusting that the host group will define it with the right value for the context.

Your Turn

In this chapter, we took a second look at the main ways to structure your examples into groups. You saw how important it is to take the time to get the words right, and use terms in your specs like context or specify where they make more sense than describe or it.

We also dove into ways to move duplicated setup code out of your specs: let definitions, hooks, and helper methods. Although we've had brief encounters with these techniques in prior chapters, you saw how to get the most out of them here.

Finally, we talked about how to share examples or entire contexts. Now, it's time to bring these techniques to bear on your own code.

Exercise

In this exercise, you've inherited specs for two different URI parsers. The implementations have similar, but not identical, behavior. Your task will be to figure out what the common functionality is, and then extract it to shared specs using the techniques in this chapter. First, here's a spec file for Ruby's built-in URI library:

`07-structuring-code-examples/exercises/shared_examples_exercise/spec/uri_spec.rb`

```ruby
require 'uri'

RSpec.describe URI do
  it 'parses the host' do
    expect(URI.parse('http://foo.com/').host).to eq 'foo.com'
  end

  it 'parses the port' do
    expect(URI.parse('http://example.com:9876').port).to eq 9876
  end

  it 'defaults the port for an http URI to 80' do
    expect(URI.parse('http://example.com/').port).to eq 80
  end

  it 'defaults the port for an https URI to 443' do
    expect(URI.parse('https://example.com/').port).to eq 443
  end
end
```

Next, here's one for `Addressable`, an alternative to URI that's more standards-compliant:[6]

`07-structuring-code-examples/exercises//shared_examples_exercise/spec/addressable_spec.rb`

```ruby
require 'addressable'

RSpec.describe Addressable do
  it 'parses the scheme' do
    expect(Addressable::URI.parse('https://a.com/').scheme).to eq 'https'
  end

  it 'parses the host' do
    expect(Addressable::URI.parse('https://foo.com/').host).to eq 'foo.com'
  end

  it 'parses the port' do
    expect(Addressable::URI.parse('http://example.com:9876').port).to eq 9876
  end

  it 'parses the path' do
    expect(Addressable::URI.parse('http://a.com/foo').path).to eq '/foo'
  end
end
```

---

6. https://github.com/sporkmonger/addressable

Note that the specs are not identical and don't even cover all the same behavior. As you investigate what these libraries have in common and what's different about them, you may find yourself writing new specs. You'll need to make a judgment call about each new example as to whether it should go into an implementation-specific spec file or into the shared specs.

In this chapter, you'll see:

- What kind of information RSpec stores about each spec
- How you can tag your examples with custom information
- How to perform expensive setup only when you need to
- How to run just a subset of your specs

CHAPTER 8

Slicing and Dicing Specs with Metadata

Over the course of this book, you've followed a key principle that has made your specs faster, more reliable, and easier to use: *run just the code you need.* This principle shows up in several practices you've been using as you've followed along with the code examples:

- When you're isolating a failure, run just the failing example.
- When you're modifying a class, run just its unit tests.
- When you've got expensive setup code, only run it for the specs where you need it.

A key piece of RSpec that's made many of these practices possible is its powerful metadata system. Metadata undergirds many of RSpec's features, and RSpec exposes the same system for your use.

You've used metadata several times so far in your examples. In this chapter, we'll take a closer look into how it works. By the end, you'll understand enough to dictate exactly when and how your specs run.

Defining Metadata

RSpec's metadata solves a very specific problem: *where do I keep information about the context my specs are running in?* By *context*, we mean things like:

- Example configuration (for example, marked as skipped or pending)
- Source code locations
- Status of the previous run
- How one example runs differently than others (for example, needing a web browser or a database)

Without some way of attaching data to examples, you (and the RSpec maintainers!) would be stuck juggling global variables and writing a bunch of bookkeeping code.

RSpec's solution to this problem couldn't be simpler: a plain Ruby hash. Every example and example group gets its own such hash, known as the *metadata hash*. RSpec populates this hash with any metadata you've explicitly tagged the example with, plus some useful entries of its own.

Metadata Defined By RSpec

A good example is worth a thousand words, so let's jump right into one. In a fresh directory, create a file called metadata_spec.rb with the following contents:

08-metadata/01/spec/metadata_spec.rb
```
require 'pp'

RSpec.describe Hash do
  it 'is used by RSpec for metadata' do |example|
    pp example.metadata
  end
end
```

This snippet shows something we haven't talked about before: getting access to your example's properties at runtime. You can do so by having your it block take an argument. RSpec will pass an object representing the currently running example. We'll revisit this topic later in the chapter.

The call to example.metadata returns a hash containing all the metadata. We're using the pp (short for *pretty-print*) function from Ruby's standard library to dump the contents of the hash in an easy-to-read format.

Go ahead and run the example:

```
$ rspec spec/metadata_spec.rb
{:block=>
  #<Proc:0x007fa6fc07e6a8@~/code/metadata/spec/metadata_spec.rb:4>,
 :description_args=>["is used by RSpec for metadata"],
 :description=>"is used by RSpec for metadata",
 :full_description=>"Hash is used by RSpec for metadata",
 :described_class=>Hash,
 :file_path=>"./spec/metadata_spec.rb",
 :line_number=>4,
 :location=>"./spec/metadata_spec.rb:4",
 :absolute_file_path=>
  "~/code/metadata/spec/metadata_spec.rb",
 :rerun_file_path=>"./spec/metadata_spec.rb",
 :scoped_id=>"1:1",
 :execution_result=>
  #<RSpec::Core::Example::ExecutionResult:0x007ffda2846a78
   @started_at=2017-06-13 13:34:00 -0700>,
 :example_group=>
  {:block=>
    #<Proc:0x007fa6fb914bb0@~/code/metadata/spec/metadata_spec.rb:3>,
```

```
« truncated »
 :shared_group_inclusion_backtrace=>[],
 :last_run_status=>"unknown"}
```

```
Finished in 0.00279 seconds (files took 0.09431 seconds to load)
1 example, 0 failures
```

Even before we've defined any metadata, RSpec has attached plenty of its own! Most of the keys in this hash are self-explanatory, but a few merit a closer look:

:description

Just the string we passed to it; in this case, "is used by RSpec..."

:full_description

Includes the text passed to describe as well; in this case, "Hash is used by RSpec..."

:described_class

The class we passed to the outermost describe block; also available inside any example via RSpec's described_class method

:file_path

Directory and filename where the example is defined, relative to your project root; useful for filtering examples by location

:example_group

Gives you access to metadata from the enclosing example group

:last_run_status

Will be "passed", "pending", "failed", or "unknown"; the latter value appears if you haven't configured RSpec to record the pass/fail status or if the example has never been run

As you'll see in the coming sections, having this information at runtime will come in handy.

Custom Metadata

You can count on the keys in the previous section to be present in every metadata hash. Other keys may also be present, depending on metadata you've set explicitly. Update metadata_spec.rb to add a fast: true metadata entry:

08-metadata/02/spec/metadata_spec.rb
```
require 'pp'

RSpec.describe Hash do
```

```
➤    it 'is used by RSpec for metadata', fast: true do |example|
       pp example.metadata
     end
   end
```

This particular style of use—passing a key whose value is true, as in fast: true—is so common that RSpec provides a shortcut. You can just pass the key by itself:

08-metadata/03/spec/metadata_spec.rb
```
require 'pp'

RSpec.describe Hash do
➤    it 'is used by RSpec for metadata', :fast do |example|
       pp example.metadata
     end
   end
```

In either case, when you run this spec, you should see :fast=>true in the pretty-printed output.

You can even pass multiple keys:

08-metadata/04/spec/metadata_spec.rb
```
require 'pp'

RSpec.describe Hash do
➤    it 'is used by RSpec for metadata', :fast, :focus do |example|
       pp example.metadata
     end
   end
```

You'll see both :fast=>true and :focus=>true when you run this example.

Finally, when you set custom metadata on an example group, the contained examples and nested groups will inherit it:

08-metadata/04/spec/metadata_inheritance_spec.rb
```
require 'pp'

➤  RSpec.describe Hash, :outer_group do
     it 'is used by RSpec for metadata', :fast, :focus do |example|
       pp example.metadata
     end

➤    context 'on a nested group' do
➤      it 'is also inherited' do |example|
➤        pp example.metadata
➤      end
➤    end
   end
```

As you'd expect, these specs will print :outer_group=>true twice—once for the example in the outer group, and once for the example in the inner group.

Before we turn our attention to *using* metadata, let's talk about one more way to set custom metadata.

Derived Metadata

As you've worked through the examples in this book, you've always set metadata on one example or group at a time. Sometimes, though, you want to set metadata on *many* examples at once.

For instance, you can mark your quickest-running examples as :fast, and then run just those specs using RSpec's --tag option:

```
$ rspec --tag fast
```

This command would give you a quick overview of your code's health. The set of fast specs would consist of certain hand-picked integration specs, plus everything in spec/unit (since your unit specs are meant to run quickly).

It'd be nice to not have to manually tag each example group in spec/unit with :fast. Fortunately, RSpec supports setting metadata on many examples or groups at once, via its configuration API.

If you add the following code to spec/spec_helper.rb:

```
08-metadata/05/spec/spec_helper.rb
RSpec.configure do |config|
  config.define_derived_metadata(file_path: /spec\/unit/) do |meta|
    meta[:fast] = true
  end
end
```

...RSpec will add the :fast metadata to every example in the spec/unit folder. Let's break down how this code works.

RSpec's define_derived_metdata method checks every example against the *filter expression* we give it. Here, the filter expression is file_path: /spec\/unit/, which means, "match examples defined inside the spec/unit directory."

When the filter expression matches, RSpec calls the passed block. Inside the block, we can modify the metadata hash however we like. Here, we're adding fast: true to the metadata of every matching example. In effect, we're filtering by one piece of metadata (:file_path) in order to set another one (:fast).

In this case, you used a regular expression to find all filenames containing spec/unit. At other times, you may need the values to match exactly. In the following snippet, we want to match all the specs tagged with type: :model to indicate they are testing our Rails models:

```
08-metadata/06/spec/spec_helper.rb
RSpec.configure do |config|
  config.define_derived_metadata(type: :model) do |meta|
    # ...
  end
end
```

Behind the scenes, RSpec uses the === operator to compare values for your filter expression. You'll hear more about this operator in *How Matchers Match Objects*, on page 176. For now, we'll just say that this style of comparison enables all kinds of things—like using a Ruby lambda in your filter expression. Most of the time, though, we find that regular expressions and exact matches are powerful enough.

Default Metadata

In the previous section, you used metadata to tag some of the examples automatically. Now, we'll do a twist on this concept: we're going to show you how to enable something by default on *all* of your examples, but allow individual examples to opt out.

Back in *Testing Ledger Behavior*, on page 84, you set the :aggregate_failures metadata on your integration specs to get more useful failure output. RSpec typically stops an example at the first failing expectation. With this tag in place, your integration specs would soldier on and report *every* failed expectation.

This aspect of RSpec is so useful that you may be tempted to enable it for every example:

```
08-metadata/07/aggregate_failures.rb
RSpec.configure do |config|
  config.define_derived_metadata do |meta|
    # Sets the flag unconditionally;
    # doesn't allow examples to opt out
    meta[:aggregate_failures] = true
  end
end
```

Switching on a feature globally can be extremely handy in situations like this. However, it's a good idea to let individual examples opt out of the behavior.

For instance, you might have some billing specs that hit a fake payment gateway. As an extra safety check, you define a before hook that stops any spec attempting to use the real gateway:

```
08-metadata/07/aggregate_failures.rb
RSpec.describe 'Billing', aggregate_failures: false do
  context 'using the fake payment service' do
    before do
      expect(MyApp.config.payment_gateway).to include('sandbox')
    end

    # ...
  end
end
```

Even though aggregate_failures is set to false here, it's getting overridden by the global setting. That means that if one of your examples is accidentally configured to talk to the real payment gateway (instead of the sandbox), the before hook won't stop it.

The fix is easy: in your call to define_derived_metadata, check to see if the key exists first before overriding it:

```
08-metadata/08/spec/spec_helper.rb
RSpec.configure do |config|
  config.define_derived_metadata do |meta|
    meta[:aggregate_failures] = true unless meta.key?(:aggregate_failures)
  end
end
```

Now, you're able to set the flag globally, but still switch it off for individual cases where you don't want that behavior.

Next, let's talk about how to access metadata and put it to good use.

Reading Metadata

Take one more peek at the it block you wrote at the start of the chapter:

```
08-metadata/08/spec/metadata_spec.rb
it 'is used by RSpec for metadata' do |example|
  pp example.metadata
end
```

As this snippet shows, RSpec hands your block an example argument, from which you can read the metadata. RSpec passes the same kind of block argument in hooks marked as having :example scope:

```
08-metadata/09/around_hook.rb
RSpec.configure do |config|
  config.around(:example) do |example|
    pp example.metadata
  end
end
```

...and in let declarations:

```
08-metadata/10/spec/music_storage_spec.rb
RSpec.describe 'Music storage' do
  let(:s3_client) do |example|
    S3Client.for(example.metadata[:s3_adapter])
  end

  it 'stores music on the real S3', s3_adapter: :real do
    # ...
  end

  it 'stores music on an in-memory S3', s3_adapter: :memory do
    # ...
  end
end
```

These specs both rely on an S3 client, but each uses a different one. One spec will run with S3Client.for(:real), and the other with S3Client.for(:memory).

So far, we've seen how to read what metadata is defined on an example, and how to write metadata on one or more examples. The real fun starts when we fire up RSpec and actually use all this information to change its behavior.

Selecting Which Specs to Run

When you're running your specs, you often want to change *which ones* you include. In this section, we're going to show you a few different situations where this kind of slicing and dicing comes in handy.

Filtering

Most of the time when we start RSpec, we don't run the entire suite. We're either running unit specs for a specific class we're designing or we're kicking off some integration specs to catch regressions.

We first touched on running specific examples in *Running Just What You Need*, on page 20. You saw how to select examples by pass/fail status, by our need to focus on them, and by custom tags. Let's take a deeper dive into how to control which specs to run.

Excluding Examples

Sometimes, you want to exclude a set of examples from your RSpec run. For instance, when you're testing a project for compatibility across Ruby interpreters, you may have a few examples that are implementation-specific. You can give these a tag such as :jruby_only, and then use your RSpec.configure block to omit those specs when you're testing on another Ruby interpreter:

08-metadata/11/spec/spec_helper.rb
```
RSpec.configure do |config|
  config.filter_run_excluding :jruby_only unless RUBY_PLATFORM == 'java'
end
```

Here, the filter_run_excluding call indicates which examples we're leaving out.

Including Examples

The flip side to that method is filter_run_including, or just filter_run for short. As you might have guessed, this method directs RSpec to run *just* the examples with matching metadata.

This style of filtering is pretty brute-force. If no examples match the filter, RSpec will run nothing at all.

A more generally useful approach is to use filter_run_when_matching. With this method, if nothing matches the filter, RSpec just ignores it. For example, if you haven't marked any specs as *focused* (via the fdescribe/fcontext/fit methods or via the focus: true metadata), the following filter will have no effect:

08-metadata/12/spec/spec_helper.rb
```
RSpec.configure do |config|
  config.filter_run_when_matching :focus
end
```

In this section, we've used RSpec.configure to define example filters. These are permanent settings, baked into your setup code. They'll be in effect every time you run RSpec.

Sometimes, though, you want to filter examples temporarily for just one or two RSpec runs. Editing your spec_helper.rb file every time would get old quickly. Instead, you can use RSpec's command-line interface.

The Command Line

To run just the specs matching a particular piece of metadata, pass the --tag option to rspec. For example, you may want to run just the examples tagged with :fast:

```
$ rspec --tag fast
```

If you prefix the tag name with a tilde (~), RSpec treats the name as an *exclusion* filter. For example, to run all examples that *lack* the :fast tag, you could use the following command:

```
$ rspec --tag ~fast
```

Note that some shells treat ~ as a special character, and try to expand it to a directory name. You can avoid this issue by quoting the tag name:

```
$ rspec --tag '~fast'
```

The previous examples look for the tag's *truthiness*; any value besides nil or false will match. Sometimes, you care about the specific tag value. For example, you may have several specs tagged with a bug ID from your bug tracking system. If you run RSpec like so:

```
$ rspec --tag bug_id:123
```

...you can filter the examples to just the ones related to the ticket you're working on.

Sharing Code Conditionally

In *Structuring Code Examples*, we discussed three ways to share code across many example groups:

- Top-level config hooks
- Modules containing helper methods
- Shared contexts containing RSpec constructs (such as hooks and let blocks)

You've used all of these techniques throughout this book. By default, they all share code unconditionally. If you define, say, a before hook in your RSpec.configure block, the hook will run for *every* example.

Often, though, you want to use a certain bit of shared code only for specific examples. For instance, in *Isolating Your Specs Using Database Transactions*, on page 92, you defined an around hook to wrap a database transaction around only the examples tagged with :db:

```
06-integration-specs/07/expense_tracker/spec/support/db.rb
c.around(:example, :db) do |example|
  DB.transaction(rollback: :always) { example.run }
end
```

Metadata is what enables this flexibility, and you can use it with all of the code-sharing techniques listed earlier. Here's how:

Config hooks

Pass a filter expression as the second argument to config.before, config.after, or config.around to run that hook only for examples matching the filter.

Modules

Add a filter expression to the end of your config.include call in order to include a module (and its helper methods) conditionally. This also works with RSpec's similar config.extend and config.prepend methods, which are covered in the docs.[1]

Shared contexts

Just as with modules, add a filter expression when calling config.include_con-text. This will bring in your shared let constructs (among other things) into just the example groups you want.

All the techniques in this section help you selectively share behavior among your examples, based on metadata. Before we wrap up this chapter, let's take a look at one more way to use RSpec metadata: to control *how* your specs run.

Changing How Your Specs Run

RSpec allows you to change the way your specs behave using metadata. You've already used this ability several times as you've worked through this book. Here are the metadata options that affect how RSpec runs your examples:

:aggregate_failures

Changes how RSpec reacts to failure so that each example runs to completion (instead of stopping at the first failed expectation)

:pending

Indicates that you expect the example to fail; RSpec will run it and report it as *pending* if it did fail, or report it as a *failure* if it passed

:skip

Tells RSpec to skip the example entirely but still list the example in the output (unlike with filtering, which omits the example from the output)

:order

Sets the order in which RSpec runs your specs (can be the same order as they're defined, random order, or a custom order)

Both :pending and :skip take an optional explanation for *why* this spec shouldn't be run normally, which RSpec will print in the output.

As we discussed in *Testing the Invalid Case*, on page 89, RSpec is capable of running your specs in :random order, and we generally recommend you do that. The main alternative is :defined, meaning that RSpec runs your examples in the order that it sees their definitions.

---

1. http://rspec.info/documentation/3.6/rspec-core/RSpec/Core/Configuration.html#extend-instance_method

The choice between :defined and :random doesn't need to be either/or. If you're migrating an entire RSpec suite from the former to the latter, it can be difficult to make the switch all at once. As you saw in the expense tracker exercise, examples can have hidden order dependencies.

You can use metadata to make the transition to random ordering more gradual. By tagging an example group with order: :random, you can run just the examples in that group randomly:

08-metadata/13/random_order.rb
```
RSpec.describe SomeNewExampleGroup, order: :random do
  # ...
end
```

Once you've transitioned all your groups to random ordering, you can remove this metadata and then turn on randomness for the entire suite in your RSpec.configure block.

On rare occasions, you'll need even more fine-grained control over spec ordering. For example, you may want to run all your unit specs first, or run all your specs in order from fastest to slowest. In these cases, you can set the :order metadata to a custom ordering. The RSpec docs explain how to do so.[2]

Your Turn

In this chapter, you've seen how to slice and dice your specs by just about any way you can think of. You can run just the fastest examples, or the ones for a specific platform, or the ones you're focusing for a particular task. The result is that you spend less time waiting for your specs to run, and more time writing code.

We've also peeled back the curtain to show you that the magic behind this flexibility is an ordinary Ruby hash. You can easily define cross-sections of your specs to fit any situation.

Now, it's time to put this newfound experience to the test.

Exercise

When we are trying to find bottlenecks in our specs, we often look at SQL operations, one of the main sources of test slowness. It can be really useful to know which SQL statements came from which examples. With your knowledge of how metadata works, you can configure RSpec to report this information.

---

2. http://rspec.info/documentation/3.6/rspec-core/RSpec/Core/Configuration.html#register_ordering-instance_method

In *Isolating Your Specs Using Database Transactions*, on page 92, you tagged several examples with the :db metadata to indicate that they use the database via the Sequel library. In this exercise, you're going to modify RSpec's behavior based on this metadata.

First, open spec/support/db.rb and add the following lines to the before(:suite) hook:

08-metadata/exercises/expense_tracker/spec/support/db.rb
```
FileUtils.mkdir_p('log')
require 'logger'
DB.loggers << Logger.new('log/sequel.log')
```

This code will configure Sequel to record each executed SQL statement to the log file.

Now, use the techniques from this chapter to make sure Sequel also writes the example descriptions into its log:

- Before each example runs, write: Starting example: #{example_description}
- After each example runs, write: Ending example: #{example_description}

Hint: DB.log_info('some message') will write whatever text you need into the Sequel log.

In this chapter, you'll see:

- How to change RSpec's behavior at the command line
- How to customize RSpec's output
- Where to save your commonly used command-line options
- How to configure RSpec in code
- Which configuration options will be useful on your projects

CHAPTER 9

Configuring RSpec

As you've worked through the exercises in this book, you've often changed RSpec's behavior to make it a better tool for your needs. Here are just a few of the things you've customized RSpec to do for you:

- Set up and tear down a test database, but only for the examples that require one

- Report *every* failing expectation in an example, not just the first one

- Run just the examples that you're focusing on at the moment

In this chapter, we're going to connect the dots between all these individual customizations. By the end, you'll know how to configure much more than a few individual settings. You'll have a solid overview of RSpec's configuration system. Instead of having a general-purpose tool, you'll have a testing environment tailor-made to fit your workflow.

You can configure RSpec in two basic ways:

- *An RSpec.configure block*: Provides access to *all* configuration options; since this block lives in your code, you'll typically use it to make permanent changes

- *Command-line options*: Provides access to *some* configuration options, typically one-off settings that will affect a specific rspec run

We're going to take a closer look at both of these categories, beginning with command-line options.

Command-Line Configuration

To see all the available command-line options, run rspec --help. You'll get a pretty big list of settings, some of which you've already used in this book.

We're not going to go over them all here, but there are a few we'd like to highlight.

Environment Options

Sometimes, you need to control how RSpec loads your Ruby code. For instance, you may be experimenting with a locally modified version of a library—in that case, you'd want RSpec to load your custom version of that library instead of the default one.

The first two options listed in the --help output are for these kinds of environment customizations:

```
-I PATH                         Specify PATH to add to $LOAD_PATH (may    ↵
                                be used more than once).
-r, --require PATH              Require a file.
```

If you've ever passed the -I or -r options to the ruby executable, these RSpec switches may look familiar—they were designed to match the ones for Ruby.

The second option, -r or --require, makes it easy to use supporting libraries while you're testing. For example, you may want to use the byebug debugger to troubleshoot a failing spec.[1] You can easily enable debugging for a single RSpec run by using the -r option together with the library name:

```
$ rspec -rbyebug
```

The other option in this group, -I, adds a directory to Ruby's load path.[2] This helps Ruby find libraries that you load from a require statement or the --require switch.

RSpec already adds the two most important directories to the load path: your project's lib and spec folders. But sometimes you may want to use a particular library without going through Bundler or RubyGems; that's where this flag comes in handy.

Filtering Options

Now that we've covered options that configure the environment for your specs, let's talk about the options that govern which of your specs RSpec will run. Running just the specs you need at any given time will make you much more productive. To that end, RSpec supports a number of filtering options, listed further down in the --help output:

---

1. https://github.com/deivid-rodriguez/byebug
2. http://webapps-for-beginners.rubymonstas.org/libraries/load_path.html

```
**** Filtering/tags ****
```

In addition to the following options for selecting specific files,
groups, or examples, you can select individual examples by appending
the line number(s) to the filename:

```
rspec path/to/a_spec.rb:37:87
```

You can also pass example ids enclosed in square brackets:

```
rspec path/to/a_spec.rb[1:5,1:6] # run the 5th and 6th examples/groups
                                   defined in the 1st group
```

```
  --only-failures              Filter to just the examples that
                               failed the last time they ran.
  --next-failure               Apply `--only-failures` and abort
                               after one failure. (Equivalent to
                               `--only-failures --fail-fast --order
                               defined`)
-P, --pattern PATTERN          Load files matching pattern (default:
                               "spec/**/*_spec.rb").
  --exclude-pattern PATTERN    Load files except those matching
                               pattern. Opposite effect of --pattern.
-e, --example STRING           Run examples whose full nested names
                               include STRING (may be used more than
                               once)
-t, --tag TAG[:VALUE]          Run examples with the specified tag,
                               or exclude examples by adding ~ before
                               the tag.
                                 - e.g. ~slow
                                 - TAG is always converted to a symbol
  --default-path PATH          Set the default path where RSpec looks
                               for examples (can be a path to a file
                               or a directory).
```

You've used several of these options throughout this book. For instance, you
passed --only-failures to run just the specs that failed the previous RSpec run.
You saw how to use --tag to run only the specs that were tagged with a piece
of metadata, such as :fast.

We're not going to spend too much time going back over these flags in detail
a second time. But it's worth gathering the most common options into one
place and explaining when each one comes in handy:

rspec path/to/a_spec.rb:37

Appending a line number to your filenames is the simplest way to run a
particular example or group, particularly if you've configured your text
editor to do so with a keystroke.

--only-failures

Any time you have failed specs, those are usually the ones you want to focus your attention on. This option makes it easy to rerun just the failures.

--next-failure

A more surgical form of --only-failures, this option is nice when you want to fix and test each failure one by one.

--example 'part of a description'

This option comes in handy when you want to run a particular example or group, and you can remember part of the description but not what line it's on.

--tag tag_name

If you carefully tag your examples and groups with appropriate metadata, this powerful option will let you run arbitrary cross-sections of your suite.

By running exactly the specs you need, you minimize how long you have to wait to get feedback on your code changes.

Output Options

Different situations call for different levels of detail in your test suite output. Elsewhere in the --help text, you'll see a number of output options:

```
**** Output ****
  -f, --format FORMATTER        Choose a formatter.
                                  [p]rogress (default - dots)
                                  [d]ocumentation (group and example  ↵
                                    names)
                                  [h]tml
                                  [j]son
                                  custom formatter class name
  -o, --out FILE                Write output to a file instead of     ↵
                                $stdout. This option applies to the   ↵
                                previously specified --format, or the ↵
                                default format if no format is        ↵
                                specified.
      --deprecation-out FILE    Write deprecation warnings to a file  ↵
                                instead of $stderr.
  -b, --backtrace               Enable full backtrace.
      --force-color, --force-colour  Force the output to be in color, even ↵
                                if the output is not a TTY
      --no-color, --no-colour   Force the output to not be in color,  ↵
                                even if the output is a TTY
  -p, --[no-]profile [COUNT]    Enable profiling of examples and list ↵
                                the slowest examples (default: 10).
```

--dry-run	Print the formatter output of your ↩	
	suite without running any examples or ↩	
	hooks	
-w, --warnings	Enable ruby warnings	

We'll get to formatters in a moment. For now, let's take a closer look at three of the other options in this section:

--backtrace

> RSpec normally tries to keep error backtraces short; it excludes lines from RSpec itself and from any gems you've configured. When you need more context for debugging, you can pass --backtrace (or just -b) and see the entire call stack.

--dry-run

> This option, combined with --format doc, is a useful way to quickly get documentation-like output for your project—as long as you've taken care to phrase your example and group descriptions well.

--warnings

> Ruby's warning mode can point out some common mistakes, such as instance variable misspellings. Unfortunately, Ruby will print warnings for *all* running code, including gems. If you're developing an app with lots of dependencies, you'll likely get a lot of noise in the output. But if you're developing a simple library, this option can be useful.

These options will help you drill down into details when you're diagnosing a failure, without cluttering up the output of every test run.

Setting Command-Line Defaults

We've brought these command-line options together in one chapter so that you can refer to them whenever you want to do something special for a single test run. Sometimes, though, you may need custom behavior for every run.

Rather than wasting time typing the same options over and over, you can save a set of arguments as *command-line defaults*. As the term implies, RSpec will use these by default for every run—but you can still override them.

To set defaults, save your desired options in a text file at any of the following three paths:

~/.rspec

> Use this file in your home directory to store *global personal preferences*. RSpec will use it for any project on your machine. For instance, you may prefer to stop your test run on the first failed example, while your

teammates might not. In this case, you could put --fail-fast in your ~/.rspec file, and this setting would apply just for you.

./.rspec

This file in a project's root directory is for *project-level defaults*. Use restraint here; only put options that are necessary for the suite to run correctly, or for standards that your team agrees upon. For example, if there's a file you always want loaded, you can --require it automatically. (Indeed, when you generate a new project with rspec --init, RSpec puts --require spec_helper into the project's .rspec file for you.)

./.rspec-local

This file, which lives alongside a project's .rspec file, is for your *personal preferences* for that project. Since everyone may have their own version of this file, make sure to exclude it from your source control system.

Options take precedence in the order we've listed them here, meaning that local options will override more global ones. For instance, if your project has --profile 5 set in its .rspec file, you could override this setting by putting --no-profile in the project's .rspec-local file.

You can also set command-line defaults in the SPEC_OPTS environment variable; values set here will override ones set in text files.

Before we move on to the next way to configure RSpec, let's take a moment to put this knowledge into practice. We're going to set up RSpec to use a custom formatter to get the exact report output we want.

Using a Custom Formatter

In *Customizing Your Specs' Output*, on page 16, you used RSpec's built-in formatters to view different levels of detail in your specs' output. Now, you're going to use a *custom formatter* to make one small tweak to the way RSpec reports failures.

A custom formatter is a regular Ruby class that registers itself with RSpec to receive *notifications*. As your suite runs, RSpec notifies the formatter of the events it's subscribed to, such as starting an example group, running an example, or encountering a failure. This flexible system gives you room for all sorts of creative changes to the output. Here, we're going to change how RSpec reports failures.

RSpec's built-in formatters display failure details—messages and back-traces—at the very end of the run. This is a good default, since it puts a handy work list at the end of the output where it's easy to find.

However, as your spec suite grows and starts taking longer to complete, it can be nice to see failure details as soon as they occur. That way, you can start investigating a failure while the rest of the suite continues to run.

We've built a custom formatter for you that makes this change to RSpec's output. In this section, you're going to install the formatter and configure RSpec to use it. Afterward, we'll dig into how the formatter works.

Setting Up the Formatter

The new formatter is called rspec-print_failures_eagerly. We've made it available as a gem, but you're going to clone its source onto your machine instead of using gem install. This way, you'll be able to use it for all projects on your machine, rather than just the ones that mention it in their Gemfile.

First, clone the formatter's source code into your home directory:

```
$ git clone https://github.com/rspec-3-book/rspec-print_failures_eagerly.git
```

Now, to load the new library for every RSpec project, put the following content into a file called .rspec in your home directory:

```
09-configuring-rspec/02/configuring_rspec/.rspec
-I<%= ENV['HOME'] %>/rspec-print_failures_eagerly/lib
--require 'rspec/print_failures_eagerly'
```

Since you won't be relying on Bundler or RubyGems to manage Ruby's $LOAD_PATH, you'll have to do so here. The first line, starting with -I, makes the formatter's code available to RSpec. The second line actually loads the library.

RSpec supports the ERB (embedded Ruby) template syntax in this file, and we're using it to read the value of the HOME environment variable.[3]

With the setup done, you can run rspec and see the formatter in action. Here's what the output looks like on a suite with two passing examples and two failures:

```
$ rspec a_spec.rb
F

  1) A group with a failure has an example that fails
     Failure/Error: expect(1).to eq 2

       expected: 2
            got: 1

       (compared using ==)
     # ./a_spec.rb:3:in `block (2 levels) in <top (required)>'
```

---

3.   https://codingbee.net/tutorials/ruby/ruby-the-erb-templating-system

```
.F
  2) Another group with a failure has an example that fails
     Failure/Error: expect(1).to eq 2

       expected: 2
            got: 1

       (compared using ==)
     # ./a_spec.rb:13:in `block (2 levels) in <top (required)>'


.

Finished in 0.0307 seconds (files took 0.08058 seconds to load)
4 examples, 2 failures

Failed examples:

rspec ./a_spec.rb:2 # A group with a failure has an example that fails
rspec ./a_spec.rb:12 # Another group with a failure has an example that fails
```

RSpec used its default progress formatter (with dots for passing specs and F
for failing ones). But check out where the first failure message appears: after
the F but before the dot marking the second example. Thanks to the new
custom formatter, RSpec is printing failures as soon as they happen.

The new formatter also works with RSpec's built-in documentation formatter:

```
$ rspec a_spec.rb --format doc

A group with a failure
  has an example that fails (FAILED - 1)

  1) A group with a failure has an example that fails
     Failure/Error: expect(1).to eq 2

       expected: 2
            got: 1

       (compared using ==)
     # ./a_spec.rb:3:in `block (2 levels) in <top (required)>'
  has an example that succeeds
Another group with a failure
  has an example that fails (FAILED - 2)

  2) Another group with a failure has an example that fails
     Failure/Error: expect(1).to eq 2

       expected: 2
            got: 1

       (compared using ==)
```

```
     # ./a_spec.rb:13:in `block (2 levels) in <top (required)>'
  has an example that succeeds
```

```
Finished in 0.03249 seconds (files took 0.08034 seconds to load)
4 examples, 2 failures
```

```
Failed examples:
```

```
rspec ./a_spec.rb:2 # A group with a failure has an example that fails
rspec ./a_spec.rb:12 # Another group with a failure has an example that fails
```

As before, we're seeing failure messages interspersed with the rest of the output, instead of gathered at the end. Now that you've configured RSpec to use this formatter, and have seen it in action, let's walk through how it actually works.

How Formatters Work

A formatter goes through three main steps:

1. Register itself with RSpec to receive specific notifications

2. Initialize itself at the beginning of the RSpec run

3. React to events as they occur

As we talk about those steps in detail, you may want to look at the formatter's source code. If you open rspec-print_failures_eagerly/lib/rspec/print_failures_eagerly.rb from your home directory, you'll see the following Ruby class:

```
09-configuring-rspec/02/configuring_rspec/rspec/print_failures_eagerly.rb
Line 1  module RSpec
   -      module PrintFailuresEagerly
   -        class Formatter
   -          RSpec::Core::Formatters.register self, :example_failed
   5
   -          def initialize(output)
   -            @output = output
   -            @last_failure_index = 0
   -          end
   10
   -          def example_failed(notification)
   -            @output.puts
   -            @output.puts notification.fully_formatted(@last_failure_index += 1)
   -            @output.puts
   15        end
   -        end
   -      end
   -    end
```

Let's take a closer look at how this class works:

1. On line 4, we register the formatter with RSpec, passing it a list of events we want notifications about. Here, we only care about the :example_failed event. To see what other event notifications are available to formatters, check the API docs.[4]

2. In the formatter's initializer on line 6, we store the output argument RSpec passes us, so that we'll know where to send error messages. This object is a standard Ruby IO instance: either the standard output stream or a file on disk. We also set up an index to track which failure we last saw—we'll need this later to number the failures in the output.

3. Line 11 is the heart of our formatter: the example_failed callback we registered earlier. RSpec will pass us a 'notification' object containing details about the event. This object also has useful formatting helpers, such as the fully_formatted method that returns the output for a specific failure.

We've now seen how the formatter works once it's running, but we haven't talked about how it gets configured to run in the first place. Let's do so now.

Getting RSpec to Use the Formatter

Users of the new formatter are going to launch RSpec with the --require 'rspec/print_failures_eagerly' option. That flag will load the PrintFailuresEagerly::Formatter class into memory, but some piece of code will need to configure RSpec to use this class as a formatter.

For simpler formatters, RSpec provides a configuration API called add_formatter. If you were using this API, you'd call the helper inside a standard RSpec.configure block like so:

09-configuring-rspec/02/configuring_rspec/spec/spec_helper.rb
```
RSpec.configure do |config|
  config.add_formatter MyFormatter
end
```

However, it will take a little more finesse to configure this formatter. The code we just looked at will print only failure messages. But we also want to see whatever other output would normally appear, such as progress dots or example descriptions.

We'll need another formatter to supply the bulk of the output. We could just rely on users to pass a formatter explicitly to RSpec via the command line,

---

4. http://rspec.info/documentation/3.6/rspec-core/RSpec/Core/Formatters/Protocol.html

as in rspec --formatter doc. But it would be nicer not to require this extra step, and instead just use RSpec's default formatter if none is passed in.

The configure block we have shown here would prevent RSpec from providing a default formatter. Instead, we need to wait until the formatter has been set, and *then* add ours. To do so, we have put our initialization code in a before(:suite) hook:

09-configuring-rspec/02/configuring_rspec/rspec/print_failures_eagerly.rb

```
RSpec.configure do |config|
  config.before(:suite) do
    config.add_formatter RSpec::PrintFailuresEagerly::Formatter
  end
end
```

This library needs to take care of one last detail: cleaning up the output—specifically, by preventing failures from being printed twice. In the next section, we're going to see how to do that.

Cleaning Up the Output

RSpec formatters typically print a list of failures at the end of their output. Since we've already shown the failure messages during the RSpec run, we don't need to show them a second time.

Both the progress and documentation formatters listen for the dump_failures formatter event that RSpec sends at the end of a test run. They react to this notification by printing a list of failures. This behavior lives in a common dump_failures method in the BaseTextFormatter class inherited by the two formatters.

We've defined our own version of this method that prints nothing so that we don't get duplicate failure messages. This new dump_failures method goes into a module called SilenceDumpFailures, which we can then prepend onto the RSpec formatter base class to get rid of the extra output:

09-configuring-rspec/02/configuring_rspec/rspec/print_failures_eagerly.rb

```
module SilenceDumpFailures
  def dump_failures(_notification)
  end

  RSpec::Core::Formatters::BaseTextFormatter.prepend(self)
end
```

To override the formatters' behavior, we needed to monkey-patch RSpec—that is, change its behavior by opening up a core RSpec class and modifying it from our code.[5] Here, the risk is minimal. The method we're modifying is part of RSpec's published formatter protocol, and therefore won't change without a major RSpec version bump. In general, though, monkey-patching should be a tool of last resort.

This small amount of Ruby code is all it takes to define and configure this formatter so that you can use it from the command line. Now, let's move on to the other major way to configure RSpec: the configure method.

RSpec.configure

You've seen how easily you can set configuration options for a particular spec run via the command line. You've also seen how to make your favorite options the default using .rspec files.

As convenient as they are, command-line flags are not available for all RSpec options—just the ones you're likely to change from run to run. For the rest, you'll need to call RSpec.configure inside one or more Ruby files. You can have multiple configure blocks in your code base; if you do, RSpec will combine the options from all of them.

On a typical project, you'll put setup in spec/spec_helper.rb and then load this file automatically by adding --require spec_helper to your .rspec file.

Be Careful What You Load from spec_helper.rb

It's easy for your spec_helper file to get bogged down with code that you don't need for every spec, turning a spec run that would normally finish in hundreds of milliseconds into a multisecond "I wonder what's interesting on Twitter?" slog.

You'll have a *much* more enjoyable TDD experience if you limit spec_helper to load just the dependencies you *always* want. If you need a library just for a subset of specs, load it conditionally by doing one of the following:

- Add a when_first_matching_example_defined hook inside your Rspec.configure block

- require your library from the top of spec files that need it

---

You've used RSpec.configure several times as you've worked through the examples in this book. We'll do a quick review of the techniques you've seen, and in the process we'll show you a few more options.

---

5.   http://culttt.com/2015/06/17/what-is-monkey-patching-in-ruby/

Hooks

Hooks allow you to declare chunks of code that run before, after, or around your specs. A hook can run for each :example, once for each :context, or globally for the entire :suite.

We looked at hooks in detail in *Hooks*, on page 113. As a reminder, here's a typical before hook defined in an RSpec.configure block:

```
09-configuring-rspec/03/rspec_configure.rb
RSpec.configure do |config|
  config.before(:example) do
    # ...
  end
end
```

We'd like to review one other special-purpose configuration hook that doesn't fit the typical before/after/around pattern. In *Isolating Your Specs Using Database Transactions*, on page 92, you saw a way to run expensive database setup code on demand, the first time it's needed:

```
09-configuring-rspec/03/rspec_configure.rb
RSpec.configure do |config|
  config.when_first_matching_example_defined(:db) do
    require 'support/db'
  end
end
```

This hook uses metadata (the :db symbol) to perform extra configuration just for the specs that need it.

While config hooks are a great way to reduce duplication and keep your examples focused, there are significant downsides if you overuse them:

- A slow test suite due to extra logic running for every example
- Specs that are harder to understand because their logic is hidden in hooks

To avoid these pitfalls while keeping your specs organized, you can use a simpler, more explicit technique: using Ruby modules inside your configure blocks.

Sharing Code Using Modules

Modules are one of Ruby's main tools for sharing code. You can add all of a module's methods into a class by calling include or prepend:

```
09-configuring-rspec/03/rspec_configure.rb
class Performer
  include Singing # won't override Performer methods
  prepend Dancing # may override Performer methods
end
```

You can even bring methods into an individual object:

09-configuring-rspec/03/rspec_configure.rb
```
average_person = AveragePerson.new
average_person.extend Singing
```

RSpec provides the same kind of interface inside RSpec.configure blocks. By calling include, prepend, or extend on the config object, you can bring extra methods into your examples or groups.

09-configuring-rspec/03/rspec_configure.rb
```
RSpec.configure do |config|
  # Brings methods into each example
  config.include ExtraExampleMethods

  # Brings methods into each example,
  # overriding methods with the same name
  # (rarely used)
  config.prepend ImportantExampleMethods

  # Brings methods into each group (alongside let/describe/etc.)
  # Useful for adding to RSpec's domain-specific language
  config.extend ExtraGroupMethods
end
```

Because they work like their Ruby counterparts that you already use, these three config methods are great for sharing Ruby methods across your specs. If you need to share more, though—such as hooks or let definitions—you'll need to define a shared example group. You can then bring in this shared group automatically inside your configure block:

09-configuring-rspec/03/rspec_configure.rb
```
RSpec.configure do |config|
  config.include_context 'My Shared Group'
end
```

Now that we've covered sharing code via a configure block, let's talk about controlling how RSpec runs.

Filtering

Several times throughout this book, you've found the need to run just some of the examples in your suite. At various points, you've used RSpec's filtering to run the following subsets of specs:

- A single example or group by name
- Only the specs matching a certain piece of metadata, such as :fast
- Just the examples you're focusing your attention on
- Only the examples that failed the last time they ran

Let's look at how these techniques tie into RSpec's configuration system. Inside a configure block, you can use the following methods to specify which specs to run:

config.example_status_persistence_file_path = 'spec/examples.txt'
> Tells RSpec where to store the passed, failed, or pending status of each example between runs, enabling the --only-failures and --next-failure options.

config.filter_run_excluding :specific_to_some_os
> *Excludes* examples from being run; useful for permanent exclusions based on environmental factors like OS, Ruby version, or an environment variable.

config.filter_run_when_matching :some_metadata
> Sets a *conditional* filter that only applies when there are matching examples; this is how, for instance, RSpec runs just the examples you've tagged with the :focus metadata.

Metadata

As we discussed in *Slicing and Dicing Specs with Metadata*, RSpec's metadata system makes it possible for you to categorize your specs in a way that makes sense to you. Metadata is deeply connected to the configuration system. Many of RSpec's configuration options we've discussed accept (or require) a metadata argument, which determines the examples or groups the config option applies to.

You can also *set* metadata using the configuration system. The following methods let you write metadata on examples or groups:

config.define_derived_metadata(file_path: /unit/) { |meta| meta[:type] = :unit }
> Derives one metadata value from another. Here, we tag all the specs in the unit directory with type: :unit. If we had left out the file_path argument, this call would have set metadata for *all* examples.

config.alias_example_to :alias_for_it, some_metadata: :value
> Defines an alternative to the built-in it method that creates an example *and* attaches metadata. This is how RSpec's built-in fit method marks examples you want to focus on.

config.alias_example_group_to :alias_for_describe, some_metadata: :value
> Like the previous alias, except that it works on example groups instead of individual examples (like RSpec's fdescribe).

Output Options

RSpec aims to provide *actionable* output—that is, output that helps you decide what to do next. To that end, it supports a number of options to make the output useful for specific situations:

config.warnings = true

> Enables Ruby's warnings mode, like the rspec --warnings flag we discussed earlier. This helps you catch some mistakes (such as method redefinitions and variable misspellings) but may report tons of extra warnings in third-party code, unless you use something like ruby_warning_filter to cut some of the noise.[6]

config.profile_examples = 2

> RSpec will measure how long each spec took and print the given number of slowest examples and groups (two, in this case). This is helpful for keeping your test suite fast.

When an expectation fails, RSpec prints the backtrace showing the chain of method calls all the way from your spec to the lowest-level code. RSpec excludes its own stack frames from this list. You can also exclude other libraries or files from the backtrace:

config.backtrace_exclusion_patterns << /vendor/

> Excludes any lines from the backtrace matching the given regular expressions; for example, lines containing the text vendor.

config.filter_gems_from_backtrace :rack, :sinatra

> Excludes stack frames from specific libraries; here, we won't see calls from inside the rack and sinatra gems.

If you ever need more detail, you can get the full backtrace (including stack frames from RSpec and any others you have configured it to ignore) by passing --backtrace on the command line.

Nearly all of RSpec's output is customizable using a *formatter*. As we've previously discussed, you can specify a formatter on the command line using the --format or -f option. You can also add a formatter in an RSpec.configure block:

09-configuring-rspec/03/rspec_configure.rb
```
RSpec.configure do |config|
  # You can use the same formatter names supported by the CLI...
  config.add_formatter 'documentation'
```

---

6.   https://github.com/semaperepelitsa/ruby_warning_filter

```
  # ...or pass _any_ formatter class, including a custom one:
  config.add_formatter Fuubar
end
```

This example uses the Fuubar formatter, which is one of the more popular and useful third-party formatters.[7]

As the add_formatter method suggests, you can add multiple formatters, directing each to a different output:

09-configuring-rspec/03/rspec_configure.rb
```
RSpec.configure do |config|
  config.add_formatter 'documentation', $stdout
  config.add_formatter 'html', 'specs.html'
end
```

If you don't call add_formatter or pick a formatter from a command-line option, RSpec will default to the progress formatter. However, you can provide a different default using config.default_formatter:

09-configuring-rspec/03/rspec_configure.rb
```
RSpec.configure do |config|
  config.default_formatter = config.files_to_run.one? ? 'doc' : 'progress'
end
```

With this snippet, RSpec will default to the more verbose documentation formatter if you're running just one spec file, or the progress formatter if you're running multiple files. Regardless, you can override this default by passing a formatter on the command line.

Library Configuration

The most common way to run RSpec is to use rspec-core to run your specs, rspec-expectations to express expected outcomes, and rspec-mocks to provide test doubles. But you don't *have* to use them together. They ship as three separate Ruby gems precisely so that you can swap any of them out. You can even use rspec-mocks or rspec-expectations with another test framework, as we discuss in *Using Parts of RSpec With Other Test Frameworks*, on page 296.

Mocks

The config.mock_with option sets which mock object framework RSpec will use. If you want to use Mocha instead of RSpec mocks, you can do so with the following code:[8]

---

7. https://jeffkreeftmeijer.com/2010/fuubar-the-instafailing-rspec-progress-bar-formatter/
8. http://gofreerange.com/mocha/docs/

09-configuring-rspec/04/configuring_rspec/mocha_spec.rb

```
RSpec.configure do |config|
  config.mock_with :mocha
end

RSpec.describe 'config.mock_with :mocha' do
  it 'allows you to use mocha instead of rspec-mocks' do
    item = stub('Book', cost: 17.50)

    credit_card = mock('CreditCard')
    credit_card.expects(:charge).with(17.50)

    PointOfSale.purchase(item, with: credit_card)
  end
end
```

RSpec also supports the :rr and :flexmock mocking libraries.[9,10]

You can pass a block to mock_with to set options for the mocking library. In the following snippet, we turn on some extra verification in rspec-mocks:

09-configuring-rspec/04/configuring_rspec/rspec_mocks_configuration_spec.rb

```
RSpec.configure do |config|
  config.mock_with :rspec do |mocks|
    mocks.verify_partial_doubles = true
    mocks.verify_doubled_constant_names = true
  end
end
```

We'll talk more about configuring your test doubles in *Using Partial Doubles Effectively*, on page 271. In case you're curious, here's what these two options do:

mocks.verify_partial_doubles = true

> Verifies that each *partial double*—a normal object that has been partially modified with test double behavior—conforms to the object's original interface.

mocks.verify_doubled_constant_names = true

> When creating a verifying double using a string such as "SomeClassName", RSpec will verify that SomeClassName actually exists.

The full configuration docs for rspec-mocks are available online.[11]

Expectations

Just as mock_with lets you configure an alternative to rspec-mocks, expect_with lets you choose a different assertion framework instead of rspec-expectations:

9.   http://rr.github.io/rr/
10. https://github.com/doudou/flexmock
11. http://rspec.info/documentation/3.6/rspec-mocks/RSpec/Mocks/Configuration.html

09-configuring-rspec/04/configuring_rspec/expect_with_spec.rb

```ruby
require 'wrong'

RSpec.configure do |config|
  config.expect_with :minitest, :rspec, Wrong
end

RSpec.describe 'Using different assertion/expectation libraries' do
  let(:result) { 2 + 2 }

  it 'works with minitest assertions' do
    assert_equal 4, result
  end

  it 'works with rspec expectations' do
    expect(result).to eq 4
  end

  it 'works with wrong' do
    # "Where 2 and 2 always makes 5..."
    assert { result == 5 }
  end
end
```

Here, we are using three different libraries: rspec-expectations, Minitest's assertions, and a great little library called Wrong.[12,13] (You will not normally need to use multiple assertion libraries; we are just demonstrating some different options.)

You can give expect_with a well-known library name—:rspec, :minitest, or :test_unit—or you can pass in a Ruby module containing the assertion methods you want to use. If you're writing your own module, your methods should signal a failure by raising an exception.

Other Useful Options

Before we wrap up this chapter, let's take a look at a few final options that don't fit into the categories we've described.

Zero Monkey-Patching Mode

The first option we'd like to highlight here is disable_monkey_patching!:

09-configuring-rspec/05/rspec_configure.rb

```ruby
RSpec.configure do |config|
  config.disable_monkey_patching!
end
```

---

12. http://docs.seattlerb.org/minitest/
13. https://github.com/sconover/wrong

This flag disables RSpec's original syntax:

```
09-configuring-rspec/05/rspec_configure.rb
# Old syntax

describe SwissArmyKnife do   # bare `describe` method
  it 'is useful' do
    knife.should be_useful   # `should` expectation
  end
end
```

...in favor of the style in RSpec 3:

```
09-configuring-rspec/05/rspec_configure.rb
# New syntax

RSpec.describe SwissArmyKnife do   # `describe` called on the `RSpec` module
  it 'is useful' do
    expect(knife).to be_useful      # `expect()`-style expectation
  end
end
```

The old syntax relied heavily on monkey-patching core Ruby objects. The new zero-monkey-patching mode does not. The result is fewer gotchas and edge cases in your specs. Moreover, your code will continue to work with future versions of RSpec. For more information about this mode, see the RSpec blog post that introduced it.[14]

Random Order

As we discussed in *Testing the Invalid Case*, on page 89, we recommend you configure RSpec to run your specs in random order:

```
09-configuring-rspec/05/rspec_configure.rb
RSpec.configure do |config|
  config.order = :random
end
```

Running your specs in random order helps surface ordering dependencies between your examples. You'll be more likely to discover these problems when they first appear, and you'll be able to fix the bug while the code is still fresh in your mind.

Adding Your Own Settings

All of the settings we've seen so far ship with RSpec. But you're not limited to those. RSpec provides an API for adding new settings, which you can then use in your own libraries that extend RSpec's behavior.

---

14. http://rspec.info/blog/2013/07/the-plan-for-rspec-3/#zero-monkey-patching-mode

For example, suppose you're writing an RSpec plugin and accompanying web service to help developers track long-term trends about their test suites. After each spec run, your plugin would report runtimes and pass/fail status to the service.

Your users will need some way to configure your plugin to use their assigned API keys for the web service. In your library, you'd call add_setting inside an RSpec.configure block, passing it the name of the setting you're creating:

09-configuring-rspec/05/rspec_configure.rb
```
RSpec.configure do |config|
  config.add_setting :spec_history_api_key
end
```

Once a developer has installed your plugin, he or she can set it up to use the API key like so:

09-configuring-rspec/05/rspec_configure.rb
```
RSpec.configure do |config|
  config.spec_history_api_key = 'a762bc901fga4b185b'
end
```

Even if you're just writing a library for your own projects, adding these kinds of configuration options can make it easier to use.

Your Turn

In this chapter, we looked at two ways to configure RSpec: the command-line options and the configure method. Command-line options are easy to discover, and they're great for one-off changes to RSpec's behavior. The configure method covers more of RSpec's behavior and gives you finer-grained control over how RSpec runs.

We're not asking anyone to memorize the entire set of configuration options. But the ones we've shown you here will help you turn RSpec into a comfortable, productive working environment.

Exercises

Now that you've seen what a wide array of configuration options RSpec offers, try your hand at using a few of them in these exercises.

Using a Custom Formatter

Find and read the documentation for the following RSpec formatters (some of which are more useful than others):

- Fivemat[15]
- Fuubar[16]
- NyanCat[17]
- Any others you can find

Install a couple of these gems onto your system. Try each formatter at the command line with one of your projects; the expense tracker app you wrote in the second part of this book would be perfect.

Once you've found a formatter you like, configure one of your projects to use it on every run. If you *really* enjoy using this formatter, you may want to configure RSpec to use it on all your projects.

Detecting Slow-Running Specs

As we've discussed before, keeping your specs running quickly is key to achieving a productive flow. In this exercise, you're going to write a library that will measure some of your specs' execution times and fail any example that's too slow.

You don't want to apply the same timing requirements to *all* your specs—after all, integration and acceptance specs are typically slower than unit specs. Your library should use a piece of configurable metadata, such as :fail_if_slower_than, to set the threshold. For instance, any example in the following group should fail if it takes longer than a hundredth of a second to run:

```
09-configuring-rspec/exercises/fail_if_slower_than_spec.rb
RSpec.describe SomeFastUnitSpecs, fail_if_slower_than: 0.01 do
  # ...
end
```

Users will be able to configure these thresholds automatically for whole sections of their suites, using the techniques in *Derived Metadata*, on page 135.

When your library first loads, it should define an around configuration hook. The hook will compare the wall clock time before and after each example runs, and then fail the example if it takes too long.

---

15. https://github.com/tpope/fivemat
16. https://github.com/thekompanee/fuubar
17. https://github.com/mattsears/nyan-cat-formatter

Part IV

RSpec Expectations

With rspec-expectations, you can easily express expected outcomes about your code. While the syntax might initially look odd or even "magical," under the covers it uses simple matcher objects that can be composed in useful, powerful ways.

In this section, we'll dig into how rspec-expectations works, how to compose matchers, and why doing so is useful. We'll take a tour of the matchers included in RSpec and then show you how to create your own domain-specific matchers for your projects.

In this chapter, you'll see:

- How to specify expected outcomes of your code with rspec-expectations
- What a matcher is
- How to match complex data structures, focusing only on the important details
- How to combine matchers with and/or operators

## CHAPTER 10

Exploring RSpec Expectations

In *RSpec Core*, we saw how rspec-core helps you structure your test code into *example groups* and *examples*. But having a sound structure is not enough for writing good tests. If our specs run code without looking at the output, we're not really testing anything—except that the code doesn't crash outright. That's where rspec-expectations comes in. It provides an API for *specifying expected outcomes*.

Each RSpec example should contain one or more *expectations*. These express what you expect to be true at a specific point in your code. If your expectations are not satisfied, RSpec will fail the example with a clear diagnostic message.

In this chapter, we will see how one crucial part of expectations—the matcher—can be combined in useful new ways. Before diving into how expectations work, let's look at a few sample expectations to see what they're capable of:

10-exploring-rspec-expectations/01/expectation_examples.rb
```
ratio = 22 / 7.0
expect(ratio).to be_within(0.1).of(Math::PI)

numbers = [13, 3, 99]
expect(numbers).to all be_odd

alphabet = ('a'..'z').to_a
expect(alphabet).to start_with('a').and end_with('z')
```

Try reading these out loud. "Expect ratio to be within 0.1 of pi." "Expect numbers to all be odd." "Expect alphabet to start with a and end with z." These expectations read exactly like what they verify.

The primary goal of rspec-expectations is *clarity*, both in the examples you write and in the output when something goes wrong. In this chapter, we're going to show you how they work and how to use them in your RSpec examples—or even without RSpec at all!

Parts of an Expectation

When you see an expectation like the following one:

10-exploring-rspec-expectations/02/parts_of_an_expectation.rb
```
expect(deck.cards.count).to eq(52), 'not playing with a full deck'
```

...you'll notice several forms of punctuation in use: parentheses, dots, and whitespace. While there's some variety here, the syntax consistently uses just a few simple parts:

- A *subject*—the thing you're testing—that is, an instance of a Ruby class

- A *matcher*—an object that specifies what you expect to be true about the subject, and provides the pass/fail logic

- (optionally) A custom failure message

These parts are held together with a bit of glue code: expect, together with either the to or not_to method.

Let's get a feel for how these parts work by trying them out in an IRB session:

```
$ irb
```

To use rspec-expectations, you have to require the library, and then include the RSpec::Matchers module. Normally, rspec-core does this for you, but when you use rspec-expectations in another context, you need to bring it in yourself:

```
>> require 'rspec/expectations'
=> true
>> include RSpec::Matchers
=> Object
```

With that done, you can now create an expectation:

```
>> expect(1).to eq(1)
=> true
>> expect(1).to eq(2)
RSpec::Expectations::ExpectationNotMetError:
expected: 2
     got: 1

(compared using ==)

   « backtrace truncated »
```

RSpec signals failure by raising an exception. Other test frameworks use a similar technique when an assertion fails.

Wrapping Your Subject With expect

Ruby begins evaluating your expectation at the expect method. We'll start there, too. Type the following code into your IRB session:

```
>> expect_one = expect(1)
=> #<RSpec::Expectations::ExpectationTarget:0x007fb4eb83a818 @target=1>
```

Here, our subject is the number 1. We've wrapped it in the expect method to give ourselves a place to attach methods like to or not_to. In other words, the expect method wraps our object in a test-friendly adapter.

What Happened to should?

If you've used earlier versions of RSpec, you're probably familiar with the older should syntax for expectations:

```
'food'.should match(/foo/)
```

While this notation was easy to read and worked well in most cases, it had a few drawbacks. To implement it, RSpec had to monkey-patch every object in the system with should and should_not methods. This caused confusing errors in certain edge cases, such as using BasicObject or delegate to proxy method calls to an underlying object.

The new expect syntax is just as readable and is much easier to use correctly. Moreover, its implementation requires no monkey-patching at all.[a]

---

a.   http://rspec.info/blog/2012/06/rspecs-new-expectation-syntax/

Using a Matcher

If expect wraps your object for testing, then the *matcher* actually performs the test. The matcher checks that the subject satisfies its criteria. Matchers can compare numbers, find patterns in text, examine deeply nested data structures, or perform any custom behavior you need.

The RSpec::Matchers module ships with built-in methods to create matchers. Here, we'll use its eq method to create a matcher that only matches the number 1:

```
>> be_one = eq(1)
=> #<RSpec::Matchers::BuiltIn::Eq:0x007fb4eb82dd98 @expected=1>
```

This matcher can't do anything on its own; we still need to combine it with the subject we saw in the previous section.

Putting the Pieces Together

At this point, we have a subject, 1, that we've wrapped inside the expect method to make it testable. We also have a matcher, be_one. We can put them together using the to or not_to method:

```
>> expect_one.to(be_one)
=> true
>> expect_one.not_to(be_one)
RSpec::Expectations::ExpectationNotMetError:
expected: value != 1
     got: 1

(compared using ==)

    « backtrace truncated »
```

The to method tries to match the subject (in this case, the integer 1) against the provided matcher. If there's a match, the method returns true; if not, it bails with a detailed failure message.

The not_to method does the opposite: it fails if the subject *does* match. If you like to boldly split infinitives, you can also use to_not in place of not_to:

```
>> expect(1).not_to eq(2)
=> true
>> expect(1).to_not eq(2)
=> true
```

When you think of RSpec expectations as being just a couple of simple Ruby objects glued together, the syntax becomes clear. You'll use parentheses with the expect method call, a dot to attach the to or not_to method, and a space leading up to the matcher.

When an Expectation Fails

When the code you're testing does not behave as you expect, it's essential to have good, detailed error information to quickly diagnose what's going on. As you've seen, RSpec's matchers provide helpful failure messages right out of the box. Sometimes, though, you need a little more detail.

For example, consider the following expectation:

```
>> resp = Struct.new(:status, :body).new(400, 'unknown query param `sort`')
=> #<struct status=400, body="unknown query param `sort`">

>> expect(resp.status).to eq(200)
RSpec::Expectations::ExpectationNotMetError:
expected: 200
     got: 400
```

```
(compared using ==)
    « backtrace truncated »
```

"Expected 200; got 400" is technically correct, but it does not provide enough information to understand *why* we got a 400 "Bad Request" response. The HTTP server is telling us what we did wrong in the response body, but that information is not included in the failure message. To include this extra information, you can pass an alternate failure message along with the matcher to to or not_to:

```
>> expect(resp.status).to eq(200), "Got a #{resp.status}: #{resp.body}"
RSpec::Expectations::ExpectationNotMetError: Got a 400: unknown query param ↩
`sort`
    « backtrace truncated »
```

If the failure message is expensive to generate (for example, scanning a large core dump file), you can pass in a callable object such as a Proc or a Method object. That way, you only pay the cost if the spec fails:

```
>> expect(resp.status).to eq(200), resp.method(:body)
RSpec::Expectations::ExpectationNotMetError: unknown query param `sort`
    « backtrace truncated »
```

Clear Failure Messages Save You Time

We can't tell you how many times we've seen "failed assertion, no message given" in legacy test suites. When you encounter a vague failure message like that, the best you can do is add a bunch of puts calls with debugging info and then rerun your tests.

A good error message tells you exactly what went wrong so that you can start fixing it right away. Time saved diagnosing failures can translate directly to lower project costs.

When the matcher's default failure message doesn't provide enough detail, a custom message may be just what you need. If you find yourself using the same message repeatedly, you can save time by writing your own matcher instead. We'll show you how to do that in *Creating Custom Matchers*.

RSpec Expectations vs. Traditional Assertions

It might feel like RSpec's expectations have a lot of moving parts. If you've used traditional assertions in an xUnit testing framework such as Ruby's built-in Minitest, you may be wondering if the added complexity is worth it. In fact, expectations and assertions are same basic concept, just with different emphases.

Assertions are simpler to explain than RSpec's expectations—and simplicity is a good thing—but that doesn't necessarily make one better than the other. RSpec's complexity provides a number of advantages over simple assert methods.

- Composability: *Matchers* are first-class objects that can be combined and used in flexible ways that simple assert methods can't.

- Negation: Matchers can be automatically negated by passing them to expect(object).not_to, with no need for you to write an assert_not_xyz or refute_xyz method to pair with assert_xyz.

- Readability: We've chosen to use a syntax that, when read out loud, sounds like an English description of the outcome you expect.

- More useful errors. For example, the expectation for the following collection of numbers:

10-exploring-rspec-expectations/02/good_failure_messages.rb
```
expect([13, 2, 3, 99]).to all be_odd
```

...tells you exactly which item in the collection failed:

```
expected [13, 2, 3, 99] to all be odd

   object at index 1 failed to match:
      expected `2.odd?` to return true, got false
```

The equivalent xUnit-style assertion, assert [13, 2, 3, 99].all?(&:odd), merely reports Expected false to be truthy.

Though we love using expectations, we will be the first to say they are not right for every project. You can easily use RSpec with a less complex library such as Minitest's assertions, as we demonstrated in *Library Configuration*, on page 161.

How Matchers Work

Earlier, we saw that matchers are objects that carry pass/fail logic. Let's take a closer look at how they work.

A matcher is a bit like a regular expression. Just as the regular expression /^\[warn\]/ defines a category of strings (those beginning with [warn] followed by a space), a matcher defines a category of *objects*.

The resemblance doesn't end there. As you'll see in a moment, matchers implement one of the same protocols that regular expressions do, allowing them to be used in similar ways.

Any Ruby object can be used as a matcher as long as it implements a minimal set of methods. This protocol is so simple that you can even build up a matcher object in IRB. Over the next few code examples, we're going to do just that.

Back in your IRB session, type in the following code (if you're starting a new session, don't forget to rerun the setup code):

```
>> matcher = Object.new
=> #<Object:0x007fe2e213ea58>
```

Let's see how RSpec tries to use this object when we pass it as a matcher:

```
>> expect(1).to matcher
NoMethodError: undefined method `matches?' for #<Object:0x007feff9326f18>
    « backtrace truncated »
```

This expectation has triggered a NoMethodError exception. RSpec expects every matcher to implement a matches? method, which takes an object and returns true if the object matches (and false otherwise). Let's define that now, and try the matcher again:

```
>> def matcher.matches?(actual)
>>    actual == 1
>> end
=> :matches?
>> expect(1).to matcher
=> true
```

Success! What about when the match fails? Let's try matching against 2 now:

```
>> expect(2).to matcher
NoMethodError: undefined method `failure_message' for            ↵
#<Object:0x007fe2e213ea58>
    « backtrace truncated »
```

When the provided object does not match, RSpec calls the matcher's failure_message method to get an appropriate message to display to the user. Let's define that now:

```
>> def matcher.failure_message
>>    'expected object to equal 1'
>> end
=> :failure_message
>> expect(2).to matcher
RSpec::Expectations::ExpectationNotMetError: expected object to equal 1
    « backtrace truncated »
```

With that method in place, RSpec now throws an ExpectationNotMetError containing our message.

These two methods—matches? and failure_message—are all you need to define a simple matcher. The protocol contains several optional methods you can use to customize your matcher's behavior further; we'll discuss those in *Using the Matcher DSL*, on page 220.

Composing Matchers

Even on their own, matchers are powerful tools for your tests. But they really shine when you *compose* them with other matchers to specify *exactly* what you expect (and nothing more). The result is more robust tests and fewer false failures.

There are a few different ways to compose matchers:

- Pass one matcher directly into another
- Embed matchers in Array and Hash data structures
- Combine matchers with logical and/or operators

Before we consider these three cases, let's look at how matchers determine whether or not the subject matches.

How Matchers Match Objects

Matchers build on top of one of Ruby's standard protocols in order to provide composability: the humble === method. This method, often called "three-quals" or "case equality," defines a *category* to which other objects may (or may not) belong. Ruby's built-in regular expressions, ranges, and classes define this operator, and you can add it to your own objects as well.

Let's see how case equality works in an IRB session:

```
>> /^\[warn\] / === '[warn] Disk space low'
=> true
>> /^\[warn\] / === '[error] Out of memory'
=> false
>> (1..10) === 5
=> true
>> (1..10) === 15
=> false
```

We're playing with === here just to get a feel for how Ruby (and RSpec) use it internally. Most of the time, you won't call it directly from production code. Instead, Ruby will call it for you inside each when clause of a case expression.

Just to drive home the point that matchers are plain old Ruby objects that implement ===, here's what a matcher would look like inside a case expression:

```
>> def describe_value(value)
>>   case value
>>   when be_within(0.1).of(Math::PI) then 'Pi'
>>   when be_within(0.1).of(2 * Math::PI) then 'Double Pi'
>>   end
>> end
=> :describe_value
>> describe_value(3.14159)
=> "Pi"
>> describe_value(6.28319)
=> "Double Pi"
```

RSpec expectations perform the same check internally that Ruby's case statement does: they call === on the object you pass in. That object can be anything—including another matcher.

Passing One Matcher Into Another

It may not be obvious why you'd need to pass a matcher to another matcher.
Let's say you expect a particular array to start with a value that's near π. With
RSpec, you can pass the be_within(0.1).of(Math::PI) matcher into the start_with
matcher to specify this behavior:

```
>> numbers = [3.14159, 1.734, 4.273]
=> [3.14159, 1.734, 4.273]
>> expect(numbers).to start_with( be_within(0.1).of(Math::PI) )
=> true
```

It just works! Now, let's see what the message looks like when the expectation fails:

```
>> expect([]).to start_with( be_within(0.1).of(Math::PI) )
RSpec::Expectations::ExpectationNotMetError: expected [] to start with be    ↵
within 0.1 of 3.141592653589793
    « backtrace truncated »
```

Unfortunately, the failure message is the grammatically awkward "expected
[] to start with be within 0.1 of π." Luckily, RSpec provides aliases (generally
in the form of a *noun phrase*) for the built-in matchers that read much better
in situations like these:

```
>> expect([]).to start_with( a_value_within(0.1).of(Math::PI) )
RSpec::Expectations::ExpectationNotMetError: expected [] to start with a    ↵
value within 0.1 of 3.141592653589793
    « backtrace truncated »
```

Much better. This actually reads like English, and is much more intelligible:
"expected [] to start with a value within 0.1 of π."

The a_value_within matcher is an alias for be_within that acts identically, except for how it describes itself. RSpec provides a number of aliases like this for each of the built-in matchers.[1] As we'll see in *Defining Matcher Aliases*, on page 218, it's trivial to define your own aliases as well.

Embedding Matchers in Array and Hash Data Structures

In addition to passing one matcher into another, you can also embed matchers within an array at any position, or within a hash in place of a value. RSpec will compare the corresponding items using ===. This technique works at any level of nesting. Let's look at an example:

```
10-exploring-rspec-expectations/04/composing_matchers.rb
presidents = [
  { name: 'George Washington', birth_year: 1732 },
  { name: 'John Adams',        birth_year: 1735 },
  { name: 'Thomas Jefferson',  birth_year: 1743 },
  # ...
]
expect(presidents).to start_with(
  { name: 'George Washington', birth_year: a_value_between(1730, 1740) },
  { name: 'John Adams',        birth_year: a_value_between(1730, 1740) }
)
```

Here, we're using a_value_between(1730, 1740) for the birth years of George Washington and John Adams instead of a specific number. Of course, we know their birth years were exactly 1732 and 1735, respectively. But not all your real-world values are going to be so precise. If you test for behavior more specific than what you actually need, or if you're testing nondeterministic logic, your specs may break if the implementation changes slightly.

This ability to compose matchers—by passing them into one another, or by embedding them in data structures—lets you be as precise or as vague as you need to be. When you specify exactly the behavior you expect (and nothing more), your tests become less brittle.

Combining Matchers With Logical and/or Operators

There's another way to combine matchers: *compound matcher expressions*. Every built-in matcher has two methods (and and or) that allow you to logically combine any two matchers into a compound matcher:

```
10-exploring-rspec-expectations/04/composing_matchers.rb
alphabet = ('a'..'z').to_a
expect(alphabet).to start_with('a').and end_with('z')
```

---

1. http://rspec.info/documentation/3.6/rspec-expectations/RSpec/Matchers.html

```
stoplight_color = %w[ green red yellow ].sample
expect(stoplight_color).to eq('green').or eq('red').or eq('yellow')
```

As we see in the stoplight_color example, you can string matchers together into arbitrarily long chains. You can use the words and/or, or you can use the & and | operators:

```
alphabet = ('a'..'z').to_a
expect(alphabet).to start_with('a') & end_with('z')
```

```
stoplight_color = %w[ green red yellow ].sample
expect(stoplight_color).to eq('green') | eq('red') | eq('yellow')
```

This syntax might seem really fancy and complex, but internally, it's quite simple. These methods return a new matcher that wraps the two operands. The and matcher only succeeds if both of its operands match. The or matcher succeeds if either operand matches.

Poking around in IRB will give you a sense of how these work:

```
>> start_with_a_and_end_with_z = start_with('a').and end_with('z')
=> #<RSpec::Matchers::BuiltIn::Compound::And:0x007f94dc83ba30
   @matcher_1=#<RSpec::Matchers::BuiltIn::StartWith:0x007f94dc82bd38
               @actual_does_not_have_ordered_elements=false, @expected="a">,
   @matcher_2=#<RSpec::Matchers::BuiltIn::EndWith:0x007f94dc82bc20
               @actual_does_not_have_ordered_elements=false, @expected="z">>
```

Here we've created a compound matcher, an instance of RSpec::Matchers::BuiltIn::Compound::And, which keeps internal references to the original start_with and end_with matchers.

The new compound matcher works just like any other. It even provides its own error message, based on the messages of the underlying matchers:

```
>> expect(['a', 'z']).to start_with_a_and_end_with_z
=> true
>> expect(['a', 'y']).to start_with_a_and_end_with_z
RSpec::Expectations::ExpectationNotMetError: expected ["a", "y"] to end    ↵
with "z"
    « backtrace truncated »
>> expect(['b', 'y']).to start_with_a_and_end_with_z
RSpec::Expectations::ExpectationNotMetError:    expected ["b", "y"] to     ↵
start with "a"
```

```
...and:
```

```
   expected ["b", "y"] to end with "z"
   « backtrace truncated »
```

Compound matchers are smart enough to show failure messages only for the bits that failed.

Like all matchers, compound matchers can be passed as arguments to other matchers:

```
10-exploring-rspec-expectations/04/composing_matchers.rb
letter_ranges = ['N to Z', 'A to M']
expect(letter_ranges).to contain_exactly(
  a_string_starting_with('A') & ending_with('M'),
  a_string_starting_with('N') & ending_with('Z')
)
```

You can mix and match these techniques for composing matchers, all in one expectation. You can also nest them as deeply as you need. Here, we're combining matchers with logical operators, then nesting those combinations into a collection matcher. This flexibility allows you to describe complex data precisely.

Now that you've seen how to combine matchers, let's turn our attention to output.

Generated Example Descriptions

Matchers have another useful ability over simpler assert methods: they're self-describing. The matcher protocol includes the optional (but recommended) description method. All built-in matchers define this method:

```
>> start_with(1).description
=> "start with 1"
>> (start_with(1) & end_with(9)).description
=> "start with 1 and end with 9"
>> contain_exactly( a_string_starting_with(1) & ending_with(9) ).description
=> "contain exactly (a string starting with 1 and ending with 9)"
```

As you can see, the descriptions of composed and compound matchers include the description of each part. These descriptions are used in failure messages when you pass one matcher to another. They can also help you reduce duplication in your specs. Typically, each example has a string stating the intended behavior:

```
10-exploring-rspec-expectations/06/spec/cookie_recipe_spec.rb
class CookieRecipe
  attr_reader :ingredients

  def initialize
    @ingredients = [:butter, :milk, :flour, :sugar, :eggs, :chocolate_chips]
  end
end

RSpec.describe CookieRecipe, '#ingredients' do
  it 'should include :butter, :milk and :eggs' do
    expect(CookieRecipe.new.ingredients).to include(:butter, :milk, :eggs)
  end
```

```
  it 'should not include :fish_oil' do
    expect(CookieRecipe.new.ingredients).not_to include(:fish_oil)
  end
end
```

These appear in the output when you run your specs with the documentation formatter:

```
$ rspec spec/cookie_recipe_spec.rb --format documentation

CookieRecipe#ingredients
  should include :butter, :milk and :eggs
  should not include :fish_oil

Finished in 0.00197 seconds (files took 0.08433 seconds to load)
2 examples, 0 failures
```

Notice the duplication in the specs, though. We've explained each example twice: once in the description, and once in the code. If we remove the former, RSpec will write its own description based on the code:

```
10-exploring-rspec-expectations/06/spec/cookie_recipe_no_doc_strings_spec.rb
RSpec.describe CookieRecipe, '#ingredients' do
  specify do
    expect(CookieRecipe.new.ingredients).to include(:butter, :milk, :eggs)
  end

  specify do
    expect(CookieRecipe.new.ingredients).not_to include(:fish_oil)
  end
end
```

We've also switched to the specify alias to avoid the grammatically awkward phrase it expect. When we run this version of the specs:

```
$ rspec spec/cookie_recipe_no_doc_strings_spec.rb --format documentation

CookieRecipe#ingredients
  should include :butter, :milk, and :eggs
  should not include :fish_oil

Finished in 0.00212 seconds (files took 0.08655 seconds to load)
2 examples, 0 failures
```

...the output is exactly the same as when we wrote the descriptions by hand. This way, though, the specs are a litttle more future-proof. If we want to change an example later—to make the recipe dairy-free, for instance—we don't have to worry about keeping our English description in sync with the code.

To generate these descriptions, RSpec takes the description of the last-executed expectation and prefixes it with should or should not.

We can simplify our specs even further using the subject method from rspec-core instead of repeating the recipe-creation code. This construct is the equivalent of calling let(:subject) { ... }:

```
10-exploring-rspec-expectations/06/spec/cookie_recipe_subject_spec.rb
RSpec.describe CookieRecipe, '#ingredients' do
  subject { CookieRecipe.new.ingredients }
  it { is_expected.to include(:butter, :milk, :eggs) }
  it { is_expected.not_to include(:fish_oil) }
end
```

The subject method defines how to build the object we're testing. RSpec gives us is_expected as shorthand for expect(subject). The phrase it is_expected reads nicely in each spec here, though in larger projects we tend to favor more explicit let constructs for clarity's sake.

Once again, we get the same documentation output:

```
$ rspec spec/cookie_recipe_subject_spec.rb --format documentation

CookieRecipe#ingredients
  should include :butter, :milk, and :eggs
  should not include :fish_oil

Finished in 0.00225 seconds (files took 0.08616 seconds to load)
2 examples, 0 failures
```

Here's an alternate form of this one-liner syntax that looks even more like the generated descriptions:

```
10-exploring-rspec-expectations/06/spec/cookie_recipe_should_spec.rb
RSpec.describe CookieRecipe, '#ingredients' do
  subject { CookieRecipe.new.ingredients }
  it { should include(:butter, :milk, :eggs) }
  it { should_not include(:fish_oil) }
end
```

Wait, didn't we just say should was problematic in *What Happened to should?*, on page 171? The problem with the old should from RSpec 2 and before isn't the name; it's the fact that RSpec had to monkey-patch the core Object class to implement it.

This should is different: it's just a local alias for expect(subject).to. You can use either should or is_expected.to, whichever you prefer.

We recommend you use this one-liner syntax sparingly. It's possible to over-emphasize brevity and rely too much on one-liners. To keep our enthusiasm in check, let's go over a few of the downsides of generated descriptions:

- Since they're not available until runtime, you can't use them with the
  --example option to run a single spec.

- Your specs' output can be misleading if you change your setup code and
  forget to update the describe or context documentation.

- Specs written in a one-liner style carry extra cognitive load; you have to
  understand how subject and is_expected/should relate.

The one case when we do recommend one-liner syntax is when the generated
description is a near-exact duplicate of what you would have written by hand.
For a good example, see the specs for the Mustermann string-matching library.[2]

Your Turn

In this chapter, you've learned the major parts of an expectation: the expect
method, the subject, to/not_to, and the matcher. You wrote some simple
expectations using expect and a few of RSpec's built-in matchers. You saw
how to combine matchers by passing them into one another, and by combining
them with and/or.

In the next chapter, we'll take you on a tour of the matchers that RSpec ships
with. But first, test your newfound knowledge of expectations with a quick
exercise.

Exercise

We've prepared an unfinished spec file that will give you the chance to try
out the concepts explained in this chapter. We encourage you to download
it, run it, and edit it until you've gotten all the specs to pass consistently:

10-exploring-rspec-expectations/exercises/data_generator_spec.rb
```ruby
require 'date'

class DataGenerator
  def boolean_value
    [true, false].sample
  end

  def email_address_value
    domain = %w[ gmail.com yahoo.com aol.com hotmail.com ].sample
    username_characters = (0..9).to_a + ('a'..'z').to_a + ('A'..'Z').to_a
    username_length = rand(5) + 3
    username = Array.new(username_length) { username_characters.sample }.join

    "#{username}@#{domain}"
  end
```

---

2. https://github.com/sinatra/mustermann/blob/v0.4.0/mustermann/spec/sinatra_spec.rb

```ruby
  def date_value
    Date.new(
      (1950..1999).to_a.sample,
      (1..12).to_a.sample,
      (1..28).to_a.sample,
    )
  end

  def user_record
    {
      email_address: email_address_value,
      date_of_birth: date_value,
      active:        boolean_value
    }
  end

  def users(count)
    Array.new(count) { user_record }
  end
end

RSpec.configure do |c|
  c.fail_fast = true
  c.formatter = 'documentation'
  c.color     = true
  c.order     = :defined
end

RSpec.describe DataGenerator do
  def be_a_boolean
    # Ruby has no Boolean class so this doesn't work.
    # Is there a way we can use `or` to combine two matchers instead?
    be_a(Boolean)
  end

  it "generates boolean values" do
    value = DataGenerator.new.boolean_value
    expect(value).to be_a_boolean
  end

  def be_a_date_before_2000
    # Combine the `be_a(klass)` matcher with the `be < value` matcher
    # to create a matcher that matches dates before January 1st, 2000.
    fill_me_in
  end

  it "generates dates before January 1st, 2000" do
    value = DataGenerator.new.date_value
    expect(value).to be_a_date_before_2000
  end
```

```ruby
def be_an_email_address
  # Pass a simple regex to `match` to define a matcher for email addresses.
  # Don't worry about complete email validation; something very simple is fine.
  match(/some regex/)
end

it "generates email addresses" do
  value = DataGenerator.new.email_address_value
  expect(value).to be_an_email_address
end

def match_the_shape_of_a_user_record
  # Use `be_a_boolean`, `be_a_date_before_2000` and `be_an_email_address`
  # in the hash passed to `match` below to define this matcher.
  match(fill_this_in: "with a hash describing the shape of the data")
end

it "generates user records" do
  user = DataGenerator.new.user_record
  expect(user).to match_the_shape_of_a_user_record
end

def all_match_the_shape_of_a_user_record
  # Combine the `all` matcher and `match_the_shape_of_a_user_record` here.
  fill_me_in
end

it "generates a list of user records" do
  users = DataGenerator.new.users(4)
  expect(users).to all_match_the_shape_of_a_user_record
end
end
```

In this chapter, you'll see:

- A tour of the included matchers
- The difference between *primitive* and *higher-order* matchers
- The difference between *value* and *block* expectations

## CHAPTER 11

Matchers Included in RSpec Expectations

In the previous chapter, you learned how to write expectations to check your code's behavior. You got to know the various parts of an expectation, such as the *subject* and the *matcher*.

Now, it's time to take a closer look at matchers. You've called them in your specs and combined them with other matchers. You've even written a simple one from scratch, though most of the time you won't have to. RSpec ships with a ton of useful matchers to help you specify exactly how you want your code to behave.

In this chapter, we're going to take a tour of RSpec's built-in matchers. We won't exhaustively list every available matcher—that's what Appendix 3, *Matcher Cheat Sheet*, on page 307 is for. But we will hit the highlights so that you can choose the best matcher for each situation.

The matchers in rspec-expectations fall into three broad categories:

- *Primitive matchers* for basic data types like strings, numbers, and so on

- *Higher-order matchers* that can take other matchers as input, then (among other uses) apply them across collections

- *Block matchers* for checking properties of code, including blocks, exceptions, and side effects

We'll start our tour with the most commonly used primitive matchers.

Primitive Matchers

The word *primitive* in a programming language refers to a bread-and-butter data type that can't be broken down into smaller pieces. Booleans, integers, and floating-point numbers are all primitives.

RSpec's primitive matchers are similar. They have simple, precise definitions that can't be broken down any further. They're not meant to accept other matchers as input (but you can go the other direction, passing them into other matchers). Typically, they just pass the operation you're performing—an equality check, for example—straight through to the subject of the expectation.

Equality and Identity

RSpec's most fundamental matchers are all concerned with variations of the question, "Are these two things the same?" Depending on context, "the same" might refer to one of several things:

- *Identity*: for example, two references to one object

- *Hash key equality*: two objects of the same type and value, such as two copies of the string "hello"

- *Value equality*: two objects of compatible types with the same meaning, such as the integer 42 and the floating-point number 42.0

Most of the time, Ruby programmers are concerned with the last of these: value equality, embodied in Ruby's == operator.

Value Equality

In RSpec, you use the eq matcher to check value equality.

11-matchers-included-in-rspec-expectations/01/primitive_matchers.rb
```
expect(Math.sqrt(9)).to eq(3)

# equivalent to:
Math.sqrt(9) == 3
```

Most of the time, this matcher is the one you want. However, sometimes you have a more specific need.

Identity

Say you're testing a Permutations class that generates every possible ordering of a set of words. This operation gets expensive quickly, and so you'd like to memoize (cache) the result.

You might initially try using the eq matcher to make sure that the second call hits the cached value:

11-matchers-included-in-rspec-expectations/01/primitive_matchers.rb
```
perms       = Permutations.new
first_try   = perms.of(long_word_list)
second_try  = perms.of(long_word_list)

expect(second_try).to eq(first_try)
```

This test will likely give you false assurances. If the underlying cache is mis-behaving or was never implemented, the calculation will just run again and produce a new word list in the same order. Because both arrays have the same contents, your test will incorrectly pass.

Instead, you'd like to know whether or not first_try and second_try are actually referring to the same underlying object—not just two copies with identical contents.

For this stricter comparison, you'd use RSpec's equal matcher, which hands off to Ruby's equal? method behind the scenes:

11-matchers-included-in-rspec-expectations/01/primitive_matchers.rb
```
expect(second_try).to equal(first_try)
```

RSpec's own internal specs for the RSpec.configuration method use this technique to make sure that the method always returns the same RSpec::Core::Configuration instance:

11-matchers-included-in-rspec-expectations/01/primitive_matchers.rb
```
RSpec.describe RSpec do
  describe '.configuration' do
    it 'returns the same object every time' do
      expect(RSpec.configuration).to equal(RSpec.configuration)
    end
  end
end
```

If you prefer, you can also use be(x) as an alias for equal(x), to emphasize that this matcher is about *identity* rather than *value equality*:

11-matchers-included-in-rspec-expectations/01/primitive_matchers.rb
```
expect(RSpec.configuration).to be(RSpec.configuration)
```

The third notion of equality sits between these two in terms of strictness.

Hash Key Equality

Programmers rarely check hash key equality directly. As the name implies, it's used to check that two values should be considered the same Hash key. If you encounter a use of this method in the wild, it will likely be called from an object designed to behave like a dictionary.

RSpec's eql matcher, based on Ruby's built-in eql? method, checks for hash key equality. Generally, it behaves the same as the eq matcher (since eql? generally behaves the same as ==). One notable difference is that eql? always considers integers and floating-point numbers to be different:

11-matchers-included-in-rspec-expectations/01/primitive_matchers.rb
```
# 3 == 3.0:
expect(3).to eq(3.0)

# ...but 3.eql?(3.0) is false:
expect(3).not_to eql(3.0)
```

This behavior allows 3 and 3.0 to be used as different keys in the same hash.

When in Doubt, Use eq

 All these different ways to compare objects can seem confusing. When you're not sure which matcher is right, try eq first. In most situations, value equality is the one you need.

Variations

All three of these matchers have aliases that read better in composed matcher expressions:

- an_object_eq_to aliases eq
- an_object_equal_to aliases equal
- an_object_eql_to aliases eql

For instance, consider the following expectation that checks a list of Ruby classes:

11-matchers-included-in-rspec-expectations/01/primitive_matchers.rb
```
expect([String, Regexp]).to include(String)
```

The intent was to require the actual Ruby String class to be present. But this spec will incorrectly allow plain Ruby strings to pass as well:

11-matchers-included-in-rspec-expectations/01/primitive_matchers.rb
```
expect(['a string', Regexp]).to include(String)
```

As we saw in the previous chapter, higher-order matchers like include check their arguments with the three-quals operator, ===. In this case, RSpec ends up checking String === 'a string', which returns true.

The fix is to pass the an_object_eq_to matcher into include, to make the pass/fail criteria more precise:

11-matchers-included-in-rspec-expectations/01/primitive_matchers.rb
```
expect([String, Regexp]).to include(an_object_eq_to String)
```

The three equality matchers we've discussed will work on any Ruby object.

Truthiness

While Ruby has literal true and false values, it allows *any* object to be used in a conditional. The rules are very simple: false and nil are both treated as false, and everything else is treated as true (even the number zero!).

In a nod to comedian Stephen Colbert, Rubyists refer to these categories of values as *truthy* and *falsey* (or *falsy*; there's no standard spelling).[1] RSpec follows this lead with its truthiness matchers:

11-matchers-included-in-rspec-expectations/01/primitive_matchers.rb
```
expect(true).to be_truthy
expect(0).to be_truthy
expect(false).not_to be_truthy
expect(nil).not_to be_truthy

# ...and on the flip side:
expect(false).to be_falsey
expect(nil).to be_falsey
expect(true).not_to be_falsey
expect(0).not_to be_falsey
```

If you find the language of "be truthy" and "be falsey" distasteful, bear in mind that the naming is intentional. It's a subtle nudge that you've chosen a more informal matcher. If you want to specify that a value is *precisely* equal to true or false, simply use one of the equality matchers we described in the last section:

11-matchers-included-in-rspec-expectations/01/primitive_matchers.rb
```
expect(1.odd?).to be true
expect(2.odd?).to eq false
```

Like the equality matchers we saw earlier, truthiness matchers have aliases designed to read well in composed matcher expressions:

- be_truthy is aliased as a_truthy_value.
- be_falsey is aliased as be_falsy, a_falsey_value and a_falsy_value.

Operator Comparisons

We've used the be method with arguments before, as in expect(answer).to be(42). This method has another form, one without arguments. With it, you can perform greater-than and less-than comparisons (or use any Ruby binary operator):

---

1. http://www.cc.com/video-clips/63ite2/the-colbert-report-the-word---truthiness

11-matchers-included-in-rspec-expectations/01/primitive_matchers.rb
```
expect(1).to be == 1
expect(1).to be < 2
expect(1).to be <= 2
expect(2).to be > 1
expect(2).to be >= 1
expect(String).to be === 'a string'
expect(/foo/).to be =~ 'food'
```

In each case, RSpec uses your operator—such as == or <—to compare the actual and expected values. The matcher on the first line, be == 1, is equivalent to eq(1). Use whichever you prefer.

When passing one of these operator matchers into a different matcher, you'll probably want to use the alias a_value. For example:

11-matchers-included-in-rspec-expectations/01/primitive_matchers.rb
```
squares = 1.upto(4).map { |i| i * i }
expect(squares).to include(a_value > 15)
```

So far, we've been comparing precise values like integers and strings. Next, we'll see what happens when we drag imprecise floating-point numbers into the mix.

Delta and Range Comparisons

Floating-point numbers are an unfortunate reality in the world of binary computing with limited precision. Checking two floats for exact equality will frequently cause failures. For example, if you try this seemingly straightforward expectation:

11-matchers-included-in-rspec-expectations/01/primitive_matchers.rb
```
expect(0.1 + 0.2).to eq(0.3)
```

...then you get a failure:

```
expected: 0.3
     got: 0.30000000000000004

(compared using ==)
```

This failure may surprise you, but you'll see similar behavior in any language that uses IEEE-754 floats, as Ruby does.[2] Just as decimal math can't express most real numbers using a finite amount of digits (for example, $1/3 = 0.333...$), your computer's internal binary representation of floating-point numbers is also imperfect.

---

2. http://0.30000000000000004.com/

Absolute Difference

Instead of looking for exact equality with floats, you should use RSpec's be_within matcher:

```
11-matchers-included-in-rspec-expectations/01/primitive_matchers.rb
expect(0.1 + 0.2).to be_within(0.0001).of(0.3)
```

The value we've passed to be_within here is the *delta*, or absolute difference in either direction. This particular expectation passes as long as the value is between 0.2999 and 0.3001 (which it is, of course).

Relative Difference

Equally useful is the percent_of method, where you give a *relative* difference instead:

```
11-matchers-included-in-rspec-expectations/01/primitive_matchers.rb
town_population = 1237
expect(town_population).to be_within(25).percent_of(1000)
```

We've used integers for this example to show that range-related matchers aren't just for floating-point numbers. All the matchers in this section work just fine for both types of numbers. Integer approximation comes in handy when you're testing things that have slightly different values each time, such as memory consumption.

A single be_within matcher supports both absolute and relative values, based on which method you chain off of it. This style is called a *fluent interface*, and it helps you write expectations that read naturally: "expect [actual] to be within [delta] of [expected]."[3]

As you will see throughout the rest of this chapter, many of the other built-in matchers support this same kind of fluent interface. It is easy to add it to your custom matchers as well, as you will see in *Adding a Fluent Interface*, on page 222.

Ranges

Sometimes, it's a better fit to express your expected values in terms of a *range*, rather than a target value and delta. For these situations, you can use the be_between matcher:

```
11-matchers-included-in-rspec-expectations/01/primitive_matchers.rb
expect(town_population).to be_between(750, 1250)
```

---

3. https://martinfowler.com/bliki/FluentInterface.html

Like the be_within matcher, be_between supports a fluent interface. You can use be_between(x, y).inclusive or be_between(x, y).exclusive to explicitly choose an inclusive or exclusive range. The default is inclusive, like Ruby's Comparable#between?(x, y).

Finally, both of these matchers have aliases that are designed to read well in composed matcher expressions: be_within is aliased to a_value_within and be_between is aliased to a_value_between.

Dynamic Predicates

A *predicate* is a method that answers a question with a Boolean answer. In Ruby, predicate method names typically omit the verb and end with a question mark. For example, Ruby's Array class provides an empty? method rather than is_empty.

This convention is so common that RSpec includes special support for it in the form of *dynamic predicate matchers*.

How to Use Them

When you use an unrecognized matcher of the form be_..., RSpec strips off the be_, adds a question mark to the end, and calls that method on the subject.

For instance, for RSpec to call array.empty?, you can use be_empty in your expectation:

```
11-matchers-included-in-rspec-expectations/01/primitive_matchers.rb
expect([]).to be_empty
```

If empty? returns a truthy value (see *Truthiness*, on page 191), the expectation passes. You can alternately use a be_a_ or be_an_ prefix for predicates that are nouns. For example, if you had a user object with an admin? predicate, either of these would work:

```
11-matchers-included-in-rspec-expectations/01/primitive_matchers.rb
expect(user).to be_admin
expect(user).to be_an_admin
```

The latter reads much more nicely. For predicates that begin with has_, such as hash.has_key?(:age), you can use a dynamic predicate matcher starting with have_:

```
11-matchers-included-in-rspec-expectations/01/primitive_matchers.rb
hash = { name: 'Harry Potter', age: 17, house: 'Gryffindor' }
expect(hash).to have_key(:age)
```

This example demonstrates another feature of RSpec's dynamic predicate matchers: they support arguments and a block. If you pass arguments (or a block) to a dynamic predicate matcher, RSpec will forward them on to the predicate method when it calls it on the expectation subject.

Trade-offs

As readable and useful as dynamic predicate matchers can be, they do have some trade-offs. Like the truthiness matchers, the dynamic predicate matchers use Ruby's loose Boolean conditional semantics. Most of the time, this is what you want, but you'll need to use a different technique if you want to test for exact true or false results.

A bigger problem is documentation. Because dynamic matchers are generated on the fly, they have no documentation. Your teammates may see be_an_admin in your tests and go looking for it in vain in the RSpec docs. A simple equality matcher wouldn't have this problem:

`11-matchers-included-in-rspec-expectations/01/primitive_matchers.rb`
```
expect(user.admin?).to eq(true)
```

However, the output from the simple matcher isn't nearly as helpful:

```
expected: true
     got: false

(compared using ==)
```

The failure output from using be_an_admin is far better:

```
expected `#<User name="Daphne">.admin?` to return true, got false
```

Dynamic predicate matchers are useful in composed matcher expressions. For instance, you can customize how a collection matches based on a predicate:

`11-matchers-included-in-rspec-expectations/01/primitive_matchers.rb`
```
expect(array_of_hashes).to include(have_key(:lol))
```

The language is a little stilted here, since dynamic matchers have no built-in aliases. If you want a nice, readable noun-phrase version of a predicate matcher, you'll have to alias it yourself. Luckily, it's trivial to do so, as we'll show in *Defining Matcher Aliases*, on page 218.

Given these trade-offs, there's no slam-dunk case for or against them. Personally, we like them, but talk it over with your team before you strew these all over your specs.

Dynamic Predicate Matchers vs. Comparing to true/false

One of the goals of TDD is to help you design your APIs. For this reason, when we're writing specs *for* a predicate method, we like to call the method directly and compare the return value explicitly with true or false. If we're testing a method named success?, we'll say expect(subject.success?).to be true in our examples.

On the other hand, when a predicate method isn't what we're directly testing but instead just happens to be available on a returned object, we like to use a dynamic predicate matcher. For instance, when you tested the Ledger#record method in the expense tracker project earlier in this book, we suggested that you write an expectation like expect(result).to be_success.

Satisfaction

Sometimes, you'll have a complicated condition that can't be expressed with any of the matchers we've seen so far. For these cases, RSpec provides the satisfy matcher. To use it, you wrap up your pass/fail logic into a block and hand that block to satisfy:

11-matchers-included-in-rspec-expectations/01/primitive_matchers.rb
```
expect(1).to satisfy { |number| number.odd? }
```

RSpec passes the subject of the expectation, 1, into the block—which supports any arbitrary logic you can think up.

We like to think of satisfy as an *adapter*: it wraps any chunk of Ruby code and adapts it to RSpec's matcher protocol. This ability is useful when building a composed matcher expression:

11-matchers-included-in-rspec-expectations/01/primitive_matchers.rb
```
expect([1, 2, 3]).to include(an_object_satisfying(&:even?))
```

Here, we're using satisfy's alias, an_object_satisfying with a composed matcher expression. We're also saving a bit of verbiage by creating the block implicitly, using Ruby's Symbol#to_proc.[4]

As flexible as satisfy is, we still favor purpose-built matchers. The latter provide more specific, helpful failure messages.

---

4. http://ruby-doc.org/core-2.4.1/Symbol.html#method-i-to_proc

Higher-Order Matchers

All the matchers seen so far are primitives. Now, we're going to look at higher-order matchers—that is, matchers that you can pass other matchers into. With this technique, you can build up composed matchers that specify exactly the behavior you want.

Collections and Strings

One of the primary tasks of programming, in any language, is dealing with collections, and Ruby is no exception. RSpec ships with six different matchers for dealing with data structures:

- include requires certain items to be present (in any order).
- start_with and end_with require items to be at the beginning or end.
- all checks a common property across all items.
- match checks a data structure against a pattern.
- contain_exactly requires certain items, *and no others*, to be present (in any order).

All of these matchers also work with strings, with a few minor differences (after all, strings are just collections of characters!). In the following sections, we'll review the matchers in detail.

include

The include matcher is one of the most flexible, useful matchers RSpec provides. It's also a key defense against brittleness. By using include rather than a stricter matcher like eq or match, you can specify just the elements you care about. The collection can contain unrelated items, and your tests will still pass.

At its simplest, the include matcher works on any object with an include? method. Strings and arrays both support this method:

```
11-matchers-included-in-rspec-expectations/02/higher_order_matchers.rb
expect('a string').to include('str')
expect([1, 2, 3]).to include(3)
```

For hashes, you can check for the presence of a specific *key* or *key-value pair* (passed as a hash):

```
11-matchers-included-in-rspec-expectations/02/higher_order_matchers.rb
hash = { name: 'Harry Potter', age: 17, house: 'Gryffindor' }
expect(hash).to include(:name)
expect(hash).to include(age: 17)
```

The include matcher accepts a variable number of arguments so that you can specify multiple substrings, array items, hash keys or key-value pairs:

```
11-matchers-included-in-rspec-expectations/02/higher_order_matchers.rb
expect('a string').to include('str', 'ing')
expect([1, 2, 3]).to include(3, 2)
expect(hash).to include(:name, :age)
expect(hash).to include(name: 'Harry Potter', age: 17)
```

This works well, but there is a gotcha related to variable numbers of items. Consider this example:

```
11-matchers-included-in-rspec-expectations/02/higher_order_matchers.rb
expecteds = [3, 2]
expect([1, 2, 3]).to include(expecteds)
```

This expectation fails, even though the array clearly includes 3 and 2. Here's the failure message:

```
expected [1, 2, 3] to include [3, 2]
```

The error message gives us a clue. This matcher expects the array to include([3, 2]), rather than to include(3, 2). It would pass if the actual array was something like [1, [3, 2]].

In order for RSpec to look for the individual items, you need to extract them from the array. You can do so by prefixing the expecteds argument with the Ruby splat operator:[5]

```
11-matchers-included-in-rspec-expectations/02/higher_order_matchers.rb
expect([1, 2, 3]).to include(*expecteds)
```

The include matcher is also available as a_collection_including, a_string_including, and a_hash_including, for when you're passing it into other matchers. As a higher-order matcher, include can also receive matchers as arguments—see *Operator Comparisons*, on page 191 or *Satisfaction*, on page 196 for examples.

start_with and end_with

These two matchers are useful when you care about the contents of a string or collection at the start or end but don't care about the rest. They work exactly the way their names imply:

```
11-matchers-included-in-rspec-expectations/02/higher_order_matchers.rb
expect('a string').to start_with('a str').and end_with('ng')
expect([1, 2, 3]).to start_with(1).and end_with(3)
```

---

5. http://ruby-doc.org/core-2.4.1/doc/syntax/calling_methods_rdoc.html#label-Array+to+Arguments+Conversion

As the string example shows, you can specify as much or as little of the string as you like. The same applies to arrays; you can check for a sequence of elements at the beginning or end:

11-matchers-included-in-rspec-expectations/02/higher_order_matchers.rb
```
expect([1, 2, 3]).to start_with(1, 2)
expect([1, 2, 3]).to end_with(2, 3)
```

The same caution about using the Ruby splat operator with include applies to starts_with and ends_with as well.

Following the aliasing pattern we've seen elsewhere, these matchers have two aliases each:

- a_string_starting_with / a_string_ending_with
- a_collection_starting_with / a_collection_ending_with

You could combine these, for example:

11-matchers-included-in-rspec-expectations/02/higher_order_matchers.rb
```
expect(['list', 'of', 'words']).to start_with(
  a_string_ending_with('st')
).and end_with(
  a_string_starting_with('wo')
)
```

The outer start_with matcher checks the word 'list' using the inner a_string_ending_with, and so on.

all

The all matcher is somewhat of an oddity: it is the only built-in matcher that is not a verb, and it is the only one that *always* takes another matcher as an argument:

11-matchers-included-in-rspec-expectations/02/higher_order_matchers.rb
```
numbers = [2, 4, 6, 8]
expect(numbers).to all be_even
```

This expression does exactly what it says: it expects all the numbers in the array to be even. Here, 'be_even' is a dynamic predicate like the ones we saw in *Dynamic Predicates*, on page 194. It calls 'even?' on each element of the array.

One gotcha to be aware of is that, like Enumerable#all?, this matcher passes against an empty array. This can lead to surprises. Consider the following incorrect method for generating a list of numbers:

```
11-matchers-included-in-rspec-expectations/02/higher_order_matchers.rb
def self.evens_up_to(n = 0)
  0.upto(n).select(&:odd?)
end
```

```
expect(evens_up_to).to all be_even
```

This method generates odd numbers instead of evens, but our expectation didn't fail. We forgot to pass an argument to evens_up_to, and it returned an empty array. One solution is to use a compound matcher to ensure the array is non-empty:

```
11-matchers-included-in-rspec-expectations/02/higher_order_matchers.rb
RSpec::Matchers.define_negated_matcher :be_non_empty, :be_empty
```

```
expect(evens_up_to).to be_non_empty.and all be_even
```

We're using another RSpec feature, define_negated_matcher, to create a new be_non_empty matcher that's the opposite of be_empty. We'll learn more about define_negated_matcher in *Negating Matchers*, on page 219.

Now, the expectation correctly flags the broken method as failing:

```
expected `[].empty?` to return false, got true
```

RSpec's all matcher uses Ruby's Enumerable#all? under the hood. You may be wondering whether or not RSpec has matchers for the other similar Enumerable methods, like any or none. It doesn't, because this would lead to nonsensical code such as expect(numbers).to none be_even. Instead, you can build up easier-to-read matchers using to include or not_to include.[6]

match

If you call JSON or XML APIs, you often end up with deeply nested arrays and hashes. The match matcher is a Swiss army knife for this kind of data.

As you did with eq, you provide a data structure that's laid out like the result you're expecting. match is more flexible, however. You can substitute a matcher for any array element, or for any hash value, at any level of nesting:

```
11-matchers-included-in-rspec-expectations/02/higher_order_matchers.rb
children = [
  { name: 'Coen',   age: 6 },
  { name: 'Daphne', age: 4 },
  { name: 'Crosby', age: 2 }
]
```

---

6. That is the question.

```
expect(children).to match [
  { name: 'Coen',   age: a_value > 5 },
  { name: 'Daphne', age: a_value_between(3, 5) },
  { name: 'Crosby', age: a_value < 3 }
]
```

When you're matching against a string, match delegates to String#match, which accepts either a regular expression or a string:

11-matchers-included-in-rspec-expectations/02/higher_order_matchers.rb
```
expect('a string').to match(/str/)
expect('a string').to match('str')
```

Naturally, this matcher has an_object_matching and a_string_matching aliases.

contain_exactly

We've seen that match checks data structures more loosely than eq; contain_exactly is even looser. The difference is that match requires a specific order, whereas contain_exactly ignores ordering. For example, both of these expectations pass:

11-matchers-included-in-rspec-expectations/02/higher_order_matchers.rb
```
expect(children).to contain_exactly(
  { name: 'Daphne', age: a_value_between(3, 5) },
  { name: 'Crosby', age: a_value < 3 },
  { name: 'Coen',   age: a_value > 5 }
)

expect(children).to contain_exactly(
  { name: 'Crosby', age: a_value < 3 },
  { name: 'Coen',   age: a_value > 5 },
  { name: 'Daphne', age: a_value_between(3, 5) }
)
```

Like include, contain_exactly receives multiple array elements as separate arguments. It's also available as a_collection_containing_exactly.

Which Collection Matcher Should I Use?

With a half-dozen collection matchers to pick from, you may wonder which one is the best for your situation. In general, we recommend you use the loosest matcher that still specifies the behavior you care about.

Avoid Overspecification: Favor Loose Matchers

 Using a loose matcher makes your specs less brittle; it prevents incidental details from causing an unexpected failure.

The flowchart on page 202 provides a quick reference for the different uses of collection and string matchers.

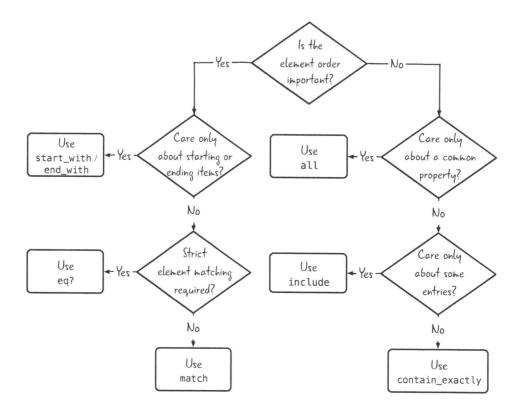

Object Attributes

Some Ruby objects act like fancier versions of hashes. Struct, OpenStruct, and ActiveRecord can all act like buckets for your data, which you read via attributes.

If you need to check an object's attributes against a template, you can use the have_attributes matcher:

```
11-matchers-included-in-rspec-expectations/02/higher_order_matchers.rb
require 'uri'
uri = URI('http://github.com/rspec/rspec')
expect(uri).to have_attributes(host: 'github.com', path: '/rspec/rspec')
```

This matcher is particularly useful as an argument to another matcher; the an_object_having_attributes form comes in handy here:

```
11-matchers-included-in-rspec-expectations/02/higher_order_matchers.rb
expect([uri]).to include(an_object_having_attributes(host: 'github.com'))
```

This comparison is more forgiving than exact equality. Your object can contain additional attributes beyond the ones you specify, and still satisfy the matcher.

Block Matchers

With all the expectations we've seen so far, we've passed regular Ruby objects into expect:

11-matchers-included-in-rspec-expectations/03/block_matchers.rb
```
expect(3).to eq(3)
```

This is fine for checking properties of your data. But sometimes you need to check properties of a *piece of code*. For example, perhaps a certain piece of code is supposed to raise an exception. In this case, you can pass a block into expect:

11-matchers-included-in-rspec-expectations/03/block_matchers.rb
```
expect { raise 'boom' }.to raise_error('boom')
```

RSpec will run the block and watch for the specific side effects you specify: exceptions, mutating variables, I/O, and so on.

Raising and Throwing

You're likely familiar with raising Ruby exceptions to jump out of your running code and report an error to the caller. Ruby also has a related concept, throwing symbols, for jumping to other parts of your program.

RSpec provides matchers for both of these situations: the appropriately named raise_error and throw_symbol.

raise_error

First, let's look at raise_error, also known as raise_exception. This matcher is very flexible, supporting multiple forms:

- raise_error with no arguments matches if *any* error is raised.

- raise_error(SomeErrorClass) matches if SomeErrorClass or a subclass is raised.

- raise_error('some message') matches if an error is raised with a message exactly equal to a given string.

- raise_error(/some regex/) matches if an error is raised with a message matching a given pattern.

You can combine these criteria if both the class and message are important, either via passing two arguments or by using a fluent interface:

- raise_error(SomeErrorClass, "some message")
- raise_error(SomeErrorClass, /some regex/)
- raise_error(SomeErrorClass).with_message("some message")
- raise_error(SomeErrorClass).with_message(/some regex/)

With any of these forms, you can pass in another RSpec matcher (such as a_string_starting_with for the message name) to control how the matching works. For example, the following expectation ensures the exception has its name attribute set:

11-matchers-included-in-rspec-expectations/03/block_matchers.rb
```
expect {
  'hello'.world
}.to raise_error(an_object_having_attributes(name: :world))
```

Checking properties of exceptions can get really fiddly. If you find yourself passing a complex nested composed matcher expression to raise_error, you'll see a really long failure message in the output. To avoid this situation, you can instead pass a block into raise_error and move your logic there:

11-matchers-included-in-rspec-expectations/03/block_matchers.rb
```
expect { 'hello'.world }.to raise_error(NoMethodError) do |ex|
  expect(ex.name).to eq(:world)
end
```

There are a couple of gotchas with raise_error that can lead to false positives. First, raise_error (with no arguments) will match *any* error—and it can't tell the difference between exceptions you *did* or *did not* mean to throw.

For example, if you rename a method but forget to update your spec, Ruby will throw a NoMethodError. An overzealous raise_error will swallow this exception, and your spec will pass even though it's no longer exercising the method you mean to test!

Likewise, you might use raise_error(ArgumentError) to make sure one of your methods correctly raises this error. If you later make a breaking change to the method signature—such as adding an argument—but forget to update a caller, Ruby will throw the same error. Your spec will pass (because all it sees is the ArgumentError it's expecting), but the code will still be broken.

We've actually run into this kind of false positive In RSpec itself.[7]

Never Check for a Bare Exception

Always include some kind of detail—either a specific custom error class or a snippet from the message—that is unique to the specific raise statement you are testing.

On the flip side, the negative form—expect { ... }.not_to raise_error(...)—has the opposite problem. If we give too much detail in our specs, we risk seeing a

___
7. https://github.com/rspec/rspec-mocks/pull/550

false positive. Consider this expectation, where an underlying age_of method is supposed to avoid a specific exception:

```
11-matchers-included-in-rspec-expectations/03/block_matchers.rb
expect { age__of(user) }.not_to raise_error(MissingDataError)
```

This snippet contains a hard-to-spot typo: we wrote age_of with two under-scores. When Ruby executes this line, it will raise a NameError, which is *not* a MissingDataError. The expectation will pass, even though our method never even runs!

Because this is such a thorny trap, RSpec 3 will warn you in this situation, and will suggest that you remove the exception class and just call not_to raise_error with no arguments. This form isn't susceptible to the false positive problem, since it will catch *any* exception.

In fact, you can often simplify your specs even further. Since RSpec in effect wraps every example with expect { example.run }.not_to raise_error, you can remove your explicit not_to raise_error check—unless you want to keep it around for clarity.

throw_symbol

Exceptions are designed for, well, exceptional situations, such as an error in program logic. They're not suited for everyday control flow, such as jumping out of a deeply nested loop or method call. For situations like these, Ruby provides the throw construct. You can test your control logic with RSpec's throw_symbol matcher:

```
11-matchers-included-in-rspec-expectations/03/block_matchers.rb
expect { throw :found }.to throw_symbol(:found)
```

Ruby allows you to include an object along with the thrown symbol, and throw_symbol can likewise be used to specify that object via an additional argument:

```
11-matchers-included-in-rspec-expectations/03/block_matchers.rb
expect { throw :found, 10 }.to throw_symbol(:found, a_value > 9)
```

Since throw_symbol is a higher-order matcher, the additional argument can be an exact value, an RSpec matcher, or any object that implements ===.

Yielding

Blocks are one of Ruby's most distinctive features. They allow you to pass around little chunks of code using an easy-to-read syntax. Any method can pass control to its caller using the yield keyword, and RSpec provides four different matchers for specifying this behavior.

yield_control

The simplest yield matcher is yield_control:

```
11-matchers-included-in-rspec-expectations/03/block_matchers.rb
def self.just_yield
  yield
end
```

```
expect { |block_checker| just_yield(&block_checker) }.to yield_control
```

In order for the expectation to pass, the just_yield method must yield control to a block, or to an object that acts like a block. RSpec provides just such an object for us: a block checker that verifies that we actually yielded to it. All of the yield matchers use this technique.

You can also specify an expected number of yields by chaining once, twice, thrice, exactly(n).times, at_least(n).times or at_most(n).times.

```
11-matchers-included-in-rspec-expectations/03/block_matchers.rb
expect { |block| 2.times(&block) }.to yield_control.twice
expect { |block| 2.times(&block) }.to yield_control.at_most(4).times
expect { |block| 4.times(&block) }.to yield_control.at_least(3).times
```

The times method is just decoration, but it helps to keep your yield_control expectations readable.

yield_with_args

When you care about which specific arguments your method is yielding, you can check them with the yield_with_args matcher:

```
11-matchers-included-in-rspec-expectations/03/block_matchers.rb
def self.just_yield_these(*args)
  yield(*args)
end
```

```
expect { |block|
  just_yield_these(10, 'food', Math::PI, &block)
}.to yield_with_args(10, /foo/, a_value_within(0.1).of(3.14))
```

As this example shows, you can use several different criteria to check a yielded object, including:

- An exact value such as the number 10
- An object implementing ===, such as the regular expression /foo/
- Any RSpec matcher, such as a_value_within()

yield_with_no_args

So far we have seen yield_control, which does not care about arguments, and yield_with_args, which requires certain arguments to be yielded. Sometimes, though, you specifically care that your code yields *no* arguments. For these cases, RSpec offers yield_with_no_args:

11-matchers-included-in-rspec-expectations/03/block_matchers.rb
```
expect { |block| just_yield_these(&block) }.to yield_with_no_args
```

yield_successive_args

Some methods, particularly those in the Enumerable module, can yield many times. To check this behavior, you'd need to combine yield_control's counting ability with yield_with_args's parameter checking.

That's exactly what yield_successive_args does. To use it, you pass one or more arguments, each of which can be an object or a list of objects. The first object or list goes with the first call to yield, and so on:

11-matchers-included-in-rspec-expectations/03/block_matchers.rb
```
expect { |block|
  ['football', 'barstool'].each_with_index(&block)
}.to yield_successive_args(
  [/foo/,                     0],
  [a_string_starting_with('bar'), 1]
)
```

The built-in Ruby function each_with_index will yield twice: first with the two values 'football' and 0, then with the two values 'barstool' and 1. As we did with yield_with_args, we're checking these results using a mix of plain Ruby values, regular expression-style objects, and RSpec matchers.

Mutation

In the wild, it's common for external actions—such as submitting a web form—to change some state inside the system. The change matcher helps you specify these sorts of mutations. Here's the matcher in its most basic form:

11-matchers-included-in-rspec-expectations/03/block_matchers.rb
```
array = [1, 2, 3]
expect { array << 4 }.to change { array.size }
```

The matcher performs the following actions in turn:

1. Run your change block and store the result, array.size, as the *before* value

2. Run the code under test, array << 4

3. Run your change block a second time and store the result, array.size, as the *after* value

4. Pass the expectation if the before and after values are different

This expectation checks *whether* or not the expectation changed, without regard to *how much*. For that, we'll need to turn to another technique.

Specifying Change Details

Like other RSpec fluent matchers, the change matcher offers an easy way to give details about the change. Specifically, you can use by, by_at_least, or by_at_most to specify the *amount* of the change:

11-matchers-included-in-rspec-expectations/03/block_matchers.rb
```
expect { array.concat([1, 2, 3]) }.to change { array.size }.by(3)
expect { array.concat([1, 2, 3]) }.to change { array.size }.by_at_least(2)
expect { array.concat([1, 2, 3]) }.to change { array.size }.by_at_most(4)
```

If you care about the exact before and after values, you can chain from and to on to your matcher (either individually or together):

11-matchers-included-in-rspec-expectations/03/block_matchers.rb
```
expect { array << 4 }.to change { array.size }.from(3)
expect { array << 5 }.to change { array.size }.to(5)
expect { array << 6 }.to change { array.size }.from(5).to(6)
expect { array << 7 }.to change { array.size }.to(7).from(6)
```

It probably doesn't surprise you to hear that you can also pass a matcher (or any object that implements the === protocol) into from and to:

11-matchers-included-in-rspec-expectations/03/block_matchers.rb
```
x = 5
expect { x += 10 }.to change { x }
  .from(a_value_between(2, 7))
  .to(a_value_between(12, 17))
```

Note that there's a bit of a gotcha to passing a matcher, at least if you only use to or from (and not both). Consider this expectation:

11-matchers-included-in-rspec-expectations/03/block_matchers.rb
```
x = 5
expect { x += 1 }.to change { x }.from(a_value_between(2, 7))
```

This expectation passes, because the value of x changed, and it was originally a value between 2 and 7. However, as this reads, you might expect that it would only pass if the final value of x was no longer between 2 and 7. If you care about both the *before* and *after* values, it's a good idea to specify both from and to.

Negative Expectations

RSpec doesn't allow you to use the three relative by... methods or the to method with the negative expectation form, expect { ... }.not_to change { ... }. After all, when you're expecting a value *not* to change, it doesn't make sense to spell out how much it *didn't* change by or a value it *didn't* change to.

Negative expectations do, however, work with from:

```
11-matchers-included-in-rspec-expectations/03/block_matchers.rb
x = 5
expect { }.not_to change { x }.from(5)
```

In this example, we want x to stay at 5 before and after the block runs.

Output

Many Ruby tools write output to stdout or stderr, and RSpec includes a matcher specifically for these cases:

```
11-matchers-included-in-rspec-expectations/03/block_matchers.rb
expect { print 'OK' }.to output('OK').to_stdout
expect { warn 'problem' }.to output(/prob/).to_stderr
```

This matcher works by temporarily replacing the global $stdout or $stderr variable with a StringIO while it runs your expect block. This generally works well but it does have some gotchas.

For example, if you use the STDOUT constant explicitly, or spawn a subprocess that writes to one of the streams, this matcher won't work properly. Instead, you can chain to_std(out|err)_from_any_process for these situations:

```
11-matchers-included-in-rspec-expectations/03/block_matchers.rb
expect { system('echo OK') }.to output("OK\n").to_stdout_from_any_process
```

The ...from_any_process form uses a different mechanism: it temporarily reopens the stream to write to a Tempfile. This works in more situations, but is much, much slower—30x, according to our benchmarks. Thus, you need to explicitly opt in to this slower version of the output matcher.

Your Turn

We've covered a lot of ground this chapter! From basic Ruby building blocks like strings and numbers, through deeply nested collections, to methods with side effects, you can find a matcher to suit your needs.

All these matchers built into RSpec are designed to help you do two things:

- Express exactly how you want the code to behave, without being too strict or too lax

- Get precise feedback when something breaks so that you can find exactly where the failure happened

It's much more important to keep these two principles in mind than it is to memorize all the different matchers. As you try your hand at the following exercises, refer to Appendix 3, *Matcher Cheat Sheet*, on page 307 to get inspiration for different matchers to try.

Exercises

Since matchers help you diagnose failures, we want to show you how to get helpful failure messages by choosing the right matcher. *We wrote the following exercises to fail on purpose.* While you're certainly welcome to fix the underlying issue in as many exercises as you like, please focus first on experimenting with different matchers.

Matching Phone Numbers

Create a new spec file with the following description for a class that matches phone numbers from a string and yields them to its caller, one by one:

```
11-matchers-included-in-rspec-expectations/exercises/phone_number_extractor_spec.rb
RSpec.describe PhoneNumberExtractor do
  let(:text) do
    <<-EOS
      Melinda: (202) 555-0168
      Bob: 202-555-0199
      Sabina: (202) 555-0176
    EOS
  end

  it 'yields phone numbers as it finds them' do
    yielded_numbers = []
    PhoneNumberExtractor.extract_from(text) do |number|
      yielded_numbers << number
    end

    expect(yielded_numbers).to eq [
      '(202) 555-0168',
      '202-555-0199',
      '(202) 555-0175'
    ]
  end
end
```

Here's a partial implementation of the spec for you to add to the top of the file—not enough to pass, but enough to show that there's room for improvement in our specs:

`11-matchers-included-in-rspec-expectations/exercises/phone_number_extractor_spec.rb`

```ruby
class PhoneNumberExtractor
  def self.extract_from(text, &block)
    # Look for patterns like (###) ###-####
    text.scan(/(d{3}) d{3}-d{4}/, &block)
  end
end
```

Run this file through RSpec. Now, take a look at the spec code. We had to do a lot of work to set up a separate collection for the yielded phone numbers, and then compare it afterward. Change this example to use a matcher better suited to how the extract_from method works. Notice how much simpler and clearer the spec is now.

Banner Year

The next two exercises will be in the same example group and will share the same implementation class. Let's start with the spec, which describes a fictional public company (named after a river) that had a good year. Add the following code to a new file:

`11-matchers-included-in-rspec-expectations/exercises/public_company_spec.rb`

```ruby
RSpec.describe PublicCompany do
  let(:company) { PublicCompany.new('Nile', 10, 100_000) }

  it 'increases its market cap when it gets better than expected revenues' do
    before_market_cap = company.market_cap
    company.got_better_than_expected_revenues
    after_market_cap = company.market_cap

    expect(after_market_cap - before_market_cap).to be >= 50_000
  end
end
```

At the top of your file, add the following (not yet correct) implementation of the PublicCompany class:

`11-matchers-included-in-rspec-expectations/exercises/public_company_spec.rb`

```ruby
PublicCompany = Struct.new(:name, :value_per_share, :share_count) do
  def got_better_than_expected_revenues
    self.value_per_share *= rand(1.05..1.10)
  end

  def market_cap
    @market_cap ||= value_per_share * share_count
  end
end
```

Run your spec, and look at the failure message: expected: >= 50000 / got: 0. It's pretty terse and doesn't really communicate the intent of the code.

Update the expectation to describe how the code should behave, rather than what the value of a variable is.

About Our Company

We also want to check that our class is correctly storing all the information investors will want to know about the company. Add the following example inside the example group from the previous exercise, just after the other example:

11-matchers-included-in-rspec-expectations/exercises/public_company_spec.rb
```
it 'provides attributes' do
  expect(company.name).to eq('Nil')
  expect(company.value_per_share).to eq(10)
  expect(company.share_count).to eq(10_000)
  expect(company.market_cap).to eq(1_000_000)
end
```

When you run this new example, RSpec stops the test at the first failure, on company.name. We don't get to see whether or not any of the other attributes were correct.

Use a different matcher here that checks *all* the attributes, and reports on any differences between what we're expecting and how the code actually behaves.

Tokenizing Words

For this exercise, we're testing a *tokenizer* that breaks text into individual words. Add the following spec to a new file:

11-matchers-included-in-rspec-expectations/exercises/tokenizer_spec.rb
```
RSpec.describe Tokenizer do
  let(:text) do
    <<-EOS
      I am Sam.
      Sam I am.
      Do you like green eggs and ham?
    EOS
  end

  it 'tokenizes multiple lines of text' do
    tokenized = Tokenizer.tokenize(text)
    expect(tokenized.first(6)).to eq ['I', 'am', 'Sam.', 'Sam', 'I', 'am']
  end
end
```

Add the following incorrect implementation of the Tokenizer class to the top of your new file:

11-matchers-included-in-rspec-expectations/exercises/tokenizer_spec.rb
```ruby
class Tokenizer
  def self.tokenize(string)
    string.split(/ +/)
  end
end
```

Run the spec, and read the failure message. Our spec caught the error, but it didn't give any context beyond just the six words we asked for. Moreover, if we ever update this spec, we have to take extra care to keep the length parameter, first(6), in sync with the list of expected words.

Change your spec to use a more future-proof matcher that doesn't require us to extract a hard-coded number of tokens.

Building Blocks of Nature

For this example, we'll be tearing apart the molecules making up our world around us. Fortunately, it's just a simulation. Create a new file with the following spec for water:

11-matchers-included-in-rspec-expectations/exercises/water_spec.rb
```ruby
RSpec.describe Water do
  it 'is H20' do
    expect(Water.elements.sort).to eq [:hydrogen, :hydrogen, :oxygen]
  end
end
```

At the top of your file, add an implementation of Water that's missing one of its hydrogen atoms:

11-matchers-included-in-rspec-expectations/exercises/water_spec.rb
```ruby
class Water
  def self.elements
    [:oxygen, :hydrogen]
  end
end
```

Run your spec. It will fail correctly, but the output leaves something to be desired. We just get two collections dumped to the console, and it's up to us to read them by hand and find out what's different. With just a few items, comparing by hand is manageable, but differences become much harder to spot as the collections get bigger.

Also, take a look at that sort call we had to add. This spec has nothing to do with sorting, but we had to sort the collection to ensure we were just comparing the elements without regard to order.

Fix our mistake here and use a matcher whose failure message clearly spells out the difference between the two collections.

Working for the Weekend

For our final example, we're going to write a calendar-related spec that determines whether any given day is on the weekend:

11-matchers-included-in-rspec-expectations/exercises/calendar_spec.rb
```ruby
RSpec.describe Calendar do
  let(:sunday_date) { Calendar.new('Sun, 11 Jun 2017') }

  it 'considers sundays to be on the weekend' do
    expect(sunday_date.on_weekend?).to be true
  end
end
```

Here's an obviously incorrect implementation of the on_weekend? method:

11-matchers-included-in-rspec-expectations/exercises/calendar_spec.rb
```ruby
require 'date'

Calendar = Struct.new(:date_string) do
  def on_weekend?
    Date.parse(date_string).saturday?
  end
end
```

When you run this spec, you get the stilted phrase "to be true" in the output. Change this matcher to one that reads more clearly in the test report.

Bonus Points

As we mentioned earlier, the main point of these exercises was to practice using matchers that express just what you want to say about your code's behavior (and no more), and that give you clear output.

So, there's no need to fix the underlying implementations. But for extra credit, feel free to make the specs pass. Post your solutions in the forums, and we'll send you a GIF of a gold star.

Either way, meet us in the next chapter to see how you can create your own matchers that are just as expressive as the built-in ones.

In this chapter, you'll see:

- How good matchers make for readable specs and helpful output
- How to define new matchers in terms of RSpec's built-in ones
- How to use RSpec's DSL to make a new matcher
- What a custom matcher class written by hand looks like

## CHAPTER 12

Creating Custom Matchers

In the previous chapter, we took a tour of the matchers that ship with RSpec. You can be productive in RSpec with just these matchers. On simpler projects, they're all you'll need.

Eventually, though, you're going to hit the limits of the built-in matchers. Because they're meant for testing general-purpose Ruby code, they require you to speak in Ruby terms rather than your project's terms.

For example, the following expectations are a jumble of Ruby method calls and hard-coded values:

12-creating-custom-matchers/01/custom_matcher/spec/event_spec.rb
```
expect(art_show.tickets_sold.count).to eq(0)
expect(u2_concert.tickets_sold.count).to eq(u2_concert.capacity)
```

It takes a lot of reading and parsing, plus understanding the ticketing API we're testing, to understand exactly what behavior we're looking for. By contrast, the following snippet expresses the same desired behavior in much clearer terms:

12-creating-custom-matchers/01/custom_matcher/spec/event_spec.rb
```
expect(art_show).to have_no_tickets_sold
expect(u2_concert).to be_sold_out
```

Much, much better. We've added two *custom matchers*—have_no_tickets_sold and be_sold_out—so that we can describe the behavior in terms of *events* and *tickets*. These are the terms that the rest of the project team would use.

When you write clear, easy-to-use custom matchers, you gain several benefits:

- You stand a greater chance of building what your stakeholders want.

- You reduce the cost of API changes (because you need only update your matchers).

- You can provide better failure messages when something goes wrong.

That final advantage—better test output—bears a closer look. The original snippet would produce failure messages like this:

```
expected: 0
     got: 2

(compared using ==)

expected: 10000
     got: 9900

(compared using ==)
```

The output just reads "expected x / got y," with no hint about the higher-level concepts. By contrast, check out the failure messages from the second snippet:

```
expected #<Event "Art Show" (capacity: 100)> to have no tickets sold, but ↵
had 2

expected #<Event "U2 Concert" (capacity: 10000)> to be sold out, but had  ↵
100 unsold tickets
```

Not only does this report speak our domain language, it also provides additional details—such as what specific events we are testing here. In this chapter, we're going to show you how to build custom matchers like these by taking tiny steps forward from the RSpec concepts you already know.

Delegating to Existing Matchers Using Helper Methods

We're going to start with a technique you've already used to keep your code organized: helper methods. RSpec provides its own matchers via built-in methods, such as contain_exactly(...). You can easily write your own methods that return the same matcher objects but using names specific to your domain. You can also add your own customizations, such as default arguments.

When you developed the expense tracker application in *Building an App With RSpec 3*, you used the matcher expression a_hash_including(id: some_id) to represent a particular expected expense. Here's an example use:

```
12-creating-custom-matchers/02/expense_tracker/spec/integration/app/ledger_spec.rb
expect(ledger.expenses_on('2017-06-10')).to contain_exactly(
  a_hash_including(id: result_1.expense_id),
  a_hash_including(id: result_2.expense_id)
)
```

This matcher got the job done. Notice, though, how it expresses the expectation in terms of Ruby objects: *hashes* and *IDs*. The object you're describing is an *expense*. It would be nice to use the domain language of the application:

```
12-creating-custom-matchers/03/expense_tracker/spec/integration/app/ledger_spec.rb
expect(ledger.expenses_on('2017-06-10')).to contain_exactly(
  an_expense_identified_by(result_1.expense_id),
  an_expense_identified_by(result_2.expense_id)
)
```

It's easy to implement this new an_expense_identified_by matcher. All you have to do is write a helper method with this name that delegates to a_hash_including. To make your new matcher available to all your specs, define it in a module inside spec/spec_helper.rb. Then, configure RSpec to include this module in all your example groups:

```
12-creating-custom-matchers/03/expense_tracker/spec/spec_helper.rb
module ExpenseTrackerMatchers
  def an_expense_identified_by(id)
    a_hash_including(id: id)
  end
end

RSpec.configure do |config|
  config.include ExpenseTrackerMatchers
  # ...rest of the config...
```

There's no magic here. It's just one method delegating to another, like you do all the time in Ruby.

There is something about this method that might give you pause, though. We've defined an_expense_identified_by to match any hash containing an id key with a particular value. For example, a completely unrelated hash—such as a user record—would fool our matcher:

```
{
  id:     1,
  email: 'john.doe@example.com',
  role:   'admin'
}
```

If this matcher claims to match only expenses, you probably want to reduce the chances of a false positive. You can do so by checking for the presence of the other keys that a valid expense would contain:

```
12-creating-custom-matchers/04/expense_tracker/spec/spec_helper.rb
def an_expense_identified_by(id)
  a_hash_including(id: id).and including(:payee, :amount, :date)
end
```

Using a domain-specific name made it obvious that our match logic was too generic. This simple improvement makes the matcher more robust, and also makes it available to your entire spec suite.

Aaron Kromer describes another great use of this technique in his blog post, "Farewell JSON API Gems."[1] In it, he uses a helper method to return a matcher that describes the exact shape of a JSON response he expects from a particular API.

Defining Matcher Aliases

In *Passing One Matcher Into Another*, on page 177, you saw how RSpec defines a_value_within as an alias of the be_within matcher. It allows you to write expectations that read smoothly like the following one:

```
12-creating-custom-matchers/05/custom_matchers.rb
expect(results).to start_with a_value_within(0.1).of(Math::PI)
```

You can use the same techniques in your own projects. Just call alias_matcher with the name of the *new* matcher first, followed by the existing one (the same order you'd use with Ruby's alias_method):

```
12-creating-custom-matchers/05/custom_matchers.rb
RSpec::Matchers.alias_matcher :an_admin, :be_an_admin
```

This snippet defines a new method, an_admin, which wraps the existing be_an_admin matcher (a dynamic predicate matcher that calls admin?; see *Dynamic Predicates*, on page 194). The new matcher will use "an admin," rather than "be an admin," in its description and failure messages:

```
>> be_an_admin.description
=> "be an admin"
>> an_admin.description
=> "an admin"
```

The alias_matcher method can also take a block, for when you want something different from the matcher's Ruby method name for your descriptions. For instance, if you wanted an_admin to show up as a superuser in the output:

```
>> an_admin.description
=> "a superuser"
```

...you could define your alias like so:

```
12-creating-custom-matchers/05/custom_matchers.rb
RSpec::Matchers.alias_matcher :an_admin, :be_an_admin do |old_description|
  old_description.sub('be an admin', 'a superuser')
end
```

Dynamic predicate matchers like these are common targets for these kinds of aliases, since RSpec doesn't ship with its own aliases for them.

---

1.   http://aaronkromer.com/blog/2014-09-29-farewell-json-api-gems.html

Negating Matchers

In *Putting the Pieces Together*, on page 172, we saw RSpec's not_to and to_not methods, which specify that a given condition should *not* hold:

```
12-creating-custom-matchers/05/custom_matchers.rb
expect(correct_grammar).to_not split_infinitives
```

If you find yourself doing this over and over again, you can define a *negated matcher* that you'd use like so:

```
12-creating-custom-matchers/05/custom_matchers.rb
expect(correct_grammar).to avoid_splitting_infinitives
```

It's easy to create your own negated matcher. All you have to do is call define_negated_matcher:

```
12-creating-custom-matchers/05/custom_matchers.rb
RSpec::Matchers.define_negated_matcher :avoid_splitting_infinitives,
                                       :split_infinitives
```

As with alias_matcher, you pass the name of the new matcher, followed by the old one. The avoid_splitting_infinitives matcher will now behave as the negation of split_infinitives.

Negative matchers come in handy for more complex cases, such as when you're combining matchers. For example, the following expectation is ambiguous, and RSpec warns us of this problem:

```
>> expect(adverb).not_to start_with('a').and end_with('z')
NotImplementedError: `expect(...).not_to matcher.and matcher` is not       ↵
supported, since it creates a bit of an ambiguity. Instead, define negated  ↵
versions of whatever matchers you wish to negate with                       ↵
`RSpec::Matchers.define_negated_matcher` and use `expect(...).to            ↵
matcher.and matcher`.
    « backtrace truncated »
```

The ambiguity is subtle: should the adverb "absolutely" match (because it satisfies the "does not end with z" condition)? Or should it fail to match (because it does not satisfy *both* conditions)?

RSpec's error message points out the ambiguity and suggests negated matchers as an alternative. Here's what those negated matchers might look like:

```
12-creating-custom-matchers/05/custom_matchers.rb
RSpec::Matchers.define_negated_matcher :start_with_something_besides,
                                       :start_with

RSpec::Matchers.define_negated_matcher :end_with_something_besides,
                                       :end_with
```

Now, we can specify the exact behavior we want, with no ambiguity:

```
12-creating-custom-matchers/05/custom_matchers.rb
# Strict: requires both conditions to be satisfied
expect('blazingly').to(
  start_with_something_besides('a').and \
    end_with_something_besides('z')
)

# Permissive: requires at least one condition to be satisfied
expect('absolutely').to(
  start_with_something_besides('a').or \
    end_with_something_besides('z')
)
```

The techniques we've seen so far—helper methods, matcher aliases, and negated matchers—are all about exposing existing matchers with new names. In the next section, we'll take the next logical step: creating a new matcher that's not based on an existing one.

Using the Matcher DSL

In *Building an App With RSpec 3*, you built an expense-tracking API. If this grows to include expense accounts, you'd end up writing specs that check account balances. In this section, we're going to build a custom have_a_balance_of matcher that helps with those expectations. Here's what the matcher will eventually look like:

```
12-creating-custom-matchers/06/custom_matcher/spec/initial_account_spec.rb
expect(account).to have_a_balance_of(30)
```

Unlike most of the other examples in the book, the code snippets in this section aren't intended for you to type in as you read. We want to focus on just the matcher, without cluttering the examples with all the supporting code. If you *do* want to run these snippets on your machine, you can get the class we're testing (as well as the matcher and some specs) from the book's source code.[2]

There are two ways to build a matcher like the one we just showed you:

Using the matcher DSL
> For most needs, RSpec provides a domain-specific language (DSL) for defining custom matchers.

Creating a Ruby class
> Any Ruby class can define a matcher if it implements the *matcher protocol*.[3]

---

2. https://github.com/rspec-3-book/book-code/blob/v1.0/12-creating-custom-matchers/06/custom_matcher/lib/account.rb
3. http://rspec.info/documentation/3.6/rspec-expectations/RSpec/Matchers/MatcherProtocol.html

We're going to show you both techniques. We'll start with the approach we generally recommend—the matcher DSL—and then show you what the same matcher would look like as a Ruby class.

A Minimal Custom Matcher

To define a matcher using the DSL, we call RSpec::Matchers.define, passing the matcher name and a block containing the matcher definition:

```
12-creating-custom-matchers/06/custom_matcher/spec/support/matchers.rb
RSpec::Matchers.define :have_a_balance_of do |amount|
  match { |account| account.current_balance == amount }
end
```

The outer block receives any arguments passed to the matcher. When a spec calls have_a_balance_of(amount), RSpec will pass the amount into this block.

The match method defines the actual match/no-match logic. The inner block receives the *subject* of the expectation (the account), and returns a truthy value if the account balance matches the expected amount.

Improving the Custom Matcher Failure Messages

This matcher was easy to write, but we shouldn't declare victory just yet. Here's the output that it produces when a spec fails:

```
1) `have_a_balance_of(amount)` fails when the balance does not match
   Failure/Error: expect(account).to have_a_balance_of(35)
     expected #<Account name="Checking"> to have a balance of 35
   # ./spec/initial_account_spec.rb:17:in `block (2 levels) in <top
```

The failure message tells us that the account *should* have had a balance of 35. But it doesn't say what the *actual* balance was. We can add this information using the failure_message and failure_message_when_negated methods:

```
12-creating-custom-matchers/07/custom_matcher/spec/support/matchers.rb
RSpec::Matchers.define :have_a_balance_of do |amount|
  match { |account| account.current_balance == amount }
➤  failure_message { |account| super() + failure_reason(account) }
➤  failure_message_when_negated { |account| super() + failure_reason(account) }

  private

➤  def failure_reason(account)
➤    ", but had a balance of #{account.current_balance}"
➤  end
end
```

We define two methods so that RSpec can supply our custom failure text both for expect(...).to(...) and for expect(...).not_to(...). As with match, these methods each take a block that receives an account value. Now, we can get the actual account balance and put it into the failure message.

We'll need to keep the first part of the failure message that's provided by RSpec—the part that reads, expected ... to have a balance of 35. By calling super(), you delegate to the existing RSpec implementation for this part.

Matchers Are Just Classes

The reason that matchers can call super() just like Ruby classes is that they *are* Ruby classes. RSpec::Matchers.define creates a Ruby class, and the block you pass to it is the class body. Inside the block, we can do anything we'd do inside a Ruby class, including defining private helper methods.

Most of the failure message will be the same for regular and negated matchers, so we've abstracted that common part into a failure_reason helper method. Take a look at the output with these changes in place:

```
1) `have_a_balance_of(amount)` fails when the balance does not match
   Failure/Error: expect(account).to have_a_balance_of(35)
     expected #<Account name="Checking"> to have a balance of 35, but had a ↵
     balance of 30
   # ./spec/initial_account_spec.rb:17:in `block (2 levels) in <top
```

Much more helpful.

Adding a Fluent Interface

Many of RSpec's built-in matchers use a *fluent interface*,[4] where you can chain one method after another to create an easy-to-understand expectation:

- be_within(0.1).of(50)
- change { ... }.from(x).to(y)
- output(/warning/).to_stderr

It's easy to add these same kind of fluent interfaces to your own custom matchers. Continuing the account balance example, suppose our Account class provides two methods for querying the balance:

- current_balance
- balance_as_of(date)

It'd be nice to support both of these methods from the same matcher, by allowing specs to tack on an optional as_of modifier with a date:

---

4.   https://martinfowler.com/bliki/FluentInterface.html

```
12-creating-custom-matchers/08/custom_matcher/spec/as_of_account_spec.rb
expect(account).to have_a_balance_of(30)
# or
expect(account).to have_a_balance_of(10).as_of(Date.new(2017, 6, 12))
```

RSpec's matcher DSL offers a chain method for defining this style of interface. Here's an updated matcher that supports chained calls to as_of:

```
12-creating-custom-matchers/08/custom_matcher/spec/support/matchers.rb
Line 1  RSpec::Matchers.define :have_a_balance_of do |amount|
   -      chain(:as_of) { |date| @as_of_date = date }
   -      match { |account| account_balance(account) == amount }
   -      failure_message { |account| super() + failure_reason(account) }
   5      failure_message_when_negated { |account| super() + failure_reason(account) }
   -
   -    private
   -
   -      def failure_reason(account)
  10        ", but had a balance of #{account_balance(account)}"
   -      end
   -
   -      def account_balance(account)
   -        if @as_of_date
  15          account.balance_as_of(@as_of_date)
   -        else
   -          account.current_balance
   -        end
   -      end
  20    end
```

Most of the lines in this snippet have changed; here's a breakdown of what's different:

- On line 2, we call chain(:as_of), which defines the as_of method for us; this method stashes the date in an instance variable so that we can pass it into the account we're testing.

- The new account_balance method on line 13 checks for a date (which will only be present if the caller used as_of), then calls the underlying balance_as_of or current_balance method accordingly.

- The match and failure_reason methods now use the new account_balance helper method.

When a spec fails, the failure message will automatically mention the as_of date if a spec calls it:

```
1) `have_a_balance_of(amount)` fails when a date's balance does not match
   Failure/Error: expect(account).to                                      ↩
   have_a_balance_of(15).as_of(Date.new(2017, 6, 12))
     expected #<Account name="Checking"> to have a balance of 15 as of    ↩
```

```
    #<Date: 2017-06-12 ((2457917j,0s,0n),+0s,2299161j)>, but had a        ↵
    balance of 10
  # ./spec/as_of_account_spec.rb:19:in `block (2 levels) in <top
```

This custom matcher is getting pretty convenient to use now. But we should take a moment to consider how it will interact with other matchers.

Making Our Matcher Composable

DSL-based matchers can be used in compound expressions via and/or, without any additional configuration. Our new account balance matcher already supports the following use:

12-creating-custom-matchers/08/custom_matcher/spec/as_of_account_spec.rb
```
expect(account).to have_a_balance_of(30).and \
                   have_attributes(name: 'Checking')
```

We can also define aliases for it…

12-creating-custom-matchers/08/custom_matcher/spec/support/matchers.rb
```
RSpec::Matchers.alias_matcher :an_account_with_a_balance_of,
                              :have_a_balance_of
```

…and then pass these aliases into other matchers:

12-creating-custom-matchers/08/custom_matcher/spec/as_of_account_spec.rb
```
expect(user_accounts).to include(an_account_with_a_balance_of(30))
```

There's one thing our matcher doesn't yet support, though: we can't pass other matchers into it. It would be nice to be able to check account balances using something other than strict equality (why fuss over nickels and dimes when we're dealing with multimillion-dollar expense accounts?):

12-creating-custom-matchers/09/custom_matcher/spec/composed_account_spec.rb
```
expect(account).to have_a_balance_of(a_value < 11_000_000)
# or
expect(account).to have_a_balance_of(a_value_within(50).of(10_500_000))
```

It takes only one small change to get this to work. The existing match block compares the amount using the == operator:

12-creating-custom-matchers/09/custom_matcher/spec/support/matchers.rb
```
account_balance(account) == account
```

Instead, we'll need to use RSpec's values_match? method:

12-creating-custom-matchers/09/custom_matcher/spec/support/matchers.rb
```
values_match?(amount, account_balance(account))
```

As with traditional assertion frameworks, the expected value goes first. If this value is a matcher, RSpec will treat it as one; otherwise, it will fall back on comparison using ==.

Here's the full match block now:

12-creating-custom-matchers/09/custom_matcher/spec/support/matchers.rb
```ruby
match { |account| values_match?(amount, account_balance(account)) }
```

The DSL methods you've seen here are all you need to get started with your own matchers. However, RSpec provides several other methods to help you fine-tune your matchers' behavior. You can print meaningful diffs between the actual and expected values, provide custom exception handling, and more. For more information, see the list of DSL methods.[5]

Defining a Matcher Class

Most of the time, you'll use the DSL for defining custom matchers. Sometimes, though, you need a little more control or might prefer to define the matcher in the most explicit way possible.

As we mentioned earlier in the chapter, any Ruby object that implements the matcher protocol can serve as an RSpec matcher. It's pretty easy to translate the DSL example from the previous section into a Ruby class that has the required methods.

The Ruby Class

This class is about a page of code, but it has a lot of similarities to the shorter DSL version we wrote. Take a look here, and then we'll call out a few highlights afterward:

12-creating-custom-matchers/10/custom_matcher/spec/support/matchers.rb
```ruby
Line 1  class HaveABalanceOf
     -    include RSpec::Matchers::Composable
     -
     -    def initialize(amount)
     5      @amount = amount
     -    end
     -
     -    def as_of(date)
     -      @as_of_date = date
    10      self
     -    end
     -
     -    def matches?(account)
```

---

5. http://rspec.info/documentation/3.6/rspec-expectations/RSpec/Matchers/DSL/Macros.html

```
     -       @account = account
    15        values_match?(@amount, account_balance)
     -      end
     -
     -      def description
     -        if @as_of_date
    20          "have a balance of #{description_of(@amount)} as of #{@as_of_date}"
     -        else
     -          "have a balance of #{description_of(@amount)}"
     -        end
     -      end
    25
     -      def failure_message
     -        "expected #{@account.inspect} to #{description}" + failure_reason
     -      end
     -
    30      def failure_message_when_negated
     -        "expected #{@account.inspect} not to #{description}" + failure_reason
     -      end
     -
     -    private
    35
     -      def failure_reason
     -        ", but had a balance of #{account_balance}"
     -      end
     -
    40      def account_balance
     -        if @as_of_date
     -          @account.balance_as_of(@as_of_date)
     -        else
     -          @account.current_balance
    45        end
     -      end
     -  end
```

Let's walk through this class from top to bottom. First, we include the
RSpec::Matchers::Composable mixin on line 2.[6] This module defines a few methods
for you that make composition possible, including and, or, and the === operator.
It also provides helpers for you to call when you're defining a higher-order
matcher, such as values_match? and description_of.

In the initializer on line 4, we store the desired amount in an instance variable
so that we have something to compare against in the matches? method.

On line 8, the as_of method provides the fluent interface that lets callers write
expect(…).to have_a_balance_of(…).as_of(…). It looks a lot like the DSL version, except
that here we have to return self explicitly. Without that line, as_of would return

---

6.   http://rspec.info/documentation/3.6/rspec-expectations/RSpec/Matchers/Composable.html

a Date object. RSpec would attempt to use the date as a matcher object, and the spec would fail.

Next, the matches? method on line 13 looks like the DSL version, except that we need to hang on to the @account so that the failure messages can access it.

We have to define the description method explicitly on line 18, rather than having RSpec generate it from the names of the matchers and modifiers. The description_of helper (from the Composable module) is like calling inspect, but with special handling for matchers. We use it here since we're defining a higher-order matcher.

The remainder of the methods—the failure messages and private helpers—are basically the same as their DSL counterparts.

RSpec Integration

So far, we've just defined a Ruby class, HaveABalanceOf. To make this code available to RSpec as a matcher, we need to define a helper method, have_a_balance_of:

12-creating-custom-matchers/10/custom_matcher/spec/support/matchers.rb
```
module AccountMatchers
  def have_a_balance_of(amount)
    HaveABalanceOf.new(amount)
  end
end

RSpec.configure do |config|
  config.include AccountMatchers
end
```

Here, we've put the helper in a module and configured RSpec to include the module, making the method available to our examples.

The matcher class looks similar to its DSL equivalent, but takes up a lot more space and has to include quite a bit of boilerplate code. In most cases, you'll be better off using the DSL to define your matchers.

However, in certain situations the custom matcher class is a better fit:

- If your matcher is going to be used hundreds or thousands of times, writing your own class avoids a bit of extra overhead inherent in how the DSL is evaluated.

- Some teams prefer more explicit code.

- If you leave out the RSpec::Matchers::Composable mixin, your matcher won't have any dependencies on RSpec and will work in non-RSpec contexts.

As an example of that last benefit, the Shoulda Matchers library defines framework-independent matchers that work with RSpec, Minitest, and Test::Unit.[7]

Use the DSL Unless You're Writing a Library

Most of the time, you'll want to use the DSL to define your matchers. It will save you space, be easier to read, and integrate automatically with other RSpec features.

If you're writing a library of matchers that people will be using to test their own (possibly non-RSpec) projects, you may want to write a custom class instead.

Your Turn

This chapter paved a gradual path into custom matchers. We started off by building custom matchers from RSpec's existing ones, using helper methods, aliases, and negation. Next, we defined a brand-new matcher using RSpec's DSL. Finally, we peeled back the curtain and showed that there's no magic behind matchers. They're just plain Ruby classes.

With a good set of custom matchers, your specs will become more readable. When there's a failure, the improved error message will save you time finding the cause.

Now, it's time to try your hand at writing your own custom matcher.

Exercises

At the top of the chapter, we looked at some hypothetical matchers for a concert ticketing API. In these exercises, you're going to implement these matchers.

To keep things simple, it's fine to put all your code for this exercise in one file. Start out with the Event class you'll be testing:

```
12-creating-custom-matchers/exercises/custom_matcher/spec/event_matchers_spec.rb
Event = Struct.new(:name, :capacity) do
  def purchase_ticket_for(guest)
    tickets_sold << guest
  end

  def tickets_sold
    @tickets_sold ||= []
  end
```

---

7.   https://github.com/thoughtbot/shoulda-matchers

```
    def inspect
      "#<Event #{name.inspect} (capacity: #{capacity})>"
    end
end
```

Now it's time to add the first specs.

When No Tickets Have Been Sold

Put the following example group after your class:

12-creating-custom-matchers/exercises/custom_matcher/spec/event_matchers_spec.rb
```
RSpec.describe '`have_no_tickets_sold` matcher' do
  example 'passing expectation' do
    art_show = Event.new('Art Show', 100)

    expect(art_show).to have_no_tickets_sold
  end

  example 'failing expectation' do
    art_show = Event.new('Art Show', 100)
    art_show.purchase_ticket_for(:a_friend)

    expect(art_show).to have_no_tickets_sold
  end
end
```

Go ahead and run your spec file. Both examples should fail, because the have_no_tickets_sold matcher doesn't exist yet.

Implement this matcher using the matcher DSL. When your match logic is correct, you'll have one passing and one failing example. Then, you can turn your attention to providing a good failure message.

Selling Out

Now that we have a handle on unsuccessful ticket sales, let's test what happens for a sold-out concert. Add the following example group:

12-creating-custom-matchers/exercises/custom_matcher/spec/event_matchers_spec.rb
```
RSpec.describe '`be_sold_out` matcher' do
  example 'passing expectation' do
    u2_concert = Event.new('U2 Concert', 10_000)
    10_000.times { u2_concert.purchase_ticket_for(:a_fan) }

    expect(u2_concert).to be_sold_out
  end
```

```ruby
  example 'failing expectation' do
    u2_concert = Event.new('U2 Concert', 10_000)
    9_900.times { u2_concert.purchase_ticket_for(:a_fan) }

    expect(u2_concert).to be_sold_out
  end
end
```

As with the previous exercise, this snippet uses a matcher, be_sold_out, that hasn't been defined. Add that definition now. As you did before, get the match logic correct before moving on to the failure message.

Bonus Points

Now that you have built this matcher using the DSL, reimplement it as a matcher class.

Part V

RSpec Mocks

A robust test suite will run fast, be deterministic, and cover all essential code paths. Unfortunately, dependencies often get in the way of these goals. Sometimes, we can't reliably test code while it's integrated with other libraries or systems.

In this part of the book, we're going to talk about test doubles, including mock objects. These allow you to tightly control the environment in which your tests run. The result will be faster, more reliable specs.

In this chapter, you'll see:

- How doubles can isolate your code from your dependencies
- The differences between mocks, stubs, spies, and null objects
- How to add test double behavior to an existing Ruby object
- How to keep your doubles and your real objects in sync

## CHAPTER 13

Understanding Test Doubles

In movies, a stunt double stands in for an actor, absorbing a punch or a fall when the actor can't or shouldn't do so. In test frameworks like RSpec, a *test double* fulfills the same role. It stands in for another object during testing.

You've used this concept before, in *Test Doubles: Mocks, Stubs, and Others*, on page 67. When you wrote your API unit specs, you treated the storage layer as if it were behaving exactly how you needed it to—even though that layer hadn't been written yet!

This ability to isolate parts of your system while you're testing them is super-powerful. With test doubles, you can:

- Exercise hard-to-reach code paths, such as error-handling code for a reliable third-party service

- Write specs for a layer of your system before you've built all its dependencies, as you did with the expense tracker

- Use an API while you're still designing it so that you can fix problems with the design before spending time on implementation

- Demonstrate how a component works *relative to its neighbors in the system*, which leads to less brittle tests

In this chapter, we're going to show you how to get started with rspec-mocks, RSpec's built-in library for creating test doubles. The techniques you learn here and in the next two chapters will make your specs faster and more resilient.

Types of Test Doubles

When we first introduced test doubles, we hinted that there are different names for doubles—mocks, spies, and so on. But we glossed over some of the differences. Let's take a closer look now.

There are a couple of different ways to think about a test double. One is the *usage mode* of the double—that is, what you're using it for and what you're expecting it to do. The other thing to consider is how the double is created. We'll call this the double's *origin*.

Here are the usage modes we'll be talking about in this chapter:

Stub

Returns canned responses, avoiding any meaningful computation or I/O

Mock

Expects specific messages; will raise an error if it *doesn't* receive them by the end of the example

Null Object

A benign test double that can stand in for any object; returns itself in response to any message

Spy

Records the messages it receives, so that you can check them later

We're basing the terms here on the vocabulary that Gerard Meszaros developed in his book, *xUnit Test Patterns [Mes07]*.

In addition to having a usage mode, a test double has an *origin*, indicating what its underlying Ruby class is. Some doubles are based on real Ruby objects, and some are totally fake:

Pure Double

A double whose behavior comes entirely from the test framework; this is what people normally think of when they talk about mock objects

Partial Double

An existing Ruby object that takes on some test double behavior; its interface is a mixture of real and fake implementations

Verifying Double

Totally fake like a pure double, but constrains its interface based on a real object like a partial double; provides a safer test double by verifying that it matches the API it's standing in for

Stubbed Constant

A Ruby constant—such as a class or module name—which you create, remove, or replace for a single test

Any given test double will have both an origin and a usage mode. For instance, you may have a pure double acting as a stub, or a verifying double acting as a spy.

We're going to explore the different kinds of doubles interactively in a live IRB session. Typically, mock object frameworks assume they're running inside an individual test, but RSpec's test doubles support a special stand-alone mode for these kinds of experiments.

To use this mode, fire up IRB and require the following file:

```
>> require 'rspec/mocks/standalone'
=> true
```

Keep this session running as you try the upcoming examples.

Usage Modes: Mocks, Stubs, and Spies

First, let's talk about the different usage modes of test doubles.

Generic Test Doubles

RSpec's double method creates a *generic test double* that you can use in any mode. The simplest way to call this method is with no arguments. Let's try that now:

```
>> ledger = double
=> #<Double (anonymous)>
```

In some ways, this double acts like an ordinary Ruby object. As you send messages to it (in other words, call methods on it), it will accept some messages and reject others.

The difference is that a generic double gives you more debugging information than a regular Ruby object. Try sending the record message to your test double now:

```
>> ledger.record(an: :expense)
RSpec::Mocks::MockExpectationError: #<Double (anonymous)> received          ↩
unexpected message :record with ({:an=>:expense})
    « backtrace truncated »
```

When we sent this message, the double raised an exception. Doubles are *strict* by default: they will reject all messages except the ones you've specifically allowed. We'll see how to do that later on.

Take a peek inside that error message. RSpec shows both the message name and arguments we sent to our double; this is already more information than a typical Ruby NoMethodError.

RSpec describes the object only as #<Double (anonymous)>, with no hint as to what we're using it for. You can get a little more detail in the error message by naming the role the double plays—just pass a name to the double method.

Since this object is standing in for a Ledger instance, let's name it 'Ledger':

```
>> ledger = double('Ledger')
=> #<Double "Ledger">
>> ledger.record(an: :expense)
RSpec::Mocks::MockExpectationError: #<Double "Ledger"> received unexpected ↵
message :record with ({:an=>:expense})
    « backtrace truncated »
```

The error message contains the role name now. This extra information comes in handy when you're using multiple doubles in the same example and need to tell them apart.

This same double method can create any of the other kinds of test doubles you'll use in your specs: stubs, mocks, spies, and null objects. Over the next few sections, we're going to take a look at each of these in turn.

Stubs

As we said at the start of this chapter, stubs are simple. They return pre-programmed, canned responses. Stubs are best for when you're simulating *query methods*—that is, methods that return a value but don't perform side effects.

The simplest way to define a stub is to pass a hash of method names and return values to the double method:

```
>> http_response = double('HTTPResponse', status: 200, body: 'OK')
=> #<Double "HTTPResponse">
>> http_response.status
=> 200
>> http_response.body
=> "OK"
```

As an alternative, you can perform these two steps (creating the stub and setting up the canned messages) separately. To do so, pass that same hash of method names and return values into allow(...).to receive_messages(...), like so:

```
>> http_response = double('HTTPResponse')
=> #<Double "HTTPResponse">
>> allow(http_response).to receive_messages(status: 200, body: 'OK')
```

```
=> {:status=>200, :body=>"OK"}
>> http_response.status
=> 200
>> http_response.body
=> "OK"
```

In fact, the hash syntax is just a shorthand for spelling out each allowed message individually:

```
>> allow(http_response).to receive(:status).and_return(200)
=> #<RSpec::Mocks::MessageExpectation #<Double "HTTPResponse">.status(any    ↵
arguments)>
>> allow(http_response).to receive(:body).and_return('OK')
=> #<RSpec::Mocks::MessageExpectation #<Double "HTTPResponse">.body(any    ↵
arguments)>
```

This more verbose syntax doesn't buy you much for simple stubs like these. But it will be vital in the next chapter, where we need more precision.

All of these stubs are simple. They watch for specific messages and return the same value each time they receive a given message. They don't act differently based on their arguments, and in fact they ignore their arguments:

```
>> http_response.status(:args, :are, :ignored)
=> 200
>> http_response.body(:blocks, :are, :also) { :ignored }
=> "OK"
```

In the next chapter, we'll talk about how to express expected parameters and return values more precisely.

Stubs like these help you test a specific kind of behavior—the kind that can be verified just by looking at return values. The method you're testing will typically do the following steps:

1. Query data from a dependency

2. Perform a computation on that data

3. Return a result

Your specs can check your object's behavior just by looking at the return value in step 3. All the stub has to do is hand back an appropriate reply to the query at step 1.

Sometimes, you need to test an object that doesn't fit into this pattern. In these situations, you can turn to another kind of test double designed for this use case: a mock object.

Mocks

Mocks are great when you're dealing with *command methods*. With these, it's not a return value that you care about, but rather a *side effect*. Here's a typical sequence:

1. Receive an event from the system

2. Make a decision based on that event

3. Perform an action that has a side effect

For instance, a chat bot's Reply feature may receive a text message, decide how to reply, and then post a message in the chat room. To test this behavior, it's not enough for your test double to provide a fixed return value at step 3. It needs to make sure the object triggered the side effect of posting a message correctly.

To use a mock object, you'll pre-program it with a set of messages it's supposed to receive. These are called *message expectations*. You declare them the same way you'd write a normal expectation in your specs: by combining the expect method with a matcher:

```
>> expect(ledger).to receive(:record)
=> #<RSpec::Mocks::MessageExpectation #<Double "Ledger">.record(any    ↩
arguments)>
```

Once you've created a mock object, you'll typically pass it into the code you're testing. At the end of each RSpec example, RSpec verifies that all mocks received their expected messages.

Since you're using rspec-mocks in stand-alone mode, you'll need to kick off the verification step manually. You can do so by calling RSpec::Mocks.verify:

```
>> RSpec::Mocks.verify
RSpec::Mocks::MockExpectationError: (Double "Ledger").record(*(any args))
    expected: 1 time with any arguments
    received: 0 times with any arguments
    « backtrace truncated »
```

Because the mock Ledger didn't receive the messages it was expecting, it raises a MockExpectationError message. If this code were running inside an RSpec example, the example would fail.

You can also specify the opposite behavior: that a mock object should *not* receive a message. To do so, negate the receive expectation with not_to, just like you'd do with any other expectation:

```
>> expect(ledger).not_to receive(:reset)
=> #<RSpec::Mocks::MessageExpectation #<Double "Ledger">.reset(any    ↩
```

```
arguments)>
>> ledger.reset
RSpec::Mocks::MockExpectationError: (Double "Ledger").reset(no args)
    expected: 0 times with any arguments
    received: 1 time
    « backtrace truncated »
```

Here, we see a failure because the mock object received a message it was specifically expecting not to receive. With rspec-mocks, you can spell out much more fine-grained expectations than just receiving or not receiving messages. Later, you'll see how.

Null Objects

The test doubles you've defined so far are *strict*: they require you to declare in advance what messages are allowed. Much of the time, this is what you want. But when your test double needs to receive several messages, having to spell each one out can make your tests brittle.

In these situations, you may want a test double that's a little more forgiving. That's where null objects come in. You can convert any test double to a null object by calling as_null_object on it:

```
>> yoshi = double('Yoshi').as_null_object
=> #<Double "Yoshi">
>> yoshi.eat(:apple)
=> #<Double "Yoshi">
```

This type of null object is known as a *black hole*; it responds to any message sent to it, and always returns itself. This means that you can chain one method call after another, for as many calls as you care to:

```
>> yoshi.eat(:apple).then_shoot(:shell).then_stomp
=> #<Double "Yoshi">
```

Null objects are the placebos of the testing world. They're benign objects that do nothing, can stand in for anything, and can satisfy any interface.

This flexibility is useful for testing objects that have multiple collaborators. If you have a ChatBot class that interacts with a room and a user, you may want to test these collaborations separately. While you're focusing on the user-related specs, you can use a null object for the room.

Spies

One downside of traditional mocks is that they disrupt the normal Arrange/ Act/Assert sequence you're used to in your tests. To see what we mean, type in the following definition of a Game class:

```
>> class Game
>>   def self.play(character)
>>     character.jump
>>   end
>> end
=> :play
```

When you're testing this class, first you'll *arrange* your test double:

```
>> mario = double('Mario')
=> #<Double "Mario">
```

...*assert* that it will receive the :jump message:

```
>> expect(mario).to receive(:jump)
=> #<RSpec::Mocks::MessageExpectation #<Double "Mario">.jump(any arguments)>
```

...and finally *act* by playing the game:

```
>> Game.play(mario)
=> nil
```

It feels a bit backwards to have to assert before acting. Spies are one way to restore the traditional flow. All you have to do is change the receive expectation to have_received, and then you can move your expectation to the end:

```
>> mario = double('Mario').as_null_object
=> #<Double "Mario">
>> Game.play(mario)
=> #<Double "Mario">
>> expect(mario).to have_received(:jump)
=> nil
```

Notice that we've had to define mario as a null object. If it had been a regular, strict double, you would have gotten a failure when you called the play method (because play would have sent it an unexpected jump message).

When you spy on objects with have_received, you'll either need to use null objects or explicitly allow the expected messages:

```
>> mario = double('Mario')
=> #<Double "Mario">
>> allow(mario).to receive(:jump)
=> #<RSpec::Mocks::MessageExpectation #<Double "Mario">.jump(any arguments)>
>> Game.play(mario)
=> nil
>> expect(mario).to have_received(:jump)
=> nil
```

Having to spell out the same message twice (once before calling Game.play and once afterward) somewhat defeats the purpose of spying. It's easier just to use a null object, and in fact RSpec provides a nice spy method for this purpose:

```
>> mario = spy('Mario')
=> #<Double "Mario">
>> Game.play(mario)
=> #<Double "Mario">
>> expect(mario).to have_received(:jump)
=> nil
```

Not only does this alias save you a bit of code, it also expresses your intent better. You're declaring up front that you're going to use this test double as a spy.

Origins: Pure, Partial, and Verifying Doubles

Now that we've seen the different usage modes of test doubles, let's look at where they come from.

Pure Doubles

All of the test doubles you've written so far in this chapter are *pure doubles*: they're purpose-built by rspec-mocks and consist entirely of behavior you add to them. You can pass them into your project code just as if they were the real thing.

Pure doubles are flexible and easy to get started with. They're best for testing code where you can pass in dependencies. Unfortunately, real-world projects are not always so tester-friendly, and you'll need to turn to more powerful techniques.

Partial Doubles

Sometimes, the code you're testing doesn't give you an easy way to inject dependencies. A hard-coded class name may be lurking three layers deep in that API method you're calling. For instance, a lot of Ruby projects call Time.now without providing a way to override this behavior during testing.

To test these kinds of codebases, you can use a *partial double*. These add mocking and stubbing behavior to existing Ruby objects. That means any object in your system can be a partial double. All you have to do is expect or allow a specific message, just like you'd do for a pure double:

```
>> random = Random.new
=> #<Random:0x007ff2389554e8>
>> allow(random).to receive(:rand).and_return(0.1234)
=> #<RSpec::Mocks::MessageExpectation #<Random:0x007ff2389554e8>.rand(any ↵
arguments)>
>> random.rand
=> 0.1234
```

In this snippet, you've created an instance of Ruby's random number generator, and then replaced its rand method with one that returns a canned value. All its other methods will behave normally.

You can also use a partial double as a spy, using the expect(...).to have_received form you saw earlier:

```
>> allow(Dir).to receive(:mktmpdir).and_yield('/path/to/tmp')
=> #<RSpec::Mocks::MessageExpectation #<Dir (class)>.mktmpdir(any arguments)>
>> Dir.mktmpdir { |dir| puts "Dir is: #{dir}" }
Dir is: /path/to/tmp
=> nil
>> expect(Dir).to have_received(:mktmpdir)
=> nil
```

When you used a pure double as a spy, you had a choice of how to specify up front which messages the spy should allow. You could permit *any* message (using spy or as_null_object), or explicitly allow just the messages you want. With partial doubles, you can only do the latter. RSpec doesn't support the notion of a "partial spy," because it can't spy on all of a real object's methods in a performant way.

When you use partial doubles inside your specs, RSpec will revert all your changes at the end of each example. The Ruby object will go back to its original behavior. That way, you won't have to worry about the test double behavior leaking into other specs.

Since you are experimenting in stand-alone mode, you will need to call RSpec::Mocks.teardown explicitly to get this same cleanup to happen:

```
>> RSpec::Mocks.teardown
=> #<RSpec::Mocks::RootSpace:0x007ff2389bccb0>
>> random.rand
=> 0.9385928886462153
```

This call also exits from the stand-alone mode you've been experimenting in. If you want to keep exploring in the same IRB session, you'll need to call RSpec::Mocks.setup to go back into stand-alone mode.

Test Doubles Have Short Lifetimes

 RSpec tears down all your test doubles at the end of each example. That means they won't play well with RSpec features that live outside the typical per-example scope, such as before(:context) hooks. You can work around some of these limitations with a method named with_temporary_scope.[1]

---

1. https://relishapp.com/rspec/rspec-mocks/v/3-6/docs/basics/scope

Partial doubles are useful, but we consider them a *code smell,* a superficial sign that might lead you to a deeper design issue.[2] In *Using Partial Doubles Effectively,* on page 271, we'll explain some of these underlying issues and how to address them.

Verifying Doubles

The upside of test doubles is that they can stand in for a dependency you don't want to drag into your test. The downside is that the double and the dependency can drift out of sync with each other.[3] *Verifying doubles* can protect you from this kind of drift.

In *Test Doubles: Mocks, Stubs, and Others,* on page 67, you created a test double to help you test a high-level API when your lower-level Ledger class didn't exist yet. We later explained that you were using a verifying double for that spec; let's take a closer look at why it was important to do so.

Here's a simplified version of a similar double, *without* verification:

```
13-understanding-test-doubles/02/expense_tracker/spec/unit/ledger_double_spec.rb
ledger = double('ExpenseTracker::Ledger')
allow(ledger).to receive(:record)
```

When you tested your system's public API, your routing code called Ledger#record:

```
13-understanding-test-doubles/02/expense_tracker/app/api.rb
post '/expenses' do
  expense = JSON.parse(request.body.read)
➤ result = @ledger.record(expense)
  JSON.generate('expense_id' => result.expense_id)
end
```

The Ledger class didn't exist yet; the test double provided enough of an implementation for your routing specs to pass. Later, you built the real thing.

Consider what would happen if at some point you renamed the Ledger#record method to Ledger#record_expense but forgot to update the routing code. Your specs would still pass, since they're still providing a fake record method. But your code would fail in real-world use, because it's trying to call a method that no longer exists. These kinds of false positives can kill confidence in your unit specs.

You avoided this trap in the expense tracker project by using a verifying double. To do so, you called instance_double in place of double, passing the name of the Ledger class. Here's a stripped-down version of the code:

---

2. https://martinfowler.com/bliki/CodeSmell.html
3. https://www.thoughtworks.com/insights/blog/mockists-are-dead-long-live-classicists

13-understanding-test-doubles/02/expense_tracker/spec/unit/ledger_double_spec.rb
```
ledger = instance_double('ExpenseTracker::Ledger')
allow(ledger).to receive(:record)
```

With this double in place, RSpec checks that the real Ledger class (if it's loaded) actually responds to the record message with the same signature. If you rename this method to record_expense, or add or remove arguments, your specs will correctly fail until you update your use of the method *and* your test double setup.

Use Verifying Doubles to Catch Problems Earlier

 Although your unit specs would have had a false positive here, your acceptance specs would still have caught this regression. That's because they use the real versions of the objects, rather than counting on test doubles.

By using verifying doubles in your unit specs, you get the best of both worlds. You'll catch errors earlier and at less cost, while writing specs that behave correctly when APIs change.

RSpec gives you a few different ways to create verifying doubles, based on what it will use as an interface template for the double:

instance_double('SomeClass')
    Constrains the double's interface using the *instance methods* of SomeClass

class_double('SomeClass')
    Constrains the double's interface using the *class methods* of SomeClass

object_double(some_object)
    Constrains the double's interface using the methods of some_object, rather than a class; handy for dynamic objects that use method_missing

In addition, each of these methods has a _spy variant (such as instance_spy) as a convenience for using a verifying double as a spy.

Stubbed Constants

Test doubles are all about controlling the environment your specs run in: what classes are available, how certain methods behave, and so on. A key piece of that environment is the set of Ruby constants available to your code. With *stubbed constants*, you can replace a constant with a different one for the duration of one example.

For instance, password hashing algorithms are slow by design for security reasons—but you may want to speed them up during testing. Algorithms like bcrypt take a tunable *cost factor* to specify how expensive the hash computation will be. If your code defines this number as a constant:

13-understanding-test-doubles/03/stubbed_constants.rb
```
class PasswordHash
  COST_FACTOR = 12

  # ...
end
```

...your specs can redefine it to 1:

13-understanding-test-doubles/03/stubbed_constants.rb
```
stub_const('PasswordHash::COST_FACTOR', 1)
```

You can use stub_const to do a number of things:

- Define a new constant
- Replace an existing constant
- Replace an entire module or class (because these are also constants)
- Avoid loading an expensive class, using a lightweight fake in its place

Sometimes, controlling your test environment means *removing* an existing constant instead of stubbing one. For example, if you're writing a library that works either with or without ActiveRecord, you can hide the ActiveRecord constant for a specific example:

13-understanding-test-doubles/03/stubbed_constants.rb
```
hide_const('ActiveRecord')
```

Hiding the ActiveRecord constant like this will cut off access to the entire module, including any nested constants like ActiveRecord::Base. Your code won't be able to accidentally use ActiveRecord. Just as with partial doubles, any constants you've changed or hidden will be restored at the end of each example.

Your Turn

In this chapter, we discussed the differences between stubs, mocks, spies, and null objects. In particular, you saw how they deal with the following situations:

- Receiving expected messages
- Receiving unexpected messages
- Not receiving expected messages

We also looked at the different ways to create test doubles. Pure doubles are entirely fake, whereas partial doubles are real Ruby objects that have fake behavior added. Verifying doubles fall in between, and have the advantages of both with few of the downsides of either. They're the ones we use most often.

Now that you understand test doubles, you'll be ready to tackle the next chapter, where you'll configure *how* and *when* your doubles respond to messages. But first, we have a simple exercise that demonstrates a few nuances of verifying doubles.

Exercise

In this guided exercise, you're going to test a Skier class that collaborates with a TrailMap class. Starting in a fresh directory, put the following code in lib/skier.rb:

13-understanding-test-doubles/exercises/mountain/lib/skier.rb
```
module Mountain
  class Skier
    def initialize(trail_map)
      @trail_map = trail_map
    end

    def ski_on(trail_name)
      difficulty = @trail_map.difficulty(trail_name)
      @tired = true if difficulty == :expert
    end

    def tired?
      @tired
    end
  end
end
```

Now, create a file called lib/trail_map.rb with the following contents:

13-understanding-test-doubles/exercises/mountain/lib/trail_map.rb
```
puts 'Loading our database query library...'
sleep(1)

module Mountain
  class TrailMap
    def difficulty_of(trail_name)
      # Look up the trail in the database
    end
  end
end
```

The TrailMap class has a difficulty_of method, but the Skier class is incorrectly trying to call difficulty instead. If we use a verifying double to stand in for a TrailMap, it should be able to catch this kind of error; let's try that out.

Trying the Verifying Double

Create a file called spec/skier_spec.rb, and put the following spec in it:

13-understanding-test-doubles/exercises/mountain/spec/skier_spec.rb

```ruby
require 'skier'

module Mountain
  RSpec.describe Skier do
    it 'gets tired after skiing a difficult slope' do
      trail_map = instance_double('TrailMap', difficulty: :expert)

      skier = Skier.new(trail_map)
      skier.ski_on('Last Hoot')
      expect(skier).to be_tired
    end
  end
end
```

This spec makes the same mistake the Skier class did with method names. It stubs the difficulty method instead of difficulty_of. However, you're using instance_double, so RSpec should catch the problem—right?

Try running your spec:

```
$ rspec
```

Surprisingly, the specs pass. RSpec can only verify against a real class if that class is actually loaded. With nothing to verify against, the verifying double acts just like a normal, non-verifying double. So, try running it again *with* the TrailMap class loaded; just pass -rtrail_map on the command line:

```
$ rspec -rtrail_map
```

The specs *still* pass. Moreover, they're running much more slowly (nearly 10x slower on our computers!) because of the time spent loading a heavyweight dependency. Before moving on, see if you can guess why RSpec isn't checking your trail_map double against the real Mountain::TrailMap class.

The Problem

The problem is that the constant name passed into instance_double doesn't match the real class. The TrailMap class's full name, including the module it's nested in, is 'Mountain::TrailMap'.

Change the instance_double call to use the correct name, and then rerun your specs (again, with -rtrail_map). This time, they should fail the way you'd expect them to: with an error message about the use of a nonexistent difficulty method.

There are two ways to catch these kinds of naming issues before they happen:

- Use Ruby classes instead of strings
- Configure RSpec to check that the class name exists

You're going to get the chance to try out both of these options. Undo the fix you just made before you start the next step of the exercise.

Using Ruby Constants

First, let's try using a Ruby constant to indicate which class you're faking. In the call to instance_double, change the string 'TrailMap' to the class TrailMap (without quotes).

Now, run your specs the same way you did at the beginning of this exercise: plain rspec with no command-line arguments. The first time you tried this, RSpec gave an incorrectly passing result. Now, you'll get an uninitialized constant Mountain::TrailMap error, because the TrailMap class isn't loaded.

To use the Ruby class directly like this, you'll have to make sure the dependency is loaded before your spec runs. If your specs use the class directly (as this one now does), you'll typically just add require 'trail_map' at the top of your spec file.

There are times, however, when you might *not* want to load your dependencies explicitly in this way:

- Your dependencies take a long time to load, like trail_map does
- You need to use a test double before the dependency even exists, as you did with the Ledger double in the expense tracker project

Now, back out the change you just made, and we'll look at the other way to catch class naming issues.

Configuring RSpec to Check Names

In *Library Configuration*, on page 161, you used an RSpec.configure block to set up rspec-mocks. Using the same kind of block, you can configure RSpec to make sure that all of your verifying doubles are based on real, loaded classes.

The setting you need is called verify_doubled_constant_names. You probably don't want to turn it on unconditionally in spec_helper.rb. If you did, you'd never be able to use a verifying double before its class existed! Instead, put the setting into a file you can load on demand; let's call it spec/support/verify_doubled_constants.rb:

13-understanding-test-doubles/exercises/mountain/spec/support/verify_doubled_constants.rb
```
RSpec.configure do |c|
  c.mock_with :rspec do |mocks|
    mocks.verify_doubled_constant_names = true
  end
end
```

When you want RSpec to be strict about your verifying doubles, just pass -rsupport/verify_doubled_constants on the command line:

```
$ rspec -rtrail_map -rsupport/verify_doubled_constants
```

Your specs will correctly fail, and RSpec will warn you that the class name doesn't exist. If you use this approach, we recommend that you develop with this setting *off*, but configure your continuous integration (CI) server to run with the setting *on*.

Make It Easy to Replicate Your CI Setup

Repeatability is important when you're setting up a CI system. Few things are more frustrating than a spec passing on your local machine but failing on the CI server.

If you're going to use certain options only with CI, such as the verify_doubled_constant_names setting, we recommend putting all of these options into a script or Rake task you can run locally. That way, when a spec fails on CI, you can just run something like ./script/ci_build and diagnose the issue on your machine.

We'll talk more about integration with Rake in Appendix 1, *RSpec and the Wider Ruby Ecosystem*, on page 293.

Wrapping Up

As we wrap up, let's look at the trade-offs we've seen. Verifying doubles do the following things:

- They raise errors when your code calls a dependency incorrectly.
- They can only do so when the dependency actually exists.
- They revert silently to regular doubles if the dependency doesn't exist.

To deal with that last item, you can create your doubles from Ruby class names instead of strings. It's only practical to do so if you've already written code for the dependency, and if it's not too expensive to load it. If you can't use a Ruby class, you can still double-check your constant names by setting verify_doubled_constant_names when you run your whole suite.

Using verifying doubles correctly takes a little extra up-front care. But the benefits to your project are well worth it.

In this chapter, you'll see:

- How to return, raise, or yield a value from your double
- How to supply custom behavior for your double
- How to ensure your double is called with the right arguments
- How to make sure your double is called the right number of times and in the right order

## CHAPTER 14

Customizing Test Doubles

Now that you've got a handle on the basic types of test doubles and when to use them, we're going to dive into the rspec-mocks API for a bit. Our goal isn't to give you an exhaustive API reference here; that's what the docs are for.[1]

Instead, we're going to show you the basics, and then give a few recipes for specific situations.

Configuring Responses

Since a test double is meant to stand in for a real object, it needs to act like one. You need to be able to configure how it *responds* to the code calling it.

When you allow or expect a message on a test double without specifying how it responds, RSpec provides a simple implementation that just returns nil. Your test doubles will often need to do something more interesting: return a given value, raise an error, yield to a block, or throw a symbol. RSpec provides ways for your doubles to do each of these:

```
14-customizing-test-doubles/01/configuring_responses.rb
allow(double).to receive(:a_message).and_return(a_return_value)
allow(double).to receive(:a_message).and_raise(AnException)
allow(double).to receive(:a_message).and_yield(a_value_to_a_block)
allow(double).to receive(:a_message).and_throw(:a_symbol, optional_value)
allow(double).to receive(:a_message) { |arg| do_something_with(arg) }

# These last two are just for partial doubles:
allow(object).to receive(:a_message).and_call_original
allow(object).to receive(:a_message).and_wrap_original { |original| }
```

Now, let's look at a couple of specific situations you may run into when you're specifying how your test doubles will behave.

---

1. https://relishapp.com/rspec/rspec-mocks/v/3-6/docs/configuring-responses

---

Method Expectations Replace Their Originals

People new to RSpec are often surprised at the behavior of expect on a partial double. The following code:

```
expect(some_existing_object).to receive(:a_message)
```

...doesn't just set up an expectation. It also *changes* the behavior of the existing object. Calls to some_existing_object.a_message will return nil and do nothing else. If you want to add a message expectation while retaining the original implementation, you'll need to use and_call_original.

Returning Multiple Values

You've already used and_return, in *Test Doubles: Mocks, Stubs, and Others*, on page 67. There, you set up your test double to return the same canned expense item each time it received the record message.

Sometimes, you need your stubbed method to do something more sophisticated than return the same value every time it's called. You might want to return one value for the first call, a different one for the second call, and so on.

For these cases, you can pass multiple values to and_return:

```
>> allow(random).to receive(:rand).and_return(0.1, 0.2, 0.3)
=> #<RSpec::Mocks::MessageExpectation #<Double "Random">.rand(any arguments)>
>> random.rand
=> 0.1
>> random.rand
=> 0.2
>> random.rand
=> 0.3
>> random.rand
=> 0.3
>> random.rand
=> 0.3
```

Here, we give three return values, and the rand method returns each one in sequence. After the third call, the method continues to return 0.3, the final value passed to and_return.

Yielding Multiple Values

Blocks are ubiquitous in Ruby, and sometimes your test doubles will need to stand in for an interface that uses blocks. The aptly named and_yield method will configure your double to yield values.

To specify a sequence of values to yield, chain together multiple calls to and_yield:

```
14-customizing-test-doubles/01/configuring_responses.rb
extractor = double('TwitterURLExtractor')

allow(extractor).to receive(:extract_urls_from_twitter_firehose)
  .and_yield('https://rspec.info/',    93284234987)
  .and_yield('https://github.com/',    43984523459)
  .and_yield('https://pragprog.com/', 33745639845)
```

We've chained together three and_yield calls. When the code we're testing calls extract_urls_from_twitter_firehose with a block, the method will yield to the block three times. Each time, the block will receive a URL and a numeric tweet ID.

Raising Exceptions Flexibly

When you're testing exception-handling code, you can raise exceptions from your test doubles using the and_raise modifier. This method has a flexible API that mirrors Ruby's raise method.[2] That means all of the following calls will work:

```
14-customizing-test-doubles/01/configuring_responses.rb
allow(dbl).to receive(:msg).and_raise(AnExceptionClass)
allow(dbl).to receive(:msg).and_raise('an error message')
allow(dbl).to receive(:msg).and_raise(AnExceptionClass, 'with a message')

an_exception_instance = AnExceptionClass.new
allow(dbl).to receive(:msg).and_raise(an_exception_instance)
```

In the examples we've shown you so far, we've been working with pure test doubles. These doubles have to be told exactly how to respond, because they don't have an existing implementation to modify.

Partial doubles are different. Since they begin as a real object with real method implementations, you can base the fake version on the real one. Let's look at how to do so.

Falling Back to the Original Implementation

When you're using a partial double to replace a method, sometimes you only want to replace it conditionally. You may want to use a fake implementation for certain parameter values but fall back on the real method the rest of the time. In these cases, you can expect or allow twice: once like you normally would, and once with and_call_original to provide the default behavior.

```
14-customizing-test-doubles/01/configuring_responses.rb
# fake implementation for specific arguments:
allow(File).to receive(:read).with('/etc/passwd').and_raise('HAHA NOPE')

# fallback:
allow(File).to receive(:read).and_call_original
```

---

2. https://ruby-doc.org/core-2.4.1/Kernel.html#method-i-raise

Here, we've used with(...) to constrain which parameter values this stub applies to. We'll talk more about with later in *Constraining Arguments*, on page 256.

Modifying the Return Value

Sometimes, you want to slightly change the behavior of the method you're stubbing, rather than replacing it outright. You may, for instance, need to modify its return value.

To do so, call RSpec's and_wrap_original method, passing it a block containing your custom behavior. Your block will take the original implementation as an argument, which you can call at any time.

Here, we use this technique to stub out a CustomerService API to return a subset of customers:

14-customizing-test-doubles/01/configuring_responses.rb
```
allow(CustomerService).to receive(:all).and_wrap_original do |original|
  all_customers = original.call
  all_customers.sort_by(&:id).take(10)
end
```

This technique can be handy for acceptance specs, where you want to test against a live service. If the vendor doesn't provide a test API that only returns a few records, you can call the real API and narrow down the records yourself. By working on just a subset of the data, your specs will remain snappy.

Tweaking Arguments

You can also use and_wrap_original to tweak the arguments you pass *into* a method. This technique comes in handy when the code you're testing uses a lot of hard-coded values.

In *Stubbed Constants*, on page 244, we used stub_const to call a hashing algorithm with a lower cost factor so that our specs kept running quickly. That approach only worked because the cost was defined as a constant.

If instead the number had been a hard-coded argument value, we could have overridden it using and_wrap_original:

14-customizing-test-doubles/01/configuring_responses.rb
```
allow(PasswordHash).to receive(:hash_password)
  .and_wrap_original do |original, cost_factor|
    original.call(1)
  end
```

If the method you're stubbing takes arguments (such as the cost_factor), RSpec passes these as additional parameters into your block.

Since both and_call_original and and_wrap_original need an existing implementation to call, they only make sense for partial doubles.

When You Need More Flexibility

So far, we've seen several different ways to customize how your test doubles behave. You can return or yield a specific sequence of values, raise an exception, and so on.

Sometimes, though, the behavior you need is slightly outside what these techniques provide. If you're not quite sure how to configure a double to do what you need, you can supply a block containing whatever custom behavior you need. Simply pass the block to the last method call in the receive expression.

For instance, you might want to simulate an intermittent network failure while you're testing. Here's an example of a weather API test double that succeeds 75 percent of the time:

```
14-customizing-test-doubles/01/configuring_responses.rb
counter = 0

allow(weather_api).to receive(:temperature) do |zip_code|
  counter = (counter + 1) % 4
  counter.zero? ? raise(Timeout::Error) : 35.0
end
```

When your code calls weather_api.temperature(some_zip_code), RSpec will run this block and, depending on how many calls you've made, either return a value or raise a timeout exception.

Don't Get Carried Away with Blocks

 If your block gets any more complex than the weather API example here, you might be better off moving it into its own Ruby class. Martin Fowler refers to this kind of stand-in as a *fake*.[3] Fakes are particularly useful when you need to preserve state across multiple method calls.

Setting Constraints

Most of the test doubles you've created will accept any input. If you stub a method named jump with no other options, RSpec will use your stub whenever your code calls jump, jump(:with, :arguments), or jump { with_a_block }.

---

3.   https://www.martinfowler.com/bliki/TestDouble.html

In this section, we're going to look at ways to set *constraints* on a test double, so that RSpec only uses it if your code calls it in a certain way.

Constraining Arguments

In your projects, you'll often want to check that your code is calling a method with the correct parameters. To constrain what arguments your mock object will accept, add a call to with to your message expectation:

14-customizing-test-doubles/02/setting_constraints.rb
```
expect(movie).to receive(:record_review).with('Great movie!')
expect(movie).to receive(:record_review).with(/Great/)
expect(movie).to receive(:record_review).with('Great movie!', 5)
```

If your code calls the method with arguments that don't match the constraint, then the expectation remains unsatisfied. RSpec will treat it the same as any other unmet expectation. In this example, we're using expect, meaning that RSpec will report a failure:

```
>> expect(movie).to receive(:record_review).with('Good')
=> #<RSpec::Mocks::MessageExpectation #<Double "Jaws">.record_review("Good")>
>> movie.record_review('Bad')
RSpec::Mocks::MockExpectationError: #<Double "Jaws"> received    ↵
:record_review with unexpected arguments
  expected: ("Good")
       got: ("Bad")
    « backtrace truncated »
```

If we had used allow instead, RSpec would have looked for another expectation that fit the passed-in arguments:

```
>> allow(imdb).to receive(:rating_for).and_return(3) # default
=> #<RSpec::Mocks::MessageExpectation #<Double "IMDB">.rating_for(any   ↵
arguments)>
>> allow(imdb).to receive(:rating_for).with('Jaws').and_return(5)
=> #<RSpec::Mocks::MessageExpectation #<Double "IMDB">.rating_for("Jaws")>
>> imdb.rating_for('Weekend at Bernies')
=> 3
>> imdb.rating_for('Jaws')
=> 5
```

RSpec gives you a ton of ways to constrain method arguments. Your test doubles can require something as simple as a specific value, or as sophisticated as any custom logic you can devise.

We won't give an exhaustive reference here, but we would like to show you a few situations you're likely to run into. For a full list of everything you can specify for your arguments, see the docs.[4]

Argument Placeholders

When a method takes several arguments, you may care more about some than others. For instance, you may be stubbing a shopping cart's add_product method that takes a name, a numeric ID, and a vendor-specific code. If you only care about the name, you can pass the anything placeholder for the others:

```
14-customizing-test-doubles/02/setting_constraints.rb
expect(cart).to receive(:add_product).with('Hoodie', anything, anything)
```

You can also represent a sequence of anything placeholders with any_args:

```
14-customizing-test-doubles/02/setting_constraints.rb
expect(cart).to receive(:add_product).with('Hoodie', any_args)
```

The any_args placeholder is a bit like the "splat" operator that you use to define a Ruby method with a flexible number of arguments. It can go anywhere in the argument list, but it can only show up once. Any of the following calls would satisfy this particular constraint:

```
14-customizing-test-doubles/02/setting_constraints.rb
cart.add_product('Hoodie')
cart.add_product('Hoodie', 27182818)
cart.add_product('Hoodie', 27182818, 'HOODIE-SERIAL-123')
```

The counterpart to any_args is no_args:

```
14-customizing-test-doubles/02/setting_constraints.rb
expect(database).to receive(:delete_all_the_things).with(no_args)
```

As you might guess from the name, this constraint only matches when you call the method with no arguments.

Hashes and Keyword Arguments

A lot of Ruby APIs, especially ones written before Ruby 2.0 came out, use an options hash to provide a flexible interface for callers:

```
14-customizing-test-doubles/02/setting_constraints.rb
class BoxOffice
  def find_showtime(options)
    # ...
  end
end
```

---

4. https://relishapp.com/rspec/rspec-mocks/v/3-6/docs/setting-constraints/matching-arguments

```
box_office.find_showtime(movie: 'Jaws')
box_office.find_showtime(movie: 'Jaws', zip_code: 97204)
box_office.find_showtime(movie: 'Jaws', city: 'Portland', state: 'OR')
```

When you're testing code that calls such a method, you can use RSpec's hash_including to specify which keys must be present. All three of these find_showtime calls would match the following constraint:

14-customizing-test-doubles/02/setting_constraints.rb
```
expect(box_office).to receive(:find_showtime)
  .with(hash_including(movie: 'Jaws'))
```

Specify Exactly the Level of Constraint You Need

 Flexible constraints like hash_including make your specs less brittle. Rather than having to give *all* the keys of your hash, you can give just the ones you care about. If the value of an unimportant key changes, your specs needn't fail.

Ruby 2.0 added *keyword arguments* to the language, which provides specific syntax for this style of API:

14-customizing-test-doubles/02/setting_constraints.rb
```
class BoxOffice
  def find_showtime(movie:, zip_code: nil, city: nil, state: nil)
    # ...
  end
end
```

The good news is that the hash_including constraint works just as well with keyword arguments as it does with old-style option hashes.

RSpec also provides a hash_excluding constraint to specify that a hash must *not* include a particular key.

Custom Logic

When you've written a bunch of constraints, you'll inevitably find yourself repeating the same complex constraint in several specs. Occasionally, you'll need logic that's too involved to express as a simple constraint. In both of these situations, you can supply your own custom logic.

For example, if you have several specs that should specifically call find_showtime with cities in Oregon, you can wrap this constraint up in a custom RSpec matcher like the one you wrote in *A Minimal Custom Matcher*, on page 221:

14-customizing-test-doubles/02/setting_constraints.rb
```
RSpec::Matchers.define :a_city_in_oregon do
  match { |options| options[:state] == 'OR' && options[:city] }
end
```

You can then pass your custom matcher to any with constraint:

14-customizing-test-doubles/02/setting_constraints.rb
```
expect(box_office).to receive(:find_showtime).with(a_city_in_oregon)
```

RSpec Compares Arguments Using ===

You can constrain arguments using an ordinary Ruby value, a regular expression, one of RSpec's provided constraints, or any built-in or custom matcher. Behind the scenes, rspec-mocks compares method arguments using the === operator. Anything that supports === can be used as an argument constraint.

Custom argument constraints can reduce repetition and make your expectations easier to understand.

Constraining How Many Times a Method Gets Called

In addition to constraining a method's arguments, you can also specify how many times it should be called. For instance, some applications use a *circuit breaker* that stops trying network calls after a certain number of failures.[5] Here's how you might test a stock ticker class that protects its network client with a circuit breaker:

14-customizing-test-doubles/02/stock_ticker.rb
```
client = instance_double('NasdaqClient')
expect(client).to receive(:current_price).thrice.and_raise(Timeout::Error)
stock_ticker = StockTicker.new(client)
100.times { stock_ticker.price('AAPL') }
```

Even though we're calling stock_ticker.price many times, we expect the circuit breaker to stop hitting the network after the third simulated timeout error.

As you might guess from the name thrice, RSpec also provides once and twice modifiers. Since the English language doesn't provide any multiplicative adverbs after 3, you'll need to switch to the more verbose exactly(n).times constraint for other numbers:

14-customizing-test-doubles/02/stock_ticker.rb
```
expect(client).to receive(:current_price).exactly(4).times
```

When you don't care about the exact number of calls but have a certain minimum or maximum in mind, you can use at_least or at_most:

14-customizing-test-doubles/02/stock_ticker.rb
```
expect(client).to receive(:current_price).at_least(3).times
expect(client).to receive(:current_price).at_most(10).times
```

---

5. https://martinfowler.com/bliki/CircuitBreaker.html

```
expect(client).to receive(:current_price).at_least(:once)
expect(client).to receive(:current_price).at_most(:thrice)
```

If your code calls the method too many or too few times, you'll get an unsat-isfied expectation:

```
>> expect(client).to receive(:current_price).at_most(:twice) \
>>   .and_return(130.0)
=> #<RSpec::Mocks::VerifyingMessageExpectation                      ↵
#<InstanceDouble(NasdaqClient) (anonymous)>.current_price(any arguments)>
>> stock_ticker = StockTicker.new(client)
=> #<StockTicker>
>> stock_ticker.price('AAPL')
=> 130.0
>> stock_ticker.price('AAPL')
=> 130.0
>> stock_ticker.price('AAPL')
RSpec::Mocks::MockExpectationError: (InstanceDouble(NasdaqClient)   ↵
(anonymous)).current_price("AAPL")
    expected: at most 2 times with any arguments
    received: 3 times with arguments: ("AAPL")
    « backtrace truncated »
```

It's worth noting that you can't combine the at_least and at_most constraints.

Ordering

Normally, RSpec doesn't care what order you send messages to a test double:

```
14-customizing-test-doubles/02/setting_constraints.rb
expect(greeter).to receive(:hello)
expect(greeter).to receive(:goodbye)

# The following will pass:
greeter.goodbye
greeter.hello
```

If you do need to enforce a specific order, add the ordered modifier:

```
14-customizing-test-doubles/02/setting_constraints.rb
expect(greeter).to receive(:hello).ordered
expect(greeter).to receive(:goodbye).ordered

# The following will fail:
greeter.goodbye
greeter.hello
```

Using ordered is a sign that your specs may be too coupled to one particular implementation. In the next chapter, we'll talk more about code smells like this one, and how to deal with them.

You Can Combine All Three Types of Constraints

 You can use all of the types of constraints we've seen here—arguments, call counts, and ordering—together in one expectation:

```
expect(catalog).to receive(:search).
  with(/term/).at_least(:twice).ordered
```

Just don't go overboard! Unless all these constraints are actually important, your specs may fail even when the code's external behavior hasn't changed.

Your Turn

In this chapter, we saw several different ways to configure how your test doubles respond to messages. We talked about how to return, raise, or yield specific values. We saw how to replace a method from a real class but still use the original implementation behind the scenes.

We also discussed how to constrain whether a double should respond at all for certain message arguments. By constraining what arguments a message expectation accepts, and how many times it must be called, you can be as specific or as loose as you need in your specs.

Exercises

For these exercises, you're going to dig a little more deeply into the block implementations from *When You Need More Flexibility*, on page 255. Block implementations are the catch-all of RSpec mocks: since you can put *any* arbitrary logic in them, you can always use a block if you can't remember what built-in API does what you need.

Block Implementations

Open exercises/block_implementation_spec.rb in this chapter's source code. It contains seven examples, each of which calls allow(test_double).to receive(:message) with a block.

The first four examples deal with configuring responses via a block:

```
14-customizing-test-doubles/exercises/block_implementation_spec.rb
RSpec.describe "Block implementations that provide responses" do
  let(:test_double) { double }

  it "can return a value" do
    allow(test_double).to receive(:message) do
      # TODO
    end

    expect(test_double.message).to eq(17)
  end
```

```ruby
  it "can raise an error" do
    allow(test_double).to receive(:message) do
      # TODO
    end

    expect { test_double.message }.to raise_error(/boom/)
  end

  it "can yield a value" do
    allow(test_double).to receive(:message) do |&block|
      # TODO
    end

    expect { |b| test_double.message(&b) }.to yield_with_args(1)
  end

  it "can throw a symbol" do
    allow(test_double).to receive(:message) do
      # TODO
    end

    expect { test_double.message }.to throw_symbol(:foo)
  end
end
```

The final three examples deal with constraining method calls via a block:

14-customizing-test-doubles/exercises/block_implementation_spec.rb
```ruby
RSpec.describe "Block implementations that check calls" do
  let(:test_double) { double }

  it "can constrain arguments" do
    allow(test_double).to receive(:message) do |arg|
      # TODO
    end

    expect { test_double.message(:valid_arg) }.not_to raise_error
    expect { test_double.message(:invalid_arg) }.to raise_error(/invalid_arg/)
  end

  it "can count how many times the message was received" do
    receive_count = 0

    allow(test_double).to receive(:message) do |&block|
      # TODO
    end

    test_double.message
    test_double.message

    expect(receive_count).to eq(2)
  end
```

```
it "can constrain the order messages were received in" do
  sequence = []

  allow(test_double).to receive(:message_1) do
    # TODO
  end

  allow(test_double).to receive(:message_2) do
    # TODO
  end

  test_double.message_1
  test_double.message_2
  test_double.message_1

  expect(sequence).to eq([:message_1, :message_2, :message_1])
  end
end
```

Your task is to fill in the body of each block (marked with # TODO) to make the specs pass.

Fluent Interface

Your solution so far has shown off how flexible your test doubles can be when you use a block implementation. Blocks are general enough to provide any behavior you need.

Now, you're going to explore RSpec's fluent interface for test doubles. Each of the blocks you wrote in the first exercise has a simpler rspec-mocks equivalent. Use the APIs you learned in this chapter to replace each block with a simpler allow or expect expression. For two of the constraint examples, you'll need to edit or remove some of the surrounding code, too.

In this chapter, you'll see:

- The importance of carefully constructing an environment for each spec
- How to provide test doubles to the code you're testing
- What the most common pitfalls are and how to avoid them
- How to improve your code by applying design feedback from your test doubles

CHAPTER 15

Using Test Doubles Effectively

Over the previous two chapters, you've tried out mocks, stubs, spies, and null objects. You've learned which situations each is best for. You've also seen how to configure their behavior, and how to check that a test double is called correctly.

Now we'd like to talk about the trade-offs. Although we frequently use doubles in our specs, we'll be the first to acknowledge that doing so incurs some risk. Here are some of the problems you can run into:

- Code that passes the tests but fails in production, because the test doubles don't behave enough like the real thing

- Brittle tests that fail after a refactoring, even though the new code is working correctly

- Do-nothing tests that only end up checking your doubles

In this chapter, we're going to show you how to use test doubles *effectively*, meaning that the benefits to your project outweigh these risks.

Constructing Your Test Environment

People new to test doubles often ask how much behavior to fake. After all, if a test is too far removed from reality, it won't give you a clear idea of how the code will run in the real world. We've definitely seen tests that have gone overboard with mocks, stubs, spies, and null objects. It can be difficult to know where to draw the line.

To cut through the confusion, we like to think of a test suite as a laboratory for carefully exercising code. Your test doubles are your scientific instruments. They help you create the environment needed for each experiment. You use them to control the factors you care about, and nothing else.

If you were performing a chemistry experiment, you'd probably care about the temperature and composition of your sample, but not the arrangement of the chairs in the hall outside. The same principle applies to your software experiments. When you set up the test environment for a trip planner, you may need to control the time zone but not the low-level database details. Test doubles help you control just the factors you care about.

Let's make these ideas more concrete with an example: testing the signup process for a web app. Like many such apps, this one requires new passwords to meet a minimum strength standard. Here's what our strength validator looks like:

15-using-test-doubles-effectively/01/password_strength_validator/lib/password_strength_validator.rb
```ruby
class PasswordStrengthValidator
  def strong_enough?
    return false unless password.length >= Acme::Config.min_password_length

    # ... more validations ...
  end
end
```

To check this code, we might write a couple of specs like the following:

15-using-test-doubles-effectively/01/password_s ... lidator/spec/password_strength_validator_spec.rb
```ruby
RSpec.describe PasswordStrengthValidator do
  it 'rejects passwords shorter than 8 characters' do
    validator = PasswordStrengthValidator.new('a8E^rd2')
    expect(validator.strong_enough?).to eq false
  end

  it 'accepts passwords 8 characters or longer' do
    validator = PasswordStrengthValidator.new('a8E^rd2i')
    expect(validator.strong_enough?).to eq true
  end
end
```

Assuming the web app is configured to require eight-character passwords, these two test cases will exercise both sides of the conditional. But if we later reconfigure the app to require twelve characters (perhaps to meet a new company guideline), one of the specs will start to fail:

```
$ rspec
.F

Failures:

  1) PasswordStrengthValidator accepts passwords 8 characters or longer
     Failure/Error: expect(validator.strong_enough?).to eq true

       expected: true
            got: false
```

```
    (compared using ==)
   # ./spec/password_strength_validator_spec.rb:11:in `block (2 levels)    ↵
   in <top (required)>'
```

Finished in 0.01002 seconds (files took 0.08962 seconds to load)
2 examples, 1 failure

Failed examples:

```
rspec ./spec/password_strength_validator_spec.rb:9 #                        ↵
PasswordStrengthValidator accepts passwords 8 characters or longer
```

The test is broken, even though the code works correctly. What should have been an easy configuration change is now requiring us to spend time fighting a broken test.

Decouple Your Tests from Incidental, Changeable Details

In *Test Doubles: Mocks, Stubs, and Others*, on page 67, you constructed your test environment using a fake Ledger that returned a canned "valid" or "invalid" status. That way, you could check how your API reported results, without getting caught up in validation rules that are likely to change.

To avoid brittle specs, use test doubles to decouple them from validation rules, configuration, and other ever-changing specifics of your application.

Instead, we can choose to configure the password requirements explicitly as part of the test environment:

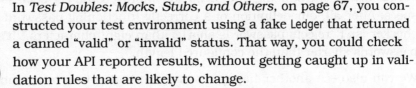
15-using-test-doubles-effectively/02/password_s ... lidator/spec/password_strength_validator_spec.rb

```ruby
RSpec.describe PasswordStrengthValidator do
  before do
    allow(Acme::Config).to receive(:min_password_length).and_return(6)
  end

  it 'rejects passwords shorter than the configured length' do
    validator = PasswordStrengthValidator.new('a8E^r')
    expect(validator.strong_enough?).to eq false
  end

  it 'accepts passwords that satisfy the configured length' do
    validator = PasswordStrengthValidator.new('a8E^rd')
    expect(validator.strong_enough?).to eq true
  end
end
```

The spec will continue to pass, no matter how many times we tweak the app's configuration. We're no longer coupled to the current value of min_password_length.

Don't Use expect When allow Is Sufficient

In this example, we *allowed* the :min_password_length message instead of *expecting* it. There are a couple of reasons for this choice:

- We prefer to use expect only when it reveals the purpose of the spec; here, the point is to check the return value of strong_enough?, not to check that we queried a specific configuration option.

- If you use expect in a before hook, an unreceived message means that *every* example in the context will fail, obscuring their actual behavior.

Paradoxically, introducing fake behavior improved the *correctness* of these specs. After all, our definition of a correctly functioning password strength checker isn't "rejects passwords shorter than eight characters." It's "rejects passwords shorter than the configured length."

We can also see another happy result: by bringing in a test double, we've made the specs easier to understand. Our code examples now clearly indicate the connection between the sample passwords and the configuration setting.

It's not always this easy to construct a test environment. In the next section, we'll see an example that blurs the line between test subject and environment. This awkwardness in our test suite will surface a design issue in our code.

Stubject (Stubbing the Subject)

You may occasionally see a test case that uses allow or expect on the same object it's testing. Sam Phippen refers to this antipattern as the *stubject* code smell, since you're stubbing methods on the test subject.[1]

For example, consider the following code for a discussion forum that sends users a summary of what's happened over the past day:

```
15-using-test-doubles-effectively/03/daily_summary_email/lib/daily_summary.rb
class DailySummary
  def send_daily_summary(user_email, todays_messages)
    message_count = todays_messages.count
    thread_count  = todays_messages.map { |m| m[:thread_id] }.uniq.count
    subject       = 'Your daily message summary'
    body          = "You missed #{message_count} messages " \
                    "in #{thread_count} threads today"
```

---

1.   https://samphippen.com/introducing-rspec-smells/#smell1stubject

```
      deliver(email: user_email, subject: subject, body: body)
    end

    def deliver(email:, subject:, body:)
      # send the message via SMTP
    end
  end
```

Here's an RSpec example for this class that checks the content of the email. We don't want to send real email from our specs, so on the highlighted lines we're mocking out the deliver method. Our version will check that we're calling it with the right body but not actually send an email:

```
15-using-test-doubles-effectively/03/daily_summary_email/spec/daily_summary_spec.rb
RSpec.describe DailySummary do
  let(:todays_messages) do
    [
      { thread_id: 1, content: 'Hello world' },
      { thread_id: 2, content: 'I think forums are great' },
      { thread_id: 2, content: 'Me too!' }
    ]
  end

  it "sends a summary of today's messages and threads" do
    summary = DailySummary.new

➤    expect(summary).to receive(:deliver).with(
➤      hash_including(body: 'You missed 3 messages in 2 threads today')
➤    )
    summary.send_daily_summary('user@example.com', todays_messages)
  end
end
```

Alas, this spec exhibits the stubject code smell. We're faking out the deliver method but testing the real send_daily_summary method on the same object.

Test doubles are intended to help you construct a test environment for a real object. Specs like this one blur the line between the subject and its environment. The temptation to fake out part of an object with allow or expect is a design signal. In other words, it's a hint that one object has two responsibilities, and might result in a better design if we split it up.

First, we can put the SMTP logic into its own EmailSender class:

```
15-using-test-doubles-effectively/04/daily_summary_email/lib/email_sender.rb
class EmailSender
  def deliver(email:, subject:, body:)
    # send the message via SMTP
  end
end
```

This class can then be provided to DailySummary as a collaborator using simple dependency injection:

15-using-test-doubles-effectively/04/daily_summary_email/lib/daily_summary.rb
```ruby
class DailySummary
➤  def initialize(email_sender: EmailSender.new)
➤    @email_sender = email_sender
➤  end

  def send_daily_summary(user_email, todays_messages)
    message_count = todays_messages.count
    thread_count  = todays_messages.map { |m| m[:thread_id] }.uniq.count
    subject       = 'Your daily message summary'
    body          = "You missed #{message_count} messages " \
                    "in #{thread_count} threads today"

➤    @email_sender.deliver(email: user_email, subject: subject, body: body)
  end
end
```

We're not suggesting you break up classes like this just to satisfy a "don't stub the subject" rule. Rather, we're saying that this guideline has told us something about the code. If we put the mail-delivery logic into its own class, we gain the following benefits:

- We can use EmailSender to send other emails besides daily summaries.
- We can test the SMTP logic independently, apart from any specific email.
- We now have a single place to add other email features such as email subscription preferences.

Once the refactoring is done, we no longer need to fake out methods on Daily-Summary itself. Instead, we can spin up a verifying double for the EmailSender:

15-using-test-doubles-effectively/04/daily_summary_email/spec/daily_summary_spec.rb
```ruby
it "sends a summary of today's messages and threads" do
➤  email_sender = instance_double(EmailSender)
  summary = DailySummary.new(email_sender: email_sender)

➤  expect(email_sender).to receive(:deliver).with(
    hash_including(body: 'You missed 3 messages in 2 threads today')
  )

  summary.send_daily_summary('user@example.com', todays_messages)
end
```

With this change, the boundary between the constructed test environment (the fake EmailSender) and the object we are testing (the DailySummary) is much clearer. A code smell in our specs has given us information we can use to improve our design.

Furthermore, moving away from the partial double allows us to improve the test, too. Maintaining the Arrange/Act/Assert flow helps to keep our tests easy to follow when we return to them months later. Let's convert the double to a spy so we can restore this flow:

```
15-using-test-doubles-effectively/05/daily_summary_email/spec/daily_summary_spec.rb
it "sends a summary of today's messages and threads" do
➤   email_sender = instance_spy(EmailSender)
    summary = DailySummary.new(email_sender: email_sender)

    summary.send_daily_summary('user@example.com', todays_messages)

➤   expect(email_sender).to have_received(:deliver).with(
➤     hash_including(body: 'You missed 3 messages in 2 threads today')
➤   )
end
```

While we could have used the partial double as a spy, it's more cumbersome, because we would have had to allow the deliver message beforehand to spy on it and stub it out. Moving to a pure double allowed us to use it as a spy with little effort.

Using Partial Doubles Effectively

Partial doubles are *really* easy to use: just stub or expect a message on any object! However, we said in *Partial Doubles*, on page 241 that we consider their usage to be a code smell. We'd like to flesh that statement out a bit now.

Most unit tests involve a mixture of two types of objects:

- Real objects: typically the subject of the example
- Fake objects: collaborating test doubles used to construct an environment for the test subject

Partial doubles don't fit neatly in this hierarchy. They are *partially* real and *partially* fake. Are they part of what you are testing or part of the environment you are constructing? When an object's roles are unclear, your tests can be harder to reason about.

We prefer not to mix these roles in the same object. In some cases, it can have some serious consequences. Let's look at an example.

Many Software as a Service (SaaS) apps use a monthly subscription model, where customers are charged every month. Here's a typical implementation, using a hypothetical billing API called CashCow:

15-using-test-doubles-effectively/06/subscription_service/lib/recurring_payment.rb
```ruby
class RecurringPayment
  def self.process_subscriptions(subscriptions)
    subscriptions.each do |subscription|
      CashCow.charge_card(subscription.credit_card, subscription.amount)
      # ...send receipt and other stuff...
    end
  end
end
```

The unit spec for this class verifies that we're charging the correct amounts:

15-using-test-doubles-effectively/07/subscription_service/spec/recurring_payment_spec.rb
```ruby
RSpec.describe RecurringPayment do
  it 'charges the credit card for each subscription' do
    card_1 = Card.new(:visa, '1234 5678 9012 3456')
    card_2 = Card.new(:mastercard, '9876 5432 1098 7654')

    subscriptions = [
      Subscription.new('John Doe', card_1, 19.99),
      Subscription.new('Jane Doe', card_2, 29.99)
    ]

    expect(CashCow).to receive(:charge_card).with(card_1, 19.99)
    expect(CashCow).to receive(:charge_card).with(card_2, 29.99)

    RecurringPayment.process_subscriptions(subscriptions)
  end
end
```

Here, we are using CashCow as a mock object. We expect it to receive the :charge_card message for each subscription. Crucially, this message expectation also serves to stub the method, preventing a real charge from going through in our tests.

Hundreds of customers later, we may find that our RecurringPayment class is spending a lot of time making a separate API call for each subscription. In this case, we can switch to CashCow's *bulk* interface, which lets us make a single API call to charge *all* of our customers' cards.

Here's an updated RecurringPayment class that uses the bulk API call:

15-using-test-doubles-effectively/08/subscription_service/lib/recurring_payment.rb
```ruby
class RecurringPayment
  def self.process_subscriptions(subscriptions)
    cards_and_amounts = subscriptions.each_with_object({}) do |sub, data|
      data[sub.credit_card] = sub.amount
    end

    CashCow.bulk_charge_cards(cards_and_amounts)
    # ...send receipts and other stuff...
  end
end
```

We haven't updated our specs yet. If we run them now, the message expectation will fail; the code is calling a different API than we've specified.

We've got a bigger problem, though. Our old specs don't stub out the bulk_charge_cards method. We'll end up sending a *real* charge request—something we don't want to do from a unit spec!

The partial double made it easy for our code to perform a costly operation for real, even though the entire point of the test double was to prevent this problem.

We can easily avoid this problem by using a pure or verifying test double instead. To do so, we'll add a new argument to process_subscriptions that lets us inject a billing object other than CashCow:

15-using-test-doubles-effectively/09/subscription_service/lib/recurring_payment.rb
```ruby
class RecurringPayment
  def self.process_subscriptions(subscriptions, bank: CashCow)
    subscriptions.each do |subscription|
      bank.charge_card(subscription.credit_card, subscription.amount)
      # ...send receipt and other stuff...
    end
  end
end
```

Now, instead of stubbing methods on the real CashCow class, our specs can just create a verifying double and pass it in instead:

15-using-test-doubles-effectively/09/subscription_service/spec/recurring_payment_spec.rb
```ruby
RSpec.describe RecurringPayment do
  it 'charges the credit card for each subscription' do
    card_1 = Card.new(:visa, '1234 5678 9012 3456')
    card_2 = Card.new(:mastercard, '9876 5432 1098 7654')

    subscriptions = [
      Subscription.new('John Doe', card_1, 19.99),
      Subscription.new('Jane Doe', card_2, 29.99)
    ]

    bank = class_double(CashCow)
    expect(bank).to receive(:charge_card).with(card_1, 19.99)
    expect(bank).to receive(:charge_card).with(card_2, 29.99)

    RecurringPayment.process_subscriptions(subscriptions, bank: bank)
  end
end
```

This kind of substitution is only feasible if you want an entirely fake object. If you find yourself needing to mix real and fake behavior in the same object, consider splitting it into multiple objects, as we did in the previous section.

That said, breaking apart objects will not always improve your design. In *Constructing Your Test Environment*, on page 265, the Acme::Config object had one simple job. Splitting it up would not have helped it do its job better, so we stubbed out one configuration method for our specs instead.

Use Partial Doubles Carefully

 Our advice to you isn't "avoid partial doubles," but rather, "listen to the feedback your doubles are giving you, and know the risks."

We recommend that you configure your projects with an additional safety check for partial doubles, in case you end up using them. The option is called verify_partial_doubles:[2]

`15-using-test-doubles-effectively/09/subscription_service/spec/spec_helper.rb`
```
RSpec.configure do |config|
  config.mock_with :rspec do |mocks|
    mocks.verify_partial_doubles = true
  end
end
```

This option will apply the same checks that RSpec uses for pure verifying doubles, providing a bit of extra safety. RSpec will set it for you in your spec_helper.rb if you use rspec --init to bootstrap your project.

While it wouldn't have prevented the credit-card problem we encountered in this section, verification will at least protect you from a mistyped or out-of-date message expectation. If you accidentally stub a method with the wrong name or wrong number of arguments, RSpec will detect this situation and report a failure.

In this section, we provided the CashCow test double by passing it as a parameter, a form of dependency injection. This technique is one of many different ways to connect each test subject to its environment. We'll explore some of these options next.

Connecting the Test Subject to Its Environment

When you construct your test environment, you also need to *connect* it to your test subject. In other words, you need to make your doubles available to the code you're testing. There are several ways to do so, including the following:

- Stubbing behavior on every instance of a class
- Stubbing factory methods

---

2. https://relishapp.com/rspec/rspec-mocks/v/3-6/docs/verifying-doubles/partial-doubles

- Treating a class as a partial double
- Using RSpec's stubbed constants
- Dependency injection, in its many forms

Each of these approaches has its advantages and trade-offs. As we look through them in turn, we'll be working with the same simple example: an APIRequestTracker class that helps API developers track simple usage statistics for each endpoint. This kind of information is handy for figuring out which features customers are engaging with the most.

For instance, in the expense tracker you built in *Building an App With RSpec 3*, you might want to count the following statistics:

- How often customers POST to /expenses, tracked as post_expense
- How often customers GET from /expenses/:date, tracked as get_expenses_on_date

Here's one way to implement APIRequestTracker:

15-using-test-doubles-effectively/10/api_request_tracker/lib/api_request_tracker.rb
```
class APIRequestTracker
  def process(request)
    endpoint_description = Endpoint.description_of(request)
    reporter = MetricsReporter.new
    reporter.increment("api.requests.#{endpoint_description}")
  end
end
```

First, we get a description of the endpoint (based on the path and whether it was a GET or POST) to use for tracking purposes. Next, we create a new instance of MetricsReporter, which will send statistics to a metrics service. Finally, we tell the reporter to increment the call count for this API endpoint. In our expense tracker example, we'd bump the api.requests.post_expense or api.requests.get_expenses_on_date metric.

The MetricsReporter collaborator is a good candidate for replacement with a mock object in our test. We'd like to run a unit spec without needing a network connection and a test account on a live metrics service.

We've got our work cut out for us if we want to use a test double with this class, though. It instantiates the reporter object from a hard-coded class name, with no easy way for a test to control which reporter gets used.

Expecting a Message on Any Instance

RSpec can get us out of difficult situations like this one, via its *any instance* feature. Instead of allowing or expecting a message on a specific instance of a class, you can do so on any of its instances:

```
15-using-test-doubles-effectively/10/api_request_tracker/spec/api_request_tracker_spec.rb
RSpec.describe APIRequestTracker do
  let(:request) { Request.new(:get, '/users') }

  it 'increments the request counter' do
    expect_any_instance_of(MetricsReporter).to receive(:increment).with(
      'api.requests.get_users'
    )

    APIRequestTracker.new.process(request)
  end
end
```

Here, we're calling expect_any_instance_of in place of plain expect, with the class as an argument. (Similarly, allow has an allow_any_instance_of counterpart.) This technique does help us get our class under test. But it definitely has significant drawbacks.

First, this tool is a *very* blunt hammer. You have no fine-grained control over how individual instances behave. Every instance of the named class (and its subclasses) will be affected, including ones you might not know about inside third-party libraries. Going back to our laboratory metaphor, when you bring a solution to a boil for an experiment, you probably don't want to boil all the liquid in the building!

Second, there are a lot of edge cases. You might wonder, for instance, whether expect_any_instance_of(MetricsReporter).to receive(:increment).twice means one instance must receive both calls to increment, or whether two different instances can each receive one call. The answer happens to be the former, but future readers may assume the latter and misunderstand your spec. Subclassing is another situation where it's easy to get mixed up, particularly when the subclass overrides a method you've stubbed.

Finally, this technique tends to calcify existing, suboptimal designs, rather than supporting you in improving the design of your code.

Stubbing a Factory Method

One slightly less far-reaching technique is to stub a factory method—typically SomeClass.new—to return a test double instead of a normal instance. Here's what that looks like for our APIRequestTracker test:

```
15-using-test-doubles-effectively/11/api_request_tracker/spec/api_request_tracker_spec.rb
it 'increments the request counter' do
➤   reporter = instance_double(MetricsReporter)
➤   allow(MetricsReporter).to receive(:new).and_return(reporter)
➤   expect(reporter).to receive(:increment).with('api.requests.get_users')

    APIRequestTracker.new.process(request)
end
```

This version gives us similar results to expect_any_instance_of, but saves us from some of its drawbacks. We've narrowed the scope to newly created instances of MetricsReporter (not including any subclasses). We can also use a pure double now, rather than a partial one.

Furthermore, this test code is more honest. The APIRequestTracker obtains its MetricsReporter instance via the new method, and our spec makes that dependency explicit. The test is awkward because the interaction in our code is awkward. Our class instantiates an object just to call one method, then discards it.

Using the Class as a Partial Double

Let's take a closer look at that short-lived reporter instance. We're not using it to track any state. We could easily avoid creating an instance by promoting the increment method to be a class method on the MetricsReporter class. Once we've updated the MetricsReporter class, we can simplify our APIRequestTracker:

15-using-test-doubles-effectively/12/api_request_tracker/lib/api_request_tracker.rb
```
class APIRequestTracker
  def process(request)
    endpoint_description = Endpoint.description_of(request)
➤   MetricsReporter.increment("api.requests.#{endpoint_description}")
  end
end
```

Define Class Methods Carefully

Not every method is a good candidate for moving to a class method. In particular, if you need to carry state around from one call to the next, you'll need an instance method.

If your method doesn't have any side effects, or at least doesn't use any internal state, you can safely turn it into a class method. Here, our increment method makes a call to an external service, but that's all it does. It's fine to make this a class method, and doing so will arguably improve the interface for callers.

Now that the MetricsReporter interface does not require us to create a disposable instance, we can just use the class as a partial double:

15-using-test-doubles-effectively/12/api_request_tracker/spec/api_request_tracker_spec.rb
```
it 'increments the request counter' do
➤   expect(MetricsReporter).to receive(:increment).with(
➤     'api.requests.get_users'
➤   )

    APIRequestTracker.new.process(request)
end
```

With this version of our test, we no longer need to deal with MetricsReporter instances. Instead, we have a simpler interface for incrementing metrics. We could potentially clean up metric-counting code all over our system. We are, however, back to using partial doubles again, something we generally avoid.

Stubbing a Constant

As we've seen in this chapter, having both real and fake behavior in the same object can cause problems. We'd prefer to use a purely fake reporter. We can achieve this goal by creating a class_double and stubbing the MetricsReporter constant to return that double:

15-using-test-doubles-effectively/13/api_request_tracker/spec/api_request_tracker_spec.rb
```
it 'increments the request counter' do
➤   reporter = class_double(MetricsReporter)
➤   stub_const('MetricsReporter', reporter)
➤   expect(reporter).to receive(:increment).with('api.requests.get_users')

    APIRequestTracker.new.process(request)
end
```

This pattern is useful enough that RSpec provides a way to implement it in one line of code. Just tack as_stubbed_const onto the end of your class double, and it will automatically replace the original class—just for the duration of the example:

15-using-test-doubles-effectively/14/api_request_tracker/spec/api_request_tracker_spec.rb
```
it 'increments the request counter' do
➤   reporter = class_double(MetricsReporter).as_stubbed_const
    expect(reporter).to receive(:increment).with('api.requests.get_users')

    APIRequestTracker.new.process(request)
end
```

We like the way that stubbed constants allow us to use a pure double. The downside is that they add their fake behavior implicitly. Someone reading the APIRequestTracker code is not going to suspect that the MetricsReporter constant might refer to a test double.

Stubbed constants can surface dependencies hiding in our code. When we hardcode the name of a class, we are tightly coupling our code to that specific class. Sandi Metz discusses ways to deal with this antipattern in *Practical Object-Oriented Design in Ruby [Met12]*.

To prevent this tight coupling, we prefer to depend on abstract roles rather than concrete classes. We'd like this API request tracker to work with *any* object that can report metrics (or pretend to report metrics), not just MetricsReporter instances.

Steve Freeman, Nat Pryce, and their co-authors refer to this as "Mock Roles, Not Objects" in their paper of the same name.[3] Steve and Nat explore related ideas in their book, *Growing Object-Oriented Software, Guided by Tests [FP09]*. For more on the importance on mocking roles rather than objects, see Gregory Moeck's RubyConf 2011 talk, "Why You Don't Get Mock Objects."[4]

Dependency Injection

To refactor the class to depend on abstract roles, we can use dependency injection. We first encountered this concept in *Connecting to Storage*, on page 65. The technique can take a few different forms, the simplest of which is *argument injection*:

15-using-test-doubles-effectively/15/api_request_tracker/lib/api_request_tracker.rb
```ruby
class APIRequestTracker
➤   def process(request, reporter: MetricsReporter)
      endpoint_description = Endpoint.description_of(request)
➤     reporter.increment("api.requests.#{endpoint_description}")
    end
end
```

Now that the process method accepts an additional reporter argument, our test can easily inject a double:

15-using-test-doubles-effectively/15/api_request_tracker/spec/api_request_tracker_spec.rb
```ruby
it 'increments the request counter' do
➤   reporter = class_double(MetricsReporter)
    expect(reporter).to receive(:increment).with('api.requests.get_users')

➤   APIRequestTracker.new.process(request, reporter: reporter)
end
```

This technique is simple and versatile. The main drawback is repetition. If you need to use the same collaborator from multiple methods, adding the same extra parameter to all of them can be cumbersome. Instead, you can use *constructor injection* to pass in your collaborator as part of the object's initial state:

15-using-test-doubles-effectively/16/api_request_tracker/lib/api_request_tracker.rb
```ruby
class APIRequestTracker
➤   def initialize(reporter: MetricsReporter.new)
➤     @reporter = reporter
➤   end
```

---

3. http://www.jmock.org/oopsla2004.pdf

4. https://www.youtube.com/watch?v=R9FOchgTtLM

```
➤    def process(request)
       endpoint_description = Endpoint.description_of(request)
➤      @reporter.increment("api.requests.#{endpoint_description}")
     end
   end
```

Now, we just need to pass in the reporter collaborator when we *create* an APIRequestTracker instance, rather than passing it as an argument to process:

15-using-test-doubles-effectively/16/api_request_tracker/spec/api_request_tracker_spec.rb
```
it 'increments the request counter' do
  reporter = class_double(MetricsReporter)
  expect(reporter).to receive(:increment).with('api.requests.get_users')
➤  APIRequestTracker.new(reporter: reporter).process(request)
   end
```

Constructor injection is our go-to technique for providing test doubles to our code. It's simple and explicit, and nicely documents what collaborators a class depends upon in the constructor. We should add that this style is not everyone's cup of tea. For a nuanced look at the advantages and disadvantages of dependency injection, see Tom Stuart's "How Testability Can Help" blog post.[5]

Sometimes, the constructor isn't available for us to modify. For example, web frameworks like Ruby on Rails often control object lifetimes, including the arguments to constructors. In these situations, we can fall back to *setter injection*:

15-using-test-doubles-effectively/17/api_request_tracker/lib/api_request_tracker.rb
```
class APIRequestTracker
➤  attr_writer :reporter
➤  def reporter
➤    @reporter ||= MetricsReporter.new
➤  end

   def process(request)
     endpoint_description = Endpoint.description_of(request)
➤     reporter.increment("api.requests.#{endpoint_description}")
   end
 end
```

Here we've exposed a *setter* (via attr_writer) for our collaborator that can be used from our test to inject the dependency:

15-using-test-doubles-effectively/17/api_request_tracker/spec/api_request_tracker_spec.rb
```
it 'increments the request counter' do
  reporter = class_double(MetricsReporter)
  expect(reporter).to receive(:increment).with('api.requests.get_users')
```

---

5. http://codon.com/how-testability-can-help

```
➤    tracker = APIRequestTracker.new
➤    tracker.reporter = reporter
➤    tracker.process(request)
   end
```

Every one of these techniques has its uses. Dependency injection is the most common technique we use, and we recommend that you favor it as well. If you'd like to use a library for this task, have a look at the dry-auto_inject project.[6]

Sometimes, dependency injection isn't practical. When you're testing a cluster of objects together, you may not have direct access to the object where you'd like to inject a dependency. Instead, you can stub a factory method or constant.

Watch out, though, for the temptation to treat each difficult situation as a puzzle to solve using more and more powerful RSpec features. When time permits, you'll get better results by refactoring your code to be easier to test with simple techniques.

Of course, refactoring has costs, which may or may not be worth paying for your project. If you do refactor, you'll likely want to get your code under test first. We reach for blunt tools like RSpec's "any instance" feature at times like these, but prefer to use them temporarily. Once we've cleaned up the code, we can drop the crutches and switch to dependency injection.

In these examples, we've been mocking MetricsReporter, a class that belongs to us. In doing so, we've been following the common testing advice, "Only mock types you own." In the next section, we'll see why that admonition is so important.

The Risks of Mocking Third-Party Code

Test doubles are great for providing fake versions of your APIs. Not only do they allow you to test your callers in isolation, they also provide design feedback on your API.

When you try to fake out someone else's API, you miss out on the design benefits of using test doubles. Moreover, you incur extra risks when you mock an interface that you don't own. Specifically, you can end up with tests that fail when they shouldn't, or worse, pass when they shouldn't.

An example will make these risks clearer. The following TwitterUserFormatter class creates a simple string describing a user of the service. Callers will obtain a Twitter::User instance from the Twitter gem (for example, by searching) and pass it to our formatter:[7]

---

6.   http://dry-rb.org/gems/dry-auto_inject/
7.   https://github.com/sferik/twitter

15-using-test-doubles-effectively/18/twitter_user_formatter/lib/twitter_user_formatter.rb
```
class TwitterUserFormatter
  def initialize(user)
    @user = user
  end

  def format
    @user.name + "'s website is " + @user.url
  end
end
```

The `name` and `url` methods come from an instance of the `Twitter::User` class. Constructing a real `User` requires multiple steps and different collaborators. It may be tempting to provide a fake implementation instead, like so:

15-using-test-doubles-effectively/18/twitter_user_formatter/spec/twitter_user_formatter_spec.rb
```
RSpec.describe TwitterUserFormatter do
  it 'describes their homepage' do
    user = instance_double(Twitter::User,
                           name: 'RSpec',
                           url: 'http://rspec.info')

    formatter = TwitterUserFormatter.new(user)

    expect(formatter.format).to eq("RSpec's website is http://rspec.info")
  end
end
```

This code would work well on earlier versions of the Twitter gem. Starting with version 5.0, though, the `Twitter::User#url` method returns a URI object instead of a plain string.

If we were to upgrade to the latest gem version and run this spec, it would still pass. Our code expects a string, and that's what our fake url method gives it.

Once we tried to use our `TwitterUserFormatter` in production, though, we'd start seeing exceptions. Specifically, when we try to concatenate the user's URL (which is now a URI instance) onto the description string:

```
@user.name + "'s website is " + @user.url
```

...we'd get a `TypeError` with the message `no implicit conversion of URI::HTTPS into String`.

This is the nightmare scenario for testing, where specs can give false confidence. Our test doubles were designed to mimic an interface that's not under our control, and that interface moved out from underneath us. (The Twitter gem maintainers are in fact careful about deprecations, but as developers we don't always remember to read the release notes.)

One way to reduce this risk is to use verifying doubles, as we've done for this example with an `instance_double`. These will detect when a class or method gets renamed, or when a method gains or loses arguments. But in this case, a method's *return type* changed, and verifying doubles can't detect that kind of incompatibility at all.

You might give up on having your unit specs detect this kind of breaking change and depend on your end-to-end acceptance specs. These will use real dependencies as much as possible and are more likely to fail on incorrect API usage.

Falling back on acceptance specs isn't the only option, however. You do have a couple of choices for making your unit specs more robust:

- Use a high-fidelity fake for the third-party API, if one is available
- Write your own wrapper around the API, and use a test double in place of your wrapper

In the next couple of sections, we're going to look at both of these approaches.

High-Fidelity Fakes

When you work with rspec-mocks, you're using fake behavior supplied by RSpec. There are other kinds of test doubles, though. You can use an alternative implementation designed to drop into your tests in place of the real thing. Because these mimic the original library's interface *and behavior* closely, we call them *high-fidelity fakes*.

For instance, the FakeFS gem makes it easy to test code that interacts with the filesystem.[8] FakeRedis acts just like the Redis data store but doesn't require a network connection or a running server.[9] If you use Braintree for credit-card processing, Fake Braintree can stand in during testing.[10]

Sometimes, a library ships with its own high-fidelity fake. The Fog gem, which wraps cloud services like Amazon's, comes with a mocks mode built in.[11] If you're developing a library that calls external services, your users will be grateful if you provide a high-fi fake. You can write one set of specs to check both the real and fake implementations using RSpec's *shared examples*. We discussed these in *Sharing Examples*, on page 124.

Fakes are particularly useful for HTTP APIs. Alas, most API clients don't include a high-fi fake. Fortunately, you can put one together fairly quickly using the VCR gem (written by Myron, one of the co-authors of this book).[12]

---

8.   https://github.com/fakefs/fakefs
9.   http://guilleiguaran.github.io/fakeredis/
10.   https://github.com/highfidelity/fake_braintree
11.   http://www.rubydoc.info/gems/fog/1.40.0#Mocks
12.   https://relishapp.com/vcr/vcr/v/3-0-3/docs

When you first use VCR from your tests, it will record network requests to the real API together with their responses. Later test runs will use the recorded data instead of making real API calls.

In the next section, we'd like to show you what it's like to test with a high-fidelity fake—specifically, the StringIO class that ships with Ruby. With it, you can simulate I/O to the console, a disk file, the network, pipes, and more.

Faking I/O with StringIO

Long before Ruby on Rails came along, the first web applications were simple command-line scripts that wrote their content to the console. This Common Gateway Interface (CGI) architecture made it possible to build dynamic websites in nearly any language.[13] All you had to do was read your input from environment variables and write the resulting web page to stdout.

Here's a CGI script that functions as a simple little Ruby documentation server. If you were to hook this code up to a local web server and visit http://localhost/String/each, it would return a JSON array of all the String methods that begin with each: ["each_byte", "each_char", ...].

15-using-test-doubles-effectively/19/ruby_doc_server/lib/ruby_doc_server.rb
```
require 'json'

class RubyDocServer
  def initialize(output: $stdout)
    @output = output
  end

  def process_request(path)
    class_name, method_prefix = path.sub(%r{^/}, '').split('/')
    klass = Object.const_get(class_name)
    methods = klass.instance_methods.grep(/\A#{method_prefix}/).sort
    respond_with(methods)
  end

private

  def respond_with(data)
    @output.puts 'Content-Type: application/json'
    @output.puts
    @output.puts JSON.generate(data)
  end
end

if __FILE__.end_with?($PROGRAM_NAME)
  RubyDocServer.new.process_request(ENV['PATH_INFO'])
end
```

---

13. https://en.wikipedia.org/wiki/Common_Gateway_Interface

The web server puts whatever path you visit, such as /String/each, into the PATH_INFO environment variable. We break this text into the String class and the each prefix, get a list of the instance methods that belong to String, and finally narrow them down to the ones that start with each.

We've already applied the lessons from earlier in this chapter and injected the output collaborator via constructor injection. It might be tempting to pass in a spy from our tests so that we could check that the CGI script was writing the correct results:

15-using-test-doubles-effectively/19/ruby_doc_server/spec/ruby_doc_server_spec.rb
```ruby
require 'ruby_doc_server'

RSpec.describe RubyDocServer do
  it 'finds matching ruby methods' do
    out = get('/Array/max')

    expect(out).to have_received(:puts).with('Content-Type: application/json')
    expect(out).to have_received(:puts).with('["max","max_by"]')
  end

  def get(path)
    output = object_spy($stdout)
    RubyDocServer.new(output: output).process_request(path)
    output
  end
end
```

Unfortunately, this spec is quite brittle. It's coupled not just to the content of the web response, but also to exactly *how* it gets written.

Ruby's IO interface is large. It provides several methods just for writing output: puts, print, write, and more. If we refactor our implementation to call write, or even to call puts just once with the entire response, our specs will break. Recall that one of the goals of TDD is to support refactoring. Instead, these specs will stand in our way.

Test Doubles Are Best for Small, Simple, Stable Interfaces

Large interfaces aren't the only ones that are hard to replace with a double. We also see problems in the following cases:

- *Complex interfaces:* The more complex the interface, the harder it is to mimic accurately; we like to use test doubles to steer our design toward simplicity.

- *Unstable interfaces:* Every message you expect or allow is a detail your specs are coupled to; the more the interface changes, the more you're going to have to update your doubles.

Instead of expecting specific IO method calls, we can use the StringIO high-fidelity fake from the Ruby standard library. StringIO objects exist in memory, but act like any other Ruby IO object, such as an open file or Unix pipe.

You can test input-handling code by initializing a StringIO with data and letting your code read from it. Or you can test your output code by letting your code write to a StringIO, and then inspecting the contents via its string method. Here's how this test looks with a StringIO object injected into the RubyDocServer:

```
15-using-test-doubles-effectively/20/ruby_doc_server/spec/ruby_doc_server_spec.rb
require 'ruby_doc_server'
require 'stringio'

RSpec.describe RubyDocServer do
  it 'finds matching ruby methods' do
    result = get('/Array/min')

    expect(result.split("\n")).to eq [
      'Content-Type: application/json',
      '',
      '["min","min_by","minmax","minmax_by"]'
    ]
  end

  def get(path)
    output = StringIO.new
    RubyDocServer.new(output: output).process_request(path)
    output.string
  end
end
```

Now, we're setting expectations on the *contents* of the response, rather than on how it was produced. This practice results in much less brittle specs.

Wrapping a Third-Party Dependency

While high-fidelity fakes can save a lot of trouble, they can still leave your logic coupled to a third-party API. This coupling has a few downsides:

- Your code will be exposed to the complexities of a (potentially) large API.
- Changes to the dependency's interface will ripple throughout your system.
- Testing is difficult, since you can't easily and safely replace the third-party code with a double.

To avoid these pitfalls, you can wrap the dependency—that is, write your own layer that delegates to it internally. Using a wrapper (also known as a *gateway* or *adapter* when you're wrapping an API) gives you a couple of key advantages:

- You can create a small, simple interface tailored exactly to your needs.
- You can safely replace your wrapper with a pure double in your specs.

- You have one place where you can easily add related features such as caching, metrics tracking, or logging.

Even though wrapping a dependency minimizes the risk of its interface changing from underneath you, this risk is still present. To address it, you can write a small number of integration specs that test your wrapper against the real library or service.

In the following example, we're testing an Invoice class that uses the TaxJar Ruby API client to calculate sales tax for a shopping site.[14] The initial version calls TaxJar directly, and then we'll refactor our class to use a wrapper. Here's the public interface of the class:

```
15-using-test-doubles-effectively/21/sales_tax/lib/invoice.rb
class Invoice
  def initialize(address, items, tax_client: MyApp.tax_client)
    @address = address
    @items = items
    @tax_client = tax_client
  end

  def calculate_total
    subtotal = @items.map(&:cost).inject(0, :+)
    taxes = subtotal * tax_rate
    subtotal + taxes
  end

  # ...
end
```

A new Invoice needs a shipping address and a list of items. To support testing, we're using dependency injection to pass a real or fake TaxJar implementation into the initializer. The calculate_total method tabulates the total cost of the items in the cart, and then applies the tax rate.

The tax rate lookup seems simple on the surface; once we know the ZIP code we're shipping to, we should be able to get the correct rate from TaxJar. The logic for doing so is a little convoluted, though:

```
15-using-test-doubles-effectively/22/sales_tax/lib/invoice.rb
def tax_rate
  @tax_client.rates_for_location(@address.zip).combined_rate
end
```

The TaxJar client requires more of us than a single method invocation. First, we call rates_for_location to get an object containing *all* the applicable tax rates (city, state, and so on). Then, we fetch its combined_rate to get the total sales tax.

---

14. https://github.com/taxjar/taxjar-ruby

This interface provides a lot of flexibility, but we don't need much of it in our Invoice class. It would be nice to have a simpler API that fits just the needs of our project.

Look what happens when we try to test this class. We end up creating one test double, tax_client, that returns a second double, tax_rate:

15-using-test-doubles-effectively/22/sales_tax/spec/unit/invoice_spec.rb
```ruby
require 'invoice'

RSpec.describe Invoice do
  let(:address) { Address.new(zip: '90210') }
  let(:items) { [Item.new(cost: 30), Item.new(cost: 70)] }

  it 'calculates the total' do
    tax_rate = instance_double(Taxjar::Rate, combined_rate: 0.095)
    tax_client = instance_double(Taxjar::Client, rates_for_location: tax_rate)

    invoice = Invoice.new(address, items, tax_client: tax_client)

    expect(invoice.calculate_total).to eq(109.50)
  end
end
```

Our complex mocking structure (a double that returns a double) has revealed a couple of problems with our project:

- The Invoice class is tightly coupled to the TaxJar client's object hierarchy.
- The complexity will make refactoring and maintenance more difficult.

In his blog post, "Test Isolation Is About Avoiding Mocks," Gary Bernhardt recommends that we untangle the object relationships that are made obvious by these kinds of nested doubles.[15] We can follow his advice by writing a SalesTax wrapper that decouples Invoice from TaxJar:

15-using-test-doubles-effectively/23/sales_tax/lib/sales_tax.rb
```ruby
require 'my_app'

class SalesTax
  RateUnavailableError = Class.new(StandardError)

  def initialize(tax_client = MyApp.tax_client)
    @tax_client = tax_client
  end

  def rate_for(zip)
    @tax_client.rates_for_location(zip).combined_rate
  rescue Taxjar::Error::NotFound
    raise RateUnavailableError, "Sales tax rate unavailable for zip: #{zip}"
  end
end
```

---

15. https://www.destroyallsoftware.com/blog/2014/test-isolation-is-about-avoiding-mocks

Our goal is to isolate the Invoice class completely from TaxJar—including its specific exception classes. That's why we transform any Taxjar::Error::NotFound error we see into an error type we have defined.

The rest of the application no longer needs to have any knowledge of TaxJar. If TaxJar's API changes, this class is the only piece of code we'll have to update.

When we create a new Invoice, we now pass in the wrapper instead of the original TaxJar class:

```
15-using-test-doubles-effectively/24/sales_tax/lib/invoice.rb
def initialize(address, items, sales_tax: SalesTax.new)
  @address = address
  @items = items
  @sales_tax = sales_tax
end
```

Here's what the new, simpler Invoice#tax_rate method looks like:

```
15-using-test-doubles-effectively/24/sales_tax/lib/invoice.rb
def tax_rate
  @sales_tax.rate_for(@address.zip)
end
```

Our unit spec for Invoice is also much easier to understand and maintain. We no longer need to construct a rickety structure of test doubles. A single instance double will do:

```
15-using-test-doubles-effectively/24/sales_tax/spec/unit/invoice_spec.rb
require 'invoice'

RSpec.describe Invoice do
  let(:address) { Address.new(zip: '90210') }
  let(:items) { [Item.new(cost: 30), Item.new(cost: 70)] }

  it 'calculates the total' do
    sales_tax = instance_double(SalesTax, rate_for: 0.095)

    invoice = Invoice.new(address, items, sales_tax: sales_tax)

    expect(invoice.calculate_total).to eq(109.50)
  end
end
```

By wrapping the TaxJar API, we've improved our code and specs in many ways:

- The wrapper API is simpler to call, because it omits details we don't need.

- We can switch to a different third-party sales tax service by changing just one class, leaving the rest of our project intact.

- Because we control the wrapper's interface, it won't change without our knowledge.

- The unit specs for Invoice won't break if the TaxJar API changes.

We do need to have *some* way to detect changes in TaxJar, though. The best place for that is an integration spec for our SalesTax wrapper, which is easy to write because we've kept our wrapper thin:

```
15-using-test-doubles-effectively/24/sales_tax/spec/integration/sales_tax_spec.rb
require 'sales_tax'

RSpec.describe SalesTax do
  let(:sales_tax) { SalesTax.new }

  it 'can fetch the tax rate for a given zip' do
    rate = sales_tax.rate_for('90210')
    expect(rate).to be_a(Float).and be_between(0.01, 0.5)
  end

  it 'raises an error if the tax rate cannot be found' do
    expect {
      sales_tax.rate_for('00000')
    }.to raise_error(SalesTax::RateUnavailableError)
  end
end
```

Because this spec tests against the real TaxJar classes, it will correctly fail if there are breaking changes in the API. Although the API should be stable, we expect the tax rate to fluctuate somewhat. That's why we're checking against a range rather than an exact value.

As a next step, we could use the VCR gem here to cache responses. We could then run these specs without needing real API credentials—which will be handy on our continuous integration (CI) server. We'd still want to revalidate against the real service periodically, which we can easily do by deleting the VCR recordings.

Your Turn

Whew! We gave you a lot to chew on in this chapter, from broad advice on test doubles to fine-grained design nuances. Here are just some of the principles we explored over several code examples:

- Construct your test environment carefully.
- Watch out for the "stubject."
- Know the risks of partial doubles.
- Favor explicit dependency injection over more implicit techniques.
- Avoid faking an interface you don't control.

- Look for high-fidelity fakes.
- Wrap third-party interfaces.

That's a lot to keep in your head, but we're definitely not asking you to do that! All of these bits of advice stem from one key practice: constructing your test environment carefully. Remember the laboratory metaphor when you're writing your specs, and you should be fine.

Above all else, when you find your test doubles straying from these principles, listen to what they're telling you about your code's design. Rather than looking for a different way to write the test, look for a better way to structure your code. By "better," we don't mean "more testable," although as Michael Feathers explains, good design and testability are often mutually reinforcing.[16] We mean easier to maintain, more flexible, easier to understand, and easier to get right. Justin Searls discusses these trade-offs for test doubles on his "Test Doubles" wiki page and in his SCNA 2012 talk, "To Mock or Not to Mock."[17,18]

Thank you for coming along on this journey with us! For one final time, please join us in the next section for an exercise.

Exercise

This exercise will be a little more open-ended than some of the ones from previous chapters. There's not a single best answer. We're going to prompt your creativity with a few questions, and then turn you loose on the code.

The following Ruby class implements a number-guessing game. Save this code into a new directory as lib/guessing_game.rb:

```
15-using-test-doubles-effectively/exercises/guessing_game/lib/guessing_game.rb
class GuessingGame
  def play
    @number = rand(1..100)
    @guess = nil

    5.downto(1) do |remaining_guesses|
      break if @guess == @number
      puts "Pick a number 1-100 (#{remaining_guesses} guesses left):"
      @guess = gets.to_i
      check_guess
    end

    announce_result
  end
```

---

16. https://vimeo.com/15007792
17. https://github.com/testdouble/contributing-tests/wiki/Test-Double
18. https://vimeo.com/54045166

```ruby
private

  def check_guess
    if @guess > @number
      puts "#{@guess} is too high!"
    elsif @guess < @number
      puts "#{@guess} is too low!"
    end
  end

  def announce_result
    if @guess == @number
      puts 'You won!'
    else
      puts "You lost! The number was: #{@number}"
    end
  end
end

# play the game if this file is run directly
GuessingGame.new.play if __FILE__.end_with?($PROGRAM_NAME)
```

Now, run the code with ruby lib/guessing_game.rb and try playing the game. Get a feel for how it works.

Your mission is to get this class under test. Here are some questions you might want to consider:

- What are this class's collaborators, and how can your test supply them?
- What kinds of test doubles would work best here?
- What edge cases do you need to cover in your specs?
- Should any of this class's responsibilities be extracted into a collaborator?

If you get stuck, you can have a peek at the specs and refactored class we wrote for this exercise. They're in the book's source code.[19,20]

Once you have a solution, please consider posting it in the forums.[21] We'd love to see what you came up with.

Happy testing!

19. https://github.com/rspec-3-book/book-code/blob/v1.0/15-using-test-doubles-effectively/solutions/guessing_game/spec/guessing_game_spec.rb

20. https://github.com/rspec-3-book/book-code/blob/v1.0/15-using-test-doubles-effectively/solutions/guessing_game/lib/guessing_game.rb

21. https://forums.pragprog.com/forums/385

RSpec and the Wider Ruby Ecosystem

RSpec does not exist in a vacuum. It's part of the wider Ruby ecosystem, and is designed to work well with existing Ruby tools. In this appendix, you'll see how to use RSpec effectively with two of Ruby's most important tools: Bundler and Rake. We'll also show you how to use parts of RSpec with other test frameworks.

Bundler

When you're using Bundler to manage your dependencies, there are a few different ways you can ensure that the correct versions of all your libraries get loaded:

- Call Bundler.require from your Ruby code
- Wrap every Ruby program with bundle exec at the command line
- Use Bundler's stand-alone mode

All of these techniques work with RSpec. Let's take a look at each one in turn.

The first option, Bundler.require, is convenient: it loads all your project's gems, so you don't have to remember to require each gem individually before use. But it has implications for your application's boot time and maintainability, as Myron points out in his blog post.[1]

The second option, bundle exec, is faster and avoids some of these maintainability pitfalls, but is still inefficient. Every time you run (for example) bundle exec rspec, Bundler spends time validating that you have all the right gem versions installed—even though this validation is only needed on the infrequent occasions that your project's gems change.

---

1. http://myronmars.to/n/dev-blog/2012/12/5-reasons-to-avoid-bundler-require

The final option, stand-alone mode, saves time by using Bundler only when you install gems. At runtime, you're just using plain Ruby, with Bundler cut completely out of the equation. To use this mode, pass the --standalone option to Bundler:

```
$ bundle install --standalone
```

This command generates a file in your project directory called bundle/bundler/set-up.rb, which sets up Ruby's $LOAD_PATH with the exact gem versions your project is configured to use. All you have to do is require this file from your code, *before* loading any gems. In fact, you can even skip this require step by using the --binstubs option together with --standalone:

```
$ bundle install --standalone --binstubs
```

This command generates *binstubs*—wrappers around your gems' Ruby commands like rspec and rake—inside your project's bin directory. Each of these will load bundle/bundler/setup.rb for you, and then run its original command.

This technique allows RSpec to start noticeably more quickly, especially in large projects—which gives us near-instantaneous feedback when running individual spec files. You will, however, need to remember to rerun this command any time your Gemfile or Gemfile.lock changes. We recommend creating an alias in your shell, such as bisb, and running it when you add or remove gems, pull code from someone else, change branches, and so on.

The improvement is particularly dramatic when you use the technique from *Ensuring the Application Works for Real*, on page 98 to run each of your spec files in isolation. Here's how long that task took using regular bundle exec:

```
$ time (for file in spec/**/*_spec.rb                              ↵
        do bundle exec rspec $file || exit 1                        ↵
      done) > /dev/null

1.50s user 0.17s system 98% cpu 1.707 total
```

Here's the same loop, but using the stand-alone-aware binstub instead:

```
$ time (for file in spec/**/*_spec.rb                              ↵
        do bin/rspec $file || exit 1                                ↵
      done) > /dev/null

0.85s user 0.11s system 97% cpu 0.983 total
```

From 1.7 seconds to less than a second! Stand-alone mode is nearly twice as fast, because the boot time for each rspec invocation is faster. On a project with a lot of gems (or a lot of spec files!), the difference is even more dramatic.

Rake

Throughout this book, you've run your spec suite via the rspec command. But there's another common way to run your specs: using the Rake build tool. The rspec-core gem ships with an easy-to-configure Rake task. To enable it, add the following two lines to your project's Rakefile:

A1-rspec-and-wider-ecosystem/02/expense_tracker/Rakefile
```
require 'rspec/core/rake_task'
RSpec::Core::RakeTask.new(:spec)
```

This snippet defines a simple spec task that will run rspec with your configured defaults. You can then run it like so:

```
$ rake spec
```

Running RSpec this way adds some overhead. It takes time to load Rake itself, plus any libraries you need for other tasks in your Rakefile. A canned Rake task is also less flexible than the rspec command, since it does not let you customize individual runs through command-line options. That said, testing via Rake comes in handy in some situations:

- When you have specific sets of RSpec options you use together frequently

- When you want to run RSpec as one step in a multistep build process (such as on a continuous integration server)

- As a convenience to new developers on your project, who may expect running rake with no argument to build and test the code base completely

If you want to specify additional RSpec options, you can pass a block to RakeTask.new:

A1-rspec-and-wider-ecosystem/02/expense_tracker/Rakefile
```
require 'rspec/core/rake_task'

namespace :spec do
  desc 'Runs unit specs'
  RSpec::Core::RakeTask.new(:unit) do |t|
    t.pattern = 'spec/unit/**/*_spec.rb'
    t.rspec_opts = ['--profile']
  end
end
```

Here, we've defined a spec:unit task that runs all our unit specs with profiling enabled.

Your users can also supply their own command-line arguments to your Rake tasks by setting the SPEC_OPTS environment variable. For example, they can get documentation-style output from your spec:unit task by calling it like so:

```
$ rake spec:unit SPEC_OPTS='-fd'
```

If you're developing a web app, you probably keep test-only gems like RSpec off your production servers. To use Rake in such an environment, you'll need to handle the case when RSpec isn't available:

```
A1-rspec-and-wider-ecosystem/02/expense_tracker/Rakefile
begin
  require 'rspec/core/rake_task'
  RSpec::Core::RakeTask.new(:spec)
rescue LoadError
  puts 'Spec tasks not defined since RSpec is unavailable'
end
```

Now, you'll be able to use Rake to run specs on your development machine, and to run deployment tasks (such as compiling assets) in your production environment.

Using Parts of RSpec With Other Test Frameworks

Sometimes, you'll want to use the powerful test doubles available in rspec-mocks, or the composable matchers provided by rspec-expectations, in a project where the rest of RSpec isn't a good fit. For instance, you may already have an extensive test suite written in Minitest, or you may be writing acceptance tests in Cucumber.[2,3]

Both of these parts of RSpec are easy to use with other test frameworks, or even without a test framework at all. In fact, you've already done so in *Parts of an Expectation* and throughout *Understanding Test Doubles*.

If you're using Minitest, RSpec provides a couple of conveniences for you, including the following:

- Reporting unmet expectations correctly as Minitest assertion failures

- Making sure RSpec's expect method doesn't clash with Minitest's method of the same name

- Verifying message expectations you've set on mock objects

---

2. https://github.com/seattlerb/minitest
3. https://cucumber.io

To take advantage of this integration, require either or both of the following files in your tests:

A1-rspec-and-wider-ecosystem/03/minitest_with_rspec/dinosaur_test.rb
```
require 'rspec/mocks/minitest_integration'
require 'rspec/expectations/minitest_integration'
```

Then, you can use RSpec's test doubles and expectations freely in your Minitest suite:

A1-rspec-and-wider-ecosystem/03/minitest_with_rspec/dinosaur_test.rb
```
class DinosaurTest < Minitest::Test
  def test_dinosaurs_fly_rockets
    dinosaur = Dinosaur.new
    rocket = instance_double(Rocket)
    expect(rocket).to receive(:launch!)
    dinosaur.fly(rocket)
    expect(dinosaur).to be_excited
  end
end
```

If you're writing acceptance tests using Cucumber, you don't need to do anything special to use RSpec-style expectations. Cucumber will detect when you've installed the rspec-expectations gem, and will automatically enable it.

We do not usually recommend using test doubles with the kinds of acceptance tests Cucumber is designed for, but Cucumber does offer rspec-mocks integration for those rare cases when you need it. To enable it, require 'cucumber/rspec/doubles' in your environment setup.

To use parts of RSpec with another test framework, take a peek inside the two minitest_integration files from this example. They'll give you a good starting point for integrating with your test framework.

Using RSpec with Rails

Throughout this book, we've barely mentioned Rails, even though it's the most popular Ruby framework. This lack of emphasis is intentional. We find that if your testing fundamentals are solid and if you know how to use RSpec in a non-Rails context, it's easy to apply that knowledge to a Rails app—but not the inverse. In short, everything we've covered in this book applies to Rails apps.

With that said, we'd like to show you a few conveniences RSpec offers for testing Rails applications. In this appendix, we're going to show you how to configure a Rails app for testing with RSpec. We've also prepared some cheat sheets cataloging the features provided for working with Rails apps.

For more detailed Rails-specific testing advice, we recommend Noel Rappin's book *Rails 4 Test Prescriptions: Build a Healthy Codebase [Rap14]*. Even though the title refers to Rails 4, the advice is timeless and still applies to Rails 5. As we write this appendix, Noel is working on an updated edition for Rails 5.[1]

Installation

Rails provides infrastructure for directly testing specific pieces of your application: models, views, controllers, and so on. It also supports tests that integrate multiple layers and acceptance tests that integrate all layers.

The rspec-rails gem adapts the Rails testing infrastructure for use from RSpec. To use it, add an entry like the following one to the :development and :test groups in your Gemfile:

A2-using-rspec-with-rails/01/rails_app/Gemfile
```
group :development, :test do
➤   gem 'rspec-rails', '~> 3.6'
end
```

---

1. https://pragprog.com/book/nrtest3/rails-5-test-prescriptions

Then, run bundle install to install rspec-rails. Finally, you can set your project up to use rspec-rails with the following command:

```
$ rails generate rspec:install
      create  .rspec
      create  spec
      create  spec/spec_helper.rb
      create  spec/rails_helper.rb
```

The .rspec file configures command-line arguments to pass into RSpec implicitly, just like we previously discussed in *Setting Command-Line Defaults*, on page 149. The one generated by rspec-rails will load spec_helper.rb for you on every RSpec run. The spec_helper.rb file, in turn, sets a number of helpful RSpec defaults—such as the verify_partial_doubles option we recommended in *Using Partial Doubles Effectively*, on page 271. It also provides some configuration suggestions in a commented-out section.

This installation process also creates a second configuration file, rails_helper.rb, but does *not* configure RSpec to require it by default. This file loads both Rails and rspec-rails, which sets up test features like model fixtures and database transactions.

These additional test features are useful or even essential for many specs—but not for all of them. In particular, we strive to build domain objects that have clear boundaries and don't depend directly on Rails. When we test these objects, we want the fastest feedback possible. Accordingly, we don't require rails_helper from a spec file unless it actually needs Rails.

Using rspec-rails

Once rspec-rails is installed, you'll be able to run your spec suite using either bundle exec rspec or bin/rake spec. Commands in the bin directory, like rake or rails, are Rails-generated binstubs (wrapper scripts) that save you the hassle of remembering to type bundle exec before every command.[2]

If you're used to creating binstubs via Bundler's --binstubs option as described in *Bundler*, on page 293, be aware that this option may not play nicely with Spring, a Rails preloader designed to speed up boot times.[3] You may see Rails commands hang or print warning messages from the Bundler-generated binstubs. To solve the problem, you'll need to either remove Spring or switch to the binstubs provided by Rails:

---

2.   https://github.com/rbenv/rbenv/wiki/Understanding-binstubs
3.   https://github.com/rails/spring

```
$ bundle config --delete bin
$ rails app:update:bin
```

When you generate a Rails object such as a controller or scaffold, RSpec will create a corresponding spec file for you:

```
$ rails generate model pterodactyl
     invoke  active_record
     create    db/migrate/20170613203526_create_pterodactyls.rb
     create    app/models/pterodactyl.rb
     invoke    rspec
     create      spec/models/pterodactyl_spec.rb
```

You can also generate just the spec file, if the class you're testing already exists or if you don't want to create it just yet; just prepend the item you're generating with rspec:, as in rails generate rspec:model pterodactyl.

Next, let's take a look at the different types of specs you might write to test your Rails app.

Spec Types

For the expense tracker API you built in this book, you wrote three different kinds of specs:

- Acceptance specs to test the entire app end to end
- Unit specs to test one layer in isolation
- Integration specs to test objects with real collaborators and external services

A Rails app is more complex than a tiny API. Accordingly, Rails provides infrastructure for several different kinds of tests, including the following ones:

- Integration tests that drive your app as a black box via its HTTP interface
- Functional tests to see how your controllers respond to requests
- Unit tests to drive a single object or layer
- Specific tests for models, mailers, and background jobs; any given test here may be a unit or integration test

To test one of these aspects of your app in RSpec, tag your example group with the :type metadata, passing it one of the spec types from the chart in the next section (:model, :request, :helper, and so on). For example, here's the spec file generated by the rails generate model pterodactyl command from the previous section:

A2-using-rspec-with-rails/01/rails_app/spec/models/pterodactyl_spec.rb
```
require 'rails_helper'

RSpec.describe Pterodactyl, type: :model do
  # ...
end
```

Some of these spec types, such as :request and :model, will be the bread and butter of your testing. Others are mainly there for edge cases or for backward compatibility, since rspec-rails works with all Rails versions from 3.0 up to the latest release. (Rails 5.1 came out as we were putting the finishing touches on this book, and rspec-rails 3.6+ supports it.)

Spec Types Cheat Sheet

Spec type	Use for...	What it provides	Notes
:feature	• Testing the entire app, including the in-browser UI, via Capybara	• feature/scenario aliases for describe/it • Access to the Capybara API, including visit, fill_in, and so on[4] • Named route helpers of the form some_route_path	• Requires the Capybara gem
:request	• Non-JavaScript interactions, such as APIs • Excercising all layers of your Ruby code • Multiple requests, controllers, sessions	• Request helpers like get '/index', post '/create' • Request matchers; see *Rails Matchers Cheat Sheet*, on page 304 • Named route helpers of the form some_route_path	• Uses the Rails router and Rack middleware stack • Similar to the acceptance specs you wrote for the expense tracker API
:model	• Testing your ActiveRecord models	• Database transactions and model fixtures (available for all spec types, but more relevant here)	

---

4.   http://teamcapybara.github.io/capybara/

Spec type	Use for...	What it provides	Notes
:controller	• Testing controllers in isolation	• Request helpers like get :index, post :create • Controller matchers; see *Rails Matchers Cheat Sheet*, on page 304 • controller to define an anonymous controller[5] • route to use a different route set • bypass_rescue to prevent converting errors to 500 responses • Named route helpers of the form some_route_path	• Bypasses Rack middleware • By design, does not render views by default; call render_views if you need this behavior[6]
:view	• Testing the HTML contents of your views	• assign to make instance variables available	
:helper	• Testing view helper modules in app/helpers	• assign to make instance variables available • helper.some_method to call methods from the helper module you're testing	
:mailer	• Testing Rails mailers	• Named route helpers of the form some_route_path	
:routing	• Checking that URLs route to specific controller actions	• Routing matchers; see *Rails Matchers Cheat Sheet*, on page 304 • Named route helpers of the form some_route_path	
:job	• Testing background jobs	• Database transactions and model fixtures (available for all spec types, but more relevant here)	

---

5. https://relishapp.com/rspec/rspec-rails/v/3-6/docs/controller-specs/anonymous-controller
6. https://relishapp.com/rspec/rspec-rails/v/3-6/docs/controller-specs/render-views

Rails Matchers Cheat Sheet

In addition to these spec types, rspec-rails provides some Rails-specific matchers. Some of these are available to any spec once you've required rails_helper; others are just for certain spec types.

Matcher	Passes if...	Available in...
be_a_new(model_class)	record.is_a(model_class) && record.new_record?	All spec types
be_a_new(model_class).with(attribute: 'value')	record.is_a(model_class) && record.new_record? && record.attribute == 'value'	All spec types
be_new_record	record.new_record?	All spec types
be_valid	record.valid?	All spec types
have_been_enqueued.with(some_args)	Job was enqueued with matching arguments	All spec types
have_enqueued_job(job_class).with(some_args), enqueue_job(job_class).with(some_args)	Code in an expect block enqueued a job_class job with matching arguments	All spec types
have_http_status(code)	response.status == code	All spec types
have_http_status(symbol)	response.status maps to a *kind* of response, such as :success	All spec types
redirect_to('http://some-url.example.com')	Response redirects to the specified URL	:request, :controller
be_routable	Route exists	:controller, :routing
route_to(controller: 'name', action: 'name'), route_to('controller#action')	Route leads to the specified controller/action/parameters	:controller, :routing

Please don't feel like you need to use all of these spec types in the same app! Here are a few recommendations for specific situations.

When you're doing outside-in acceptance testing:

- For HTTP-based APIs, use request specs.
- For user-facing web applications, add Capybara to the project and use feature specs; see Michael Crismali's article for setup advice.[7]

---

7. https://www.devmynd.com/blog/setting-up-rspec-and-capybara-in-rails-5-for-testing/

For checking the major components of your app:

- Use unit and integration specs, without Rails where possible, for your domain objects.

- Use model, mailer, and job specs for their respective types of Rails objects.

We tend to shy away from the following types of specs:

- View specs, which cost more effort than the value they provide; they encourage putting logic in your views, which we like to keep at a minimum

- Routing specs, which generally duplicate test coverage from your acceptance specs

- Controller specs, which give an overly simplified picture of behavior, have some gotchas around how they bypass Rack middleware, and are being phased out of current Rails practice; use request specs instead[8]

There's no need to limit yourself to just the spec types supported by rspec-rails. By writing domain objects that don't depend directly on Rails, you can test your code in the way that works best for you.

---

8. https://blog.bigbinary.com/2016/04/19/changes-to-test-controllers-in-rails-5.html

Matcher Cheat Sheet

In *Matchers Included in RSpec Expectations*, we went through the most commonly used matchers included in RSpec. Now, we'd like to show you all the matchers built-in to RSpec as of version 3.6 in a single reference that you can keep handy while you're writing specs.

The *Passes if...* column provides an expression for each matcher that's equivalent to what the matcher checks. The snippet isn't necessarily how the matcher is implemented internally, as we've glossed over a few edge cases that don't arise during daily use. If you're curious about these implementation details, you can check out the source code.[1]

Value Matchers

Given any Ruby expression a, value matchers are expressed in the form:

```
expect(a).to matcher
```

To negate a matcher, use either not_to or to_not rather than to:

```
expect(a).not_to matcher
# or
expect(a).to_not matcher
```

Equality/Identity

Matcher	Passes if...	Available aliases
eq(x)	a == x	an_object_eq_to(x)
eql(x)	a.eql?(x)	an_object_eql_to(x)
equal(x)	a.equal?(x)	be(x)
		an_object_equal_to(x)

---

1.   https://github.com/rspec/rspec-expectations

Truthiness and Nil

Matcher	Passes if...	Available aliases
be_truthy	a != nil && a != false	a_truthy_value
be true	a == true	
be_falsey	a == nil || a == false	be_falsy
		a_falsey_value
		a_falsy_value
be false	a == false	
be_nil	a.nil?	a_nil_value

Types

Matcher	Passes if...	Available aliases
be_an_instance_of(klass)	a.class == klass	be_instance_of(klass)
		an_instance_of(klass)
be_a_kind_of(klass)	a.is_a?(klass)	be_a(klass)
		be_kind_of(klass)
		a_kind_of(klass)

Operator Comparisons

Matcher	Passes if...	Available aliases
be == x	a == x	a_value == x
be < x	a < x	a_value < x
be > x	a > x	a_value > x
be <= x	a <= x	a_value <= x
be >= x	a >= x	a_value >= x
be =~ x	a =~ x	a_value =~ x
be === x	a === x	a_value === x

Delta/Range Comparisons

Matcher	Passes if...	Available aliases
be_between(1, 10).inclusive	a >= 1 && a <= 10	be_between(1, 10) a_value_between(1, 10).inclusive a_value_between(1, 10)
be_between(1, 10).exclusive	a > 1 && a < 10	a_value_between(1, 10).exclusive
be_within(0.1).of(x)	(a - x).abs <= 0.1	a_value_within(0.1).of(x)
be_within(5).percent_of(x)	(a - x).abs <= (0.05 * x)	a_value_within(5).percent_of(x)
cover(x, y)	a.cover?(x) && a.cover?(y)	a_range_covering(x, y)

Strings and Collections

Matcher	Passes if...	Available aliases
contain_exactly(2, 1, 3)	a.sort == [2, 1, 3].sort	match_array([2, 1, 3]) a_collection_containing_exactly(2, 1, 3)
start_with(x, y)	a[0] == x && a[1] == y	a_collection_starting_with(x, y) a_string_starting_with(x, y)
end_with(x, y)	a[-1] == x && a[-2] == y	a_collection_starting_with(x, y) a_string_starting_with(x, y)
include(x, y)	(a.include?(x) && a.include?(y)) || (a.key?(x) && a.key?(y))	a_collection_including(x, y) a_string_including(x, y) a_hash_including(x, y)
include(w: x, y: z)	a[:w] == :x && a[:y] == :z	a_hash_including(w: x, y: z)
all(matcher)	a.all? { |e| matcher.matches?(e) }	
match(x: matcher, y: 3)	matcher.matches?(a[:x]) && a[:y] == 3	an_object_matching(x: matcher, y: 3)
match([3, matcher])	a[0] == 3 && matcher.matches?(a[1])	an_object_matching([3, matcher])
match("pattern")	a.match("pattern")	a_string_matching("pattern")
match(/regex/)	a.match(/regex/)	match_regex(/regex/) a_string_matching(/regex/)

Duck Typing and Attributes

Matcher	Passes if...	Available aliases
have_attributes(w: x, y: z)	a.w == x && a.y == z	an_object_having_attributes(w: x, y: z)
respond_to(:x, :y)	a.respond_to?(:x) && a.respond_to?(:y)	an_object_responding_to(:x, :y)
respond_to(:x) .with(2).arguments	a.respond_to?(:x) && a.method(:x).arity == 2	an_object_responding_to(:x) .with(2).arguments

Dynamic Predicates

Matcher	Passes if...	Available aliases
be_xyz	a.xyz? || a.xyzs?	be_a_xyz be_an_xyz
be_foo(x, y, &b)	a.foo(x, y, &b)? || a.foos(x, y, &b)?	be_a_foo(x, y, &b) be_an_foo(x, y, &b)
have_xyz	a.has_xyz?	
have_foo(x, y, &b)	a.has_foo(x, y, &b)?	

Additional Matchers

Matcher	Passes if...	Available aliases
exist	a.exist? || a.exists?	an_object_existing
exist(x, y)	a.exist(x, y)? || a.exists(x, y)?	an_object_existing(x, y)
satisfy { |x| ... }	Provided block returns true	an_object_satisfying { |x| ... }
satisfy("criteria") { |x| ... }	Provided block returns true	an_object_satisfying("...") { |x| ... }

Block Matchers

Block matchers observe a block of code and are used to specify a side effect that occurs when the block runs. They take the form:

```
expect { some_code }.to matcher
```

As with value matchers, block matchers can be negated by using not_to or to_not rather than to.

Mutation

The change matcher captures a value before running the block (old_value) and again after running the block (new_value). The value can be specified in two ways:

```
expect { do_something }.to change(obj, :attr)
# or
expect { do_something }.to change { obj.attr }
```

It supports a rich fluent interface for specifying further details about the mutation:

Matcher	Passes if...
change { }	old_value != new_value
change { }.by(x)	(new_value - old_value) == x
change { }.by_at_least(x)	(new_value - old_value) >= x
change { }.by_at_most(x)	(new_value - old_value) <= x
change { }.from(x)	old_value != new_value && old_value == x
change { }.to(y)	old_value != new_value && new_value == y
change { }.from(x).to(y)	old_value != new_value && old_value == x && new_value == y

IO

Matcher	Passes if...	Available aliases
output("foo").to_stdout	"foo" is printed to $stdout from this process	a_block_outputting("foo") .to_stdout
output("foo").to_stderr	"foo" is printed to $stderr from this process	a_block_outputting("foo") .to_stderr
output(/bar/).to_stdout	A string matching /bar/ is printed to $stdout from this process	a_block_outputting(/bar/) .to_stdout
output(/bar/).to_stderr	A string matching /bar/ is printed to $stderr from this process	a_block_outputting(/bar/) .to_stderr

output("foo")
    .to_stdout_from_any_process
	"foo" is printed to $stdout from this process or a subprocess	a_block_outputting("foo")
		    .to_stdout_from_any_process

output("foo")
    .to_stderr_from_any_process
	"foo" is printed to $stderr from this process or a subprocess	a_block_outputting("foo")
		    .to_stderr_from_any_process

output(/bar/)
    .to_stdout_from_any_process
	A string matching /bar/ is printed to $stdout from this process or a subprocess	a_block_outputting(/bar/)
		    .to_stdout_from_any_process

output(/bar/)
    .to_stderr_from_any_process
	A string matching /bar/ is printed to $stderr from this process or a subprocess	a_block_outputting(/bar/)
		    .to_stderr_from_any_process

Raising/Throwing

Matcher	Passes if...	Available aliases
raise_error("message")	Block raises an error and error.message == "message"	raise_exception("message") a_block_raising("message")
raise_error(/regexp/)	Block raises an error and error.message =~ /regexp/	raise_exception("message") a_block_raising("message")
raise_error(klass)	Block raises an error and error.is_a?(klass)	raise_exception(klass) a_block_raising(klass)
raise_error(klass, "message")	Block raises an error and error.is_a?(klass) && error.message == "message"	raise_exception(klass, "message") a_block_raising(klass, "message")
raise_error(klass, /regexp/)	Block raises an error and error.is_a?(klass) && error.message =~ /regexp/	raise_exception(klass, /regexp/) a_block_raising(klass, /regexp/)
raise_error { |err| ... })	Block raises an error and raise_error block returns true	raise_exception { |err| ... } a_block_raising { |err| ... }
throw_symbol	Block throws any symbol	a_block_throwing
throw_symbol(:sym)	Block throws symbol :sym	a_block_throwing(:sym)
throw_symbol(:sym, arg)	Block throws symbol :sym with argument arg	a_block_throwing(:sym, arg)

Yielding

To use the yield matchers, your expect block must receive an argument (a "yield probe") and pass it on to the method-under-test using Ruby's &block syntax:

```
expect { |probe| obj.some_method(&probe) }.to yield_control
```

Matcher	Passes if method called in block yields...	Available aliases
yield_control	...one or more times	yield_control.at_least(:once) a_block_yielding_control
yield_control.once	...once	a_block_yielding_control.once
yield_control.twice	...twice	a_block_yielding_control.twice
yield_control.thrice	...thrice	a_block_yielding_control.thrice
yield_control .exactly(n).times	...n times	a_block_yielding_control .exactly(n).times
yield_control .at_least(n).times	...at least n times	a_block_yielding_control .at_least(n).times
yield_control .at_most(n).times	...at most n times	a_block_yielding_control .at_most(n).times
yield_with_args(x, y)	...once with arguments that match x and y	a_block_yielding_with_args(x, y)
yield_with_no_args	...once with no arguments	a_block_yielding_with_args(x, y)
yield_successive_args([a, b], [c, d])	...once with arguments that match a and b and once with arguments that match c and d	a_block_yielding_successive_args([a, b], [c, d])

Bibliography

[FP09]   Steve Freeman and Nat Pryce. *Growing Object-Oriented Software, Guided by Tests*. Addison-Wesley Longman, Boston, MA, 2009.

[Hen13]   Elisabeth Hendrickson. *Explore It! Reduce Risk and Increase Confidence with Exploratory Testing*. The Pragmatic Bookshelf, Raleigh, NC, 1st, 2013.

[HT00]   Andrew Hunt and David Thomas. *The Pragmatic Programmer: From Journeyman to Master*. Addison-Wesley, Boston, MA, 2000.

[Mes07]   Gerard Meszaros. *xUnit Test Patterns*. Addison-Wesley, Boston, MA, 2007.

[Met12]   Sandi Metz. *Practical Object-Oriented Design in Ruby*. Addison-Wesley Professional, Boston, MA, 1st, 2012.

[Rap14]   Noel Rappin. *Rails 4 Test Prescriptions: Build a Healthy Codebase*. The Pragmatic Bookshelf, Raleigh, NC, 1st, 2014.

Index

Explore Testing and Cucumber

Explore the uncharted waters of exploratory testing and delve deeper into Cucumber.

Explore It!

Uncover surprises, risks, and potentially serious bugs with exploratory testing. Rather than designing all tests in advance, explorers design and execute small, rapid experiments, using what they learned from the last little experiment to inform the next. Learn essential skills of a master explorer, including how to analyze software to discover key points of vulnerability, how to design experiments on the fly, how to hone your observation skills, and how to focus your efforts.

Elisabeth Hendrickson
(186 pages) ISBN: 9781937785024. $29
https://pragprog.com/book/ehxta

The Cucumber Book, Second Edition

Your customers want rock-solid, bug-free software that does exactly what they expect it to do. Yet they can't always articulate their ideas clearly enough for you to turn them into code. You need Cucumber: a testing, communication, and requirements tool—all rolled into one. All the code in this book is updated for Cucumber 2.4, Rails 5, and RSpec 3.5.

Matt Wynne and Aslak Hellesøy, with Steve Tooke
(334 pages) ISBN: 9781680502381. $39.95
https://pragprog.com/book/hwcuc2

Secure JavaScript and Web Testing

Secure your Node applications and see how to really test on the web.

Secure Your Node.js Web Application

Cyber-criminals have your web applications in their crosshairs. They search for and exploit common security mistakes in your web application to steal user data. Learn how you can secure your Node.js applications, database and web server to avoid these security holes. Discover the primary attack vectors against web applications, and implement security best practices and effective countermeasures. Coding securely will make you a stronger web developer and analyst, and you'll protect your users.

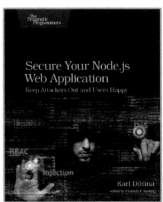

Karl Düüna
(230 pages) ISBN: 9781680500851. $36
https://pragprog.com/book/kdnodesec

The Way of the Web Tester

This book is for everyone who needs to test the web. As a tester, you'll automate your tests. As a developer, you'll build more robust solutions. And as a team, you'll gain a vocabulary and a means to coordinate how to write and organize automated tests for the web. Follow the testing pyramid and level up your skills in user interface testing, integration testing, and unit testing. Your new skills will free you up to do other, more important things while letting the computer do the one thing it's really good at: quickly running thousands of repetitive tasks.

Jonathan Rasmusson
(256 pages) ISBN: 9781680501834. $29
https://pragprog.com/book/jrtest

Pragmatic Programming

We'll show you how to be more pragmatic and effective, for new code and old.

Your Code as a Crime Scene

Jack the Ripper and legacy codebases have more in common than you'd think. Inspired by forensic psychology methods, this book teaches you strategies to predict the future of your codebase, assess refactoring direction, and understand how your team influences the design. With its unique blend of forensic psychology and code analysis, this book arms you with the strategies you need, no matter what programming language you use.

Adam Tornhill
(218 pages) ISBN: 9781680500387. $36
https://pragprog.com/book/atcrime

The Nature of Software Development

You need to get value from your software project. You need it "free, now, and perfect." We can't get you there, but we can help you get to "cheaper, sooner, and better." This book leads you from the desire for value down to the specific activities that help good Agile projects deliver better software sooner, and at a lower cost. Using simple sketches and a few words, the author invites you to follow his path of learning and understanding from a half century of software development and from his engagement with Agile methods from their very beginning.

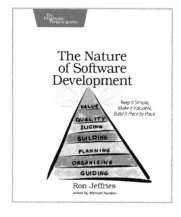

Ron Jeffries
(176 pages) ISBN: 9781941222379. $24
https://pragprog.com/book/rjnsd

More Ruby and Rails

Learn how to integrate Ruby on Rails with popular technologies and see how to improve the performance of all your Ruby programming.

Rails, Angular, Postgres, and Bootstrap, Second Edition

Achieve awesome user experiences and performance with simple, maintainable code! Embrace the full stack of web development, from styling with Bootstrap, building an interactive user interface with Angular 4, to storing data quickly and reliably in PostgreSQL. With this fully revised new edition, take a holistic view of full-stack development to create usable, high-performing applications with Rails 5.1.

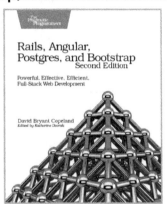

David Bryant Copeland
(342 pages) ISBN: 9781680502206. $39.95
https://pragprog.com/book/dcbang2

Ruby Performance Optimization

You don't have to accept slow Ruby or Rails performance. In this comprehensive guide to Ruby optimization, you'll learn how to write faster Ruby code—but that's just the beginning. See exactly what makes Ruby and Rails code slow, and how to fix it. Alex Dymo will guide you through perils of memory and CPU optimization, profiling, measuring, performance testing, garbage collection, and tuning. You'll find that all those "hard" things aren't so difficult after all, and your code will run orders of magnitude faster.

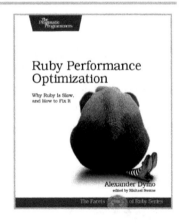

Alexander Dymo
(200 pages) ISBN: 9781680500691. $36
https://pragprog.com/book/adrpo

The Pragmatic Bookshelf

The Pragmatic Bookshelf features books written by developers for developers. The titles continue the well-known Pragmatic Programmer style and continue to garner awards and rave reviews. As development gets more and more difficult, the Pragmatic Programmers will be there with more titles and products to help you stay on top of your game.

Visit Us Online

This Book's Home Page
https://pragprog.com/book/rspec3
Source code from this book, errata, and other resources. Come give us feedback, too!

Register for Updates
https://pragprog.com/updates
Be notified when updates and new books become available.

Join the Community
https://pragprog.com/community
Read our weblogs, join our online discussions, participate in our mailing list, interact with our wiki, and benefit from the experience of other Pragmatic Programmers.

New and Noteworthy
https://pragprog.com/news
Check out the latest pragmatic developments, new titles and other offerings.

Save on the eBook

Save on the eBook versions of this title. Owning the paper version of this book entitles you to purchase the electronic versions at a terrific discount.

PDFs are great for carrying around on your laptop—they are hyperlinked, have color, and are fully searchable. Most titles are also available for the iPhone and iPod touch, Amazon Kindle, and other popular e-book readers.

Buy now at *https://pragprog.com/coupon*

Contact Us

Online Orders:	*https://pragprog.com/catalog*
Customer Service:	*support@pragprog.com*
International Rights:	*translations@pragprog.com*
Academic Use:	*academic@pragprog.com*
Write for Us:	*http://write-for-us.pragprog.com*
Or Call:	+1 800-699-7764

9 781680 501988